Donald McRae is the award-winning author of eleven non-fiction books, which have featured sporting icons, legendary trial lawyers and heart surgeons. He has twice won the prestigious William Hill Sports Book of the Year, for *Dark Trade* and *In Black & White*. He is a three-time Interviewer of the Year winner and has also won Sports Feature Writer of the Year on three separate occasions for his work in *The Guardian*. He lives in Hertfordshire.

'In this outstanding and important book, Don McRae's powerful storytelling shows the courage of Gerry Storey and the people of the North as they withstand everyday horror. These stories of bravery through boxing stay with you, and their passion comes out in every word; their strength in every unassuming anecdote.'

Andy Lee, author of *Fighter*, and former middleweight world champion

'Years of interviews and research have informed McRae's account of Storey's extraordinary courage, and those of the fighters he reared ... The result is as uplifting as it is heartbreaking.'

Emma John, *The Guardian*

'A superb tale ... His inspirational story

IN SUNSHINE OR
IN SHADOW

HOW BOXING BROUGHT
HOPE IN THE TROUBLES

Donald McRae

**SIMON &
SCHUSTER**

London · New York · Sydney · Toronto · New Delhi

A CBS COMPANY

First published in Great Britain by Simon & Schuster UK Ltd, 2019
This edition published in Great Britain by Simon & Schuster UK Ltd, 2020
A CBS COMPANY

1 3 5 7 9 10 8 6 4 2

Simon & Schuster UK Ltd
1st Floor
222 Gray's Inn Road
London WC1X 8HB

www.simonandschuster.co.uk
www.simonandschuster.com.au
www.simonandschuster.co.in

Simon & Schuster Australia, Sydney
Simon & Schuster India, New Delhi

A CIP catalogue record for this book
is available from the British Library.

Paperback ISBN: 978-1-4711-6313-5
eBook ISBN: 978-1-4711-6312-8

Typeset in Caslon by M Rules
Printed and bound by CPI Group (UK) Ltd, Croydon, CR0 4YY

MIX
Paper from
responsible sources
FSC® C020471

To my parents, Ian and Jess McRae,
and to my sister, Heather Simpson,
who died far too young on 15 September 2018

CONTENTS

The Holy Family

In the blistering summer of 2018 the vivid murals still look ominous. The brick wall facing the Holy Family Boxing Club in New Lodge, Belfast, is painted white, with green and orange trim completing the colours of the Irish flag. In its left-hand corner an IRA gunman in a balaclava looks down at the rifle that has slipped from his hands. A hooded IRA soldier stands to attention in the opposite corner. His head is bowed as he holds his gun.

In the centre of the wall two clenched fists hail the words 'Comrades in Resistance'. On either side of this slogan a stark sentence is split in two and inked into the wall:

I don't care if I fall
As long as someone else picks up my gun and keeps on shooting.

Next to it another mural depicts three gunmen, dressed in black, pointing their rifles at a blue sky. The Irish words *Tiocfaidh Ár Lá* (Our Day Will Come) and *Saoirse* (Freedom) are painted in gleaming white. Surrounded by tower blocks and rows of council housing, the murals are reminders of the violence and pain that remain in this corner of north Belfast.

Ten minutes earlier, ambling through the Cathedral Quarter, drifting past bars and cafés filled with bearded hipsters and beautiful girls showing off their tattoos and piercings, I had been in a different world – in a city full of warmth and hope for the future. It is hard to believe the Holy Family and the IRA murals are just a short walk away.

I had strolled alongside Davy Larmour, a Protestant fighter who had been trained by the venerable Gerry Storey at the Holy Family in the 1970s. Davy, a short but strapping man in his late sixties who had once been the British bantamweight champion, still cut an imposing figure. But his eyes twinkled beneath his bald head and above his boxer's nose as we left our usual café at the MAC, the Metropolitan Arts Centre, on Exchange Street.

I liked being at the MAC and at other places in this vibrant new Belfast. At the MAC you might see a Gilbert & George exhibition or work created by Irish, Croatian, Turkish or Palestinian artists. There could be stand-up comedy, video installations or a new play.

My head still hummed with the stories Davy told me. He had lived a different life to the Belfast millennials we passed. Many young people in the Cathedral Quarter would have looked at home in Berlin or Copenhagen. But Davy was rooted in Belfast. He was shaped by the past – but he had found a way to transcend the Troubles.

Davy came from near the Shankill Road, a defining marker of Protestant Belfast, but he had also been a champion amateur boxer, and then a professional fighter, with many friends in Republican Belfast. He remembered the IRA car bomb that had blown up his father's truck in 1972 on Ann Street, less than a mile from where we sat. Davy's dad had survived, but life had never been the same again. Yet there was neither bitterness nor resentment in Davy.

He was happy to hear I was on my way to see Gerry Storey at the Holy Family.

During my earliest visits to the city, not knowing the geography of Belfast despite being aware of the New Lodge's reputation, I would take a taxi from my hotel in the Cathedral Quarter to the Holy Family. It was never more than a £5 fare but we had to go the long way round. I learnt later from Gerry, who had run the gym for over 50 years, that I could walk to the Holy Family just as quickly by strolling up North Queen Street, crossing over at the McGurk's Bomb memorial and taking the walkway round the back.

The first time I took the short cut, Gerry led me down the grimy stairwell. We crossed the road under the concrete flyover and stood outside the painted exterior of McGurk's Bar. On a desolate night in 1971, Gerry had lost friends at McGurk's and his family had felt grief and rage. A week later there was a retaliatory bomb, aimed at Protestants on the Shankill Road. Four innocent people were killed; Davy Larmour just missed the explosion.

Gerry gave me these lessons in Irish history with a light touch. He also explained how his peaceful work overcame deadly bigotry. In the 1970s and '80s he had criss-crossed Belfast, moving from Republican to Loyalist no-go areas with relaxed good cheer as he trained both Catholic and Protestant boxers. Gerry and his fighters were different to anyone else during the Troubles. They were allowed to travel freely and were welcomed everywhere in a battered city. He put on boxing shows deep within gunmen territory – whether the paramilitaries were from the IRA (Irish Republican Army) or their enemies in the UDA (Ulster Defence Association) or UVF (Ulster Volunteer Force).

We moved on, walking through New Lodge, and Gerry glowed with the memory of all he had done and the men he had made, from world and British champions like Barry McGuigan and Hugh Russell to lesser-known characters he celebrated with equal fervour. The more we walked, and talked, the closer I felt to this extraordinary story. I saw the ghosts of a brutal past – and I understood the peril and hatred Gerry Storey had withstood.

I told Gerry again about my own history. I had grown up in South Africa under apartheid. When I was in my early twenties in the 1980s, we heard intricate reports about Northern Ireland on our daily news bulletins. It was almost as if the government and the state broadcaster, the SABC, wanted us to realise that other countries were afflicted by division and strife.

We heard much about Bobby Sands, the IRA hunger striker in the Maze prison near Belfast, but nothing about Nelson Mandela serving a term of life imprisonment on Robben Island. We heard much about riots and bombs in Belfast and Derry, but only controlled snippets of the dissent in the black townships of Soweto and Alexandra. We heard much about bloody conflict between Catholics and Protestants, but just censored versions of the war in the townships and along South Africa's borders with Mozambique and Angola.

Decades later, in the 21st century, lessons learnt from South Africa's post-apartheid Truth and Reconciliation Commission helped the peace process in Northern Ireland. Republicans, Loyalists and policemen from the Royal Ulster Constabulary had travelled together to Cape Town in 2012. They had once wanted to kill each other, but in South Africa they found a way to talk as they met with delegates from the TRC to discuss how they might break free from a violent history. Northern Ireland has always mirrored my old country.

I had been thinking about Storey for years – ever since I'd heard how he had taught boxing in the Maze prison in the immediate aftermath of the hunger strikes. In 1981, Sands and nine other Republicans had starved themselves to death in a battle against Margaret Thatcher's government. That crisis had gripped and appalled me 6,000 miles away in Johannesburg. I had since learnt that Storey had gone into the Maze, where the hunger strikers had died a few months earlier, and given boxing lessons to prisoners from both the Republican and Loyalist cages.

I did not know then I would spend years researching this book. In Derry, I spent many days with Charlie Nash, the first significant boxer of the Troubles, a man who fought for European and world titles despite the tragedy his family endured on Bloody Sunday.

I became friendly with Larmour and Russell, a Protestant and a Catholic who shared two bloody battles during the early 1980s. Russell was an Olympic medallist for Ireland and a British bantamweight champion. He was also one of the great photographers of the Troubles, who documented the carnage with his camera by day while sparring in the gym at night.

I became close to McGuigan, the greatest Irish boxer of the Troubles, a world champion who bridged the sectarian divide. Storey, who had trained him during some of his most significant bouts as an Olympian and Commonwealth Games champion, carved out this road before him – but McGuigan had the character and talent to showcase such unity on a world stage.

Sitting outside the Holy Family, and facing the sinister murals in the sunshine, the truth hit me again. Only boxing could have brought these peaceful men together.

The Troubles took hold of me when I met McGuigan for the first time on a beautiful afternoon in rural Kent in the spring of 2011. Even though we were far from Belfast and the peak of his boxing career, the former world champion made me feel as if we were back in the shuddering 1970s and '80s. All his bravery and glory in the ring rose up again alongside the years of bombings and kneecappings, of futility and death.

We were born in the same year, McGuigan and I, and bound together by our love of boxing. His knowledge was obviously deeper than mine, but he could tell I understood the power of the savage old fight game. We both believed in boxing and, despite the corruption and sadness that framed it, saw everything it had achieved during the Troubles.

'The sadness was unbearable for so many,' McGuigan said, 'but boxing gave people some light. It took their minds off the darkness. You know that line in "Danny Boy" my father used to sing: "I'll be there in sunshine or in shadow"? Well, the shadows ran deep. And my fights felt a little like sunshine. Both sides would say: "Leave the fighting to McGuigan." You see, it was also enter-tainment – people loved to forget the Troubles for a while.'

McGuigan offered a vivid depiction of the night he won the WBA featherweight title against Eusebio Pedroza on 8 June 1985 in front of the largest television audience in British boxing history. Twenty million viewers watched McGuigan fight a great champion.

He leapt from his chair to showcase the combination with which he dropped Pedroza in the seventh round. The little old feath-erweight danced around me, throwing big punches with rasping grunts as he imagined the formidable Panamanian in front of him again.

'Can you believe it?' McGuigan exclaimed. 'Lucian Freud, the greatest painter in Britain, was there. Incredible. Irvine Welsh is another. Have you read what he wrote in *Glue*?'

Welsh, the author of *Trainspotting*, was lost in the crowd that wild night. He has since written about the emotional response of his father, a Scottish hard man. 'Irvine Welsh went with his dad to the fight and, just before the first bell, he turned around to look at his father,' McGuigan said. 'In the ring my dad was singing "Danny Boy" and Irvine was amazed to see his own father crying. He'd never seen his dad cry before.'

That night captured McGuigan at his most powerful. As a fighter from the Republic of Ireland, who boxed for Ulster and won the British title, McGuigan was loved in both the North and the South. 'Why did I get such special support?' McGuigan asked out loud. 'The answer is simple: there was so much sadness and people were fed up.'

Daniel Day-Lewis, who played the part of a boxer in a film about the Troubles, wrote: 'Barry was compassionate in victory, coura-geous almost to his own destruction in defeat. The dove on his shorts was a symbol of the man, an exquisite paradox; the warrior and the peacemaker.'

McGuigan also suffered as his fists inadvertently ended the life of his opponent, a Nigerian called Young Ali, in 1982. 'He's never far from my mind,' McGuigan said of Ali, who fell into a coma and eventually died after their bout at the Grosvenor House Hotel in London.

There were tears in McGuigan's eyes and his face crumpled. For a few moments he could not speak for crying. 'It's impossible not to feel guilty,' he eventually said. 'I think of Young Ali every day of my life. I wonder about his wife, and the child she was pregnant with when he died. For a long time, I felt so sad I couldn't think about boxing. But my own wife was pregnant and I had to go on. Boxing was so important to me – and to all of us in Belfast.'

Two years later, in 2013, McGuigan drove me across Belfast for a couple of hours as we moved through notorious areas from the Troubles so that he could illustrate boxing's remarkable achievement in spreading peace. A familiar old slogan – End British Internment – was daubed across a wall near the Holy Family in New Lodge. The IRA murals and high-rise flats loomed darkly over the gym. But, inside, lightness lifted our mood.

It was moving that boxing brought two warring communities together. 'That was the paradox,' McGuigan said. 'Peace be with you – and you were punching someone in the mouth. Boxing was an olive branch. Boxing allowed you to do things nobody else could do. It was a horrible, terrifying time. You look back and think: "Christ Almighty, did our neighbours and friends really do such barbaric things?" But they did. It happened.'

McGuigan brightened. 'For many of us boxing was a sanctuary. It was a release, and an education. We travelled the world and became better human beings. Gerry Storey started it all. You have to meet Gerry . . . he has more soul than anyone I've ever known in boxing.'

That afternoon Gerry was out, working with young boxers in a different part of Belfast. I resolved to return and meet him.

Leaving the Holy Family, we heard something that sounded like gunfire. McGuigan swore, apologised and then laughed when I reminded him that I came from Johannesburg. It was like being home again – for both of us. We moved from New Lodge to the Falls Road, zipping past the black flags and Irish tricolours, to the Shankill Road's Union Jacks and murals dedicated to the Queen.

'I had a Falls Road and a Shankill Road Supporters' Club,' McGuigan said. 'Gerry started all that. Ask Gerry about the time he took a team of us Catholic kids to box against East Germany on the Shankill Road. It was a special time – despite so much murder and misery.'

This book makes no attempt to explore the roots of the conflict or to recount how the Troubles finally ended. That task has been completed many times before. *In Sunshine or in Shadow* focuses instead on the positive impact of boxing in Northern Ireland from 1972 to 1985. It starts with the massacre of Bloody Sunday in Derry on 30 January 1972 and ends with McGuigan winning the world title in June 1985.

These were the very worst years of the Troubles. Yet I was drawn to them because, in this period, boxing saved lives and steered countless young men away from joining paramilitary groups. I also chose this narrative arc because it coincided with the greatest years in the ring for McGuigan and Nash, Larmour and Russell. They were bound together by the debt they all owed to Gerry Storey, who trained each of them at key stages of their careers.

Boxing gave its fighters and trainers a form of diplomatic immunity to travel anywhere they chose. That was a rare privilege – not offered even to priests, poets or politicians. The liberty given to boxers still seems remarkable. I have open-minded Protestant friends in Belfast today who, because they are ordinary people rather than boxers, would still not dare step into New Lodge or another Republican area like Turf Lodge.

Boxing won the hard-bitten support of men in the street, whether they were supporters of paramilitary groups or just working-class people who yearned for a change from brutality and recession. Of course sport is meant to offer a heady distraction from real life but, in Northern Ireland, the boundaries between the personal and the political are always blurred.

Amateur fighters from Northern Ireland compete for the Republic of Ireland in the Olympics and world championships. Other sports, including rugby, hockey and cricket, also field All-Ireland teams drawn from the North and the South. Yet only rugby can rival boxing as a sport where people from Northern Ireland compete for Ireland at the very highest level. The impact of rugby during the Troubles was less powerful. Rugby in the North was played primarily in Protestant schools, and usually in more affluent areas, so it did not match boxing's cross-community appeal.

Similarly, Gaelic football and hurling, so popular in Nationalist circles, were of scant interest to Protestants. The divide was so obvious that two men carrying, respectively, a hurling stick and a hockey stick would be classified immediately as a Catholic and a Protestant.

Football's hold on people, meanwhile, diminished in the 1970s. From February 1972 until May 1975 security concerns meant Northern Ireland could not play football (or soccer) internationals at home. They played Home Internationals (against England, Scotland and Wales) at Goodison Park in Liverpool, or away, while their European Championship and World Cup qualifiers were held at English grounds as diverse as Hull, Coventry, Sheffield Wednesday and Fulham.

In later years there was fleeting harmony. The 1982 World Cup finals saw Northern Ireland perform far better than expected, even beating Spain 1–0, with a team that was an encouraging mix of Catholics and Protestants. Yet in the late 1980s and '90s, violent prejudice regained a foothold. Following Northern Ireland seemed to become a statement of Loyalist intent, as Catholic players were insulted at times by some of their own supporters. Most Catholic fans underlined their allegiance to a Republic of Ireland team that thrived under the management of Jack Charlton. It would need a different century and a post-Troubles landscape for Northern

Ireland to play football in a more vibrant and hopeful atmosphere at Windsor Park.

Boxing filled the vacuum in the Troubles – and Larmour and Russell proved that boxing had a unique ability to stage ferocious contests between Protestants and Catholics, in front of fevered and integrated crowds, without any violence outside the ring. Football was different: the tribal rivalry between opposition clubs often caused sectarian strife.

This book does not try to claim that boxing changed the political landscape because, obviously, it did not end or even defuse the Troubles. Yet, when people looked in amazement at how boxers ignored sectarian divisions, they saw acceptance and respect. It helped them believe peace and harmony would finally arrive.

In attempting to understand how Storey could do his seemingly miraculous work while criss-crossing one forbidden area after another in Belfast, I asked him often why he was given such leeway. He stressed that boxing's working-class roots echoed the background of most paramilitary leaders and that his fighters were respected for their courage and honesty.

McGuigan went further. 'Boxing was accepted and given freedom of movement, unlike any other activity, because it had street credibility,' he told me. 'Boxing has a hardness and a coldness about it. Unlike any other sport, you risk your life in the ring. And to get to the top in boxing you have to endure immense pain. Boxers often come from very harsh backgrounds and the way they deal with adversity and hurt wins them massive respect with the paramilitaries. Boxing is a violent sport and it connected with these very violent people.

'It was respected by some of the most dangerous men during the Troubles. And it's a lovely irony that a man as gentle as Gerry Storey used these special circumstances to spread peace and hope through boxing. He was the only person for a long time in Northern Ireland who could go anywhere and be accepted by everyone. In later years boxing helped me do the same. But Gerry paved the way.'

Storey is the lesser-known hero, but his experiences shape this book. McGuigan provides the culmination for he was embraced as an icon of Northern Irish sport.

Two extraordinary sportsmen from Belfast preceded him. But George Best, the amazing footballer who helped Manchester United win the European Cup in 1968, and Alex Higgins, the brilliant snooker player who won the world championship in 1972 and 1982, both succumbed to alcoholism.

Best remains one of the most gifted footballers to have played the game but even he was affected by sectarian problems. His father was a Protestant Orangeman and, as a Belfast schoolboy in the 1950s, Best was chased often by Catholic kids who wanted to beat him up because he was a 'Prod'. In the autumn of 1971, while celebrated as 'El Beatle' across Europe because of his dashing good looks and stunning skill, Best was warned he would be shot if he played for Manchester United against Newcastle United. He ignored the threat and was a weaving target the entire game, also scoring a goal. The Newcastle manager Joe Harvey made a bad joke: 'I wish they had shot the little bugger.' Despite his Protestant background, Best was loved by most Catholics in Belfast. He played only 37 times for Northern Ireland, and rarely in Belfast, and his political influence was limited – even if he called for a united Ireland team.

Higgins changed snooker for ever, making it seem dangerously glamorous when he burst into a staid sport. 'Nobody's as fast as me, or as attractive to watch,' Higgins boasted. 'I'm the Cassius Clay of snooker. Snooker needs me, somebody young, to pull in the crowds. That's what it's about, baby!' Burning with chaos and violence, he was never interested in peace or harmony. He was also a Protestant, like Best. In 1990, Higgins threatened to have Dennis Taylor shot. Taylor, a former world champion, was a Catholic from County Tyrone.

McGuigan and Storey, and all the boxing men in this book, were very different to Best and Higgins. They brought hope in a time of despair.

*

In the summer of 2018, in his gym, I show Gerry Storey my note-book, listing all our interviews. We work out that this is my 35th visit to the Holy Family. I have also interviewed Larmour, Russell, Nash and McGuigan many times. Their stories run through me like overlapping rivers, flowing with pathos and pain, human-ity and hope.

Gerry and I sit on the apron of a blue ring on a sleepy midweek afternoon. We are surrounded by black-and-white photographs of his former fighters. His latest crop of shiny-faced boys and girls, ranging in age from eight to 18, will soon tumble through the doors downstairs and race up to the gym for evening training. Thirty of them will turn the Holy Family into a stinking hothouse. Gerry will preside over everything, taking kids on the pads and watching his fellow trainers, like the passionate Seamus McCann, light up the gym with generosity and patience.

But first, Gerry taps me gently on the arm. 'Are you sure you've got all you need, Don?'

He laughs when I remind him of the hundreds of meetings and interviews, of all the stories I've heard and all the fighters and former prisoners I've met through him.

'It's quite a story,' he says eventually, sounding wistful that the telling is almost over for him. 'We lived in desperate times. But we never stopped laughing or believing we would get away from the Troubles. We had it easy compared to most people. We had boxing . . . and boxing brought us together. The shadows were long, but boxing gave us sunshine.'

CHAPTER 1

Bloody Sunday

Derry, Monday 10 January 1972

Charlie Nash had just stepped away from the guillotine when news of the first death cut him deeply. In less than three weeks, on Bloody Sunday, his life would change for ever but this new wound left him bereft. He could hardly believe boxing had taken the life of his best friend, Martin Harkin, or Mousey as everyone called him. But he knew it must be true. His trainer Tommy Donnelly, and John Daly who also worked at the St Mary's Boxing Club in Derry, looked heartbroken. They would not have walked into Charlie's workplace, the Commercial Paper Company on Guildhall Street, without a serious need to talk to him.

The steel paper cutter stood silent and empty as Charlie stared at them. Two days after he and Mousey had fought on the same amateur bill at the Ulster championships in Ballymena, Charlie felt cold and still. But his mind reeled. Mousey Harkin was dead.

Charlie had won his fight that Saturday night and he had showered and made it back to ringside in time to see Mousey face Michael Doherty from County Donegal. Mousey should have been a lightweight, like Charlie, but he lacked discipline and ate too much. So he fought Doherty at welterweight.

Charlie had perched anxiously on his seat and, unlike his usual quietness, he'd kept shouting 'Come on, Mousey, c'mon!' throughout the first two rounds of a see-sawing battle. Mousey, aged 20, was a year younger than Charlie. He wasn't as skilful, and no one expected him to win Irish titles, but he was gritty. Charlie knew Mousey was in trouble because, between rounds, he kept spitting blood into the bucket in his corner. Tommy sponged his swollen face and Charlie saw how badly he was bleeding. Mousey suffered horribly from ulcers and being hit in the face made them worse.

'Come on, Mousey, c'mon!' Charlie cried as they began the third round. But the swelling around his jaw was obvious and Mousey winced whenever he was tagged. Midway through the third the referee led him to a neutral corner. A doctor looked into Mousey's ulcerous mouth. He touched the boxer's jaw tenderly before shaking his head. The fight was over.

Doherty raised his arm, and Mousey's head slumped as he was led back to his stool.

Charlie and Damien McDermott, a bristling little featherweight from St Mary's, tried to comfort Mousey in the dressing room. But their club-mate looked disconsolate. His mouth was too sore to talk. Tommy tied a scarf around Mousey's head to support his jaw.

'The doctor thinks you've broken it,' Tommy told Mousey. 'We need to get you to hospital.'

Charlie and Damien said goodbye to Mousey, not knowing they would never see him again.

Standing next to the printer's guillotine that Monday afternoon, Tommy explained how everything had gone wrong. Once his broken jaw had been confirmed, Mousey had been moved to the Ulster Hospital in Belfast, where complications set in and he slipped into unconsciousness. Mousey Harkin had died earlier that morning from a suspected blood clot that had formed on the brain after a blow to his head. Boxing had killed him.

Charlie's mind flooded with memories of playing football with Mousey and going to dances where they looked longingly at the girls. Mousey used to make everyone laugh and bring old pictures of fighters and showbands into the gym so that Joe Louis, Sugar Ray Robinson and glamorous girl singers gazed at them from the peeling walls of St Mary's.

At the end of that week, Charlie Nash and Damien McDermott were among the pallbearers who carried the coffin of Martin Harkin through the streets of Derry.

The River Foyle had long divided Derry into two communities, with the Catholic majority on one side and the Protestant minority across the water. Even its name was a source of contention. The British and most Loyalists in Northern Ireland called it Londonderry as a way of tying the city closer to the Union Jack and the United Kingdom. Some moderate Unionists and almost everyone else called it Derry – but the city had already changed.

In August 1969 one of the Troubles' earliest riots had happened 70 miles away from Belfast, in Derry. The Battle of the Bogside lasted for two days, and over a thousand people were injured. Catholics from the Bogside fought members of the Royal Ulster Constabulary and local Loyalist groups as long-standing grievances spilled over into violence.

Charlie had spent the first five years of his life on the Bogside, before his family settled elsewhere in Derry, in Creggan. During the riot, Bogside turned into a war zone as young Catholic men and women threw stones, rocks and petrol bombs against the truncheons, rubber bullets and CS gas of the RUC. Charlie was shocked to see the falling bodies and burning barricades – and the eerie sight of children wearing gas masks as they held bottles that they turned into flaring petrol bombs in an area called Free Derry.

It became difficult to breathe and see as the tear gas choked the streets. The initial surge of adrenaline and excitement soured – but the rioting spread to Belfast and escalated when Catholic houses were burnt down by Loyalist paramilitary groups.

In 1970 and '71 new civil rights marches in Derry demanded an end to the prejudice suffered by Catholics. Nearly 70 per cent of the city's population was Catholic, but Derry had been ruled by the Ulster Unionist Party, which was staunchly Protestant, since 1925. The Republicans argued that electoral boundaries and wards were rigged to keep the Unionists in power. They also presented clear evidence that jobs and houses were awarded to the Protestant minority over the Catholic majority.

At the same time, Derry was deprived of investment and became increasingly isolated. Rail routes into the city were limited or closed and the main motorways did not reach Derry – despite it being the second-largest city in Northern Ireland. A new university was built in nearby Coleraine, a mainly Protestant community, rather than in Derry. It felt as if opportunities and basic civil rights were being denied to Catholics in Derry – and so the marches intensified.

Charlie was neither combative nor political but he had felt his family's struggle for years. It had been even harder when they were younger because, to support 13 children, his parents had to work wherever they could find employment. For his father, Alexander, this meant that, as soon as work in the docks dried up and the potato season was over, he had to become a painter and decorator in England. He would be away for months and Charlie missed his dad badly – but the money he wired home helped keep the family alive. It became easier when his brothers and sisters, and Charlie himself, began to work.

Internment blackened the mood further. From 9 August 1971 until 5 December 1975, the British army would detain 1,981 people in Northern Ireland without trial. Of those interned, 1,874 were Catholics who lived in Nationalist areas while just 107 were Protestants from Unionist neighbourhoods.

In late 1971, the doors to the Nash family home were burst open in the middle of one night and soldiers marched up the stairs with their guns. Charlie's dad pushed one of the soldiers back down the stairs. He was lucky to get away with nothing more than shouted warnings. No one was taken that night from the Nash household.

Charlie preferred to think about boxing rather than the fierce injustices. He had fallen for the ring in 1959, when he was only eight and his dad had picked him out of his bunk bed to watch the boxing late at night. Floyd Patterson fought Ingemar Johansson in New York City and only Charlie was allowed to watch the boxing with his dad. Charlie was gripped by the grainy images screened from a smoky ring on the other side of the world.

A boxing ritual began. Whenever his dad had been out for a drink, he would weave back into the crammed house and call for Charlie. He would put his mitts up and encourage little Charlie to shadow-box as if he was the hulking Johansson and his boy was the smooth-moving Patterson. 'C'mon, Charlie,' his dad would say, 'use your jab. Have a wee pop, son.'

His father was great friends with Billy 'Spider' Kelly, the Derry featherweight who won the British and Commonwealth titles in the mid-1950s. Charlie would eventually surpass the great Spider and become European champion and fight for the world title in 1980. But, first, he joined the St Mary's Club on the Lower Creggan estate.

When Charlie entered the club in 1961, aged 11, it was an old farmyard barn with the only warmth coming from a few small gas heaters meant to take the edge off the perishing cold. At least it warmed up when, on a good night, 30 boys would skip and use the worn leather punch bags that dangled from iron hooks before they took turns to spar in the ring.

Charlie soon established himself as the best fighter in the club and he won Ulster Junior titles and, eventually, the Ulster Seniors in 1969. A year later, in March 1970, Charlie won the Irish lightweight title in Dublin. He had become the first boxer from Derry to win a National amateur title.

Boxing made Charlie Nash the most famous man in Derry. Less than two years later, boxing had cost Mousey Harkin his life.

As he helped lower the coffin of his best friend into the grave, Charlie's tears fell onto the freshly dug earth. He was not sure he would ever want to fight again.

Derry was, traditionally, a football city. Yet even the sporting landscape shifted with the advent of the Troubles. In mid-August 1969 an Ulster Cup tie between Derry City and Crusaders, a Belfast team with a staunch Protestant fanbase, had been cancelled. The Irish League, based in the North, concluded that Derry's home ground of Brandywell, located in a fiercely Nationalist area of the city where the riots had occurred, was far too dangerous.

A few weeks later, on 28 August 1969, Derry City's star striker, Lynn Porter, announced his retirement. He had received a death threat and the 23-year-old told the *Belfast Telegraph* that, 'on at least two occasions, attempts have been made to assault me'. Porter would be the first, and far from the last, sportsman to be threatened during the Troubles.

Even after Derry City were allowed to stage home matches again, the club was so embedded in the community that political and social causes took precedence over football. They cancelled their home game against Crusaders on 19 August 1971 so that Brandywell could be used for a rally calling for civil disobedience against the Protestant-dominated Stormont parliament. Seven thousand people attended the rally led by John Hume. It made a striking change because football crowds at Brandywell had shrunk from a 5,000 average to a miserable 200 hardy souls who still supported Derry City at most home games in 1971.

Football was about to fade away for the next painful decade, as Brandywell became a no-go area to all other clubs in the Irish League. Riots had broken out after a teenager was run down and killed by an army vehicle and gunmen had fired at soldiers from inside the football ground. It was hard to believe that the very next day, 11 September 1971, Derry City played at home against Ballymena United – from the constituency of Ian Paisley, the vitriolic Protestant preacher and Loyalist leader. The Ballymena team bus was burnt by rioters.

Derry City were ordered by the league to play all their future home matches in Coleraine. Supporters stayed away and the club were soon forced to disband for 12 years before they re-emerged to play in the Republic of Ireland league.

Boxing avoided becoming a flashpoint for violence among its followers. Unlike football, where tribal divisions ran deep among its supporters, boxing fans generally respected the courage of any fighter who stepped into the ring. The sight of two fighters trading blows in a fair contest seemed uplifting compared to the skirmishes between Republican rioters and British soldiers. Boxing was about to move closer to the troubled heart of life in Derry.

Willie Nash was just 19 and, among 13 brothers and sisters, closest in age and character to Charlie. He was also a boxer at St Mary's, where they called him Stiff. It was an affectionate name but also an accurate indication of his lack of movement and guile in the ring. Charlie was a skilful boxer, a southpaw with slick moves, but Willie was the banger. He was a much harder puncher than Charlie, and a bigger fighter too – a natural and strong welterweight.

Charlie believed his brother was good enough to fight for Ulster Senior titles. But Willie had found a job at the docks with their dad and, after work, he preferred going out for a drink rather than sweating and aching some more at the St Mary's gym.

Willie didn't talk much but he smiled easily and danced crazily. Every Saturday night there was a dance at St Mary's and Willie made sure Charlie joined him. Even though his big brother faced a long training run in the morning, Willie insisted he come to the dance. They always ended up having a good night as Charlie sat and watched, or spoke to the people crowding around him to talk boxing, while Willie bopped away on the dance floor.

After Mousey died they had closed the boxing club for a few weeks. None of the St Mary's boys were in the mood to throw punches. Charlie could not escape so easily. Two weeks after Mousey's final fight, he represented Ireland in Cardiff. Charlie suffered a cut over his left eye but he outpointed a stocky Welshman without feeling his usual calm in the ring.

Willie helped Charlie forget about boxing on his return. They went to buy new suits for their brother James's wedding to Margaret Friel on Saturday 29 January. James, or 'Banty' as they called him, depended on them – especially on Charlie as his best man. Charlie worried that his eye would make him look like a thug but Willie reassured him. Banty wanted him as his best man and no cut eye could get in the way of a great time.

In the week of the wedding, Charlie became more cheerful. He started thinking positively about boxing again. After they reopened St Mary's, Tommy Donnelly asked Damien McDermott whether he felt ready for the Irish Junior championships in Dublin that weekend.

'I don't mind fighting,' Damien said. 'But I've put on a lot of weight.'

Tommy got out the scales and, stripped to his trunks, Damien weighed eight stone three. Rather than piling on the pounds he had lost half a stone. Charlie knew it was another consequence of Mousey's death.

'I could box at bantamweight,' Damien said.

As they discussed Damien's prospects at the lighter weight, Charlie felt an urge to support his friend in Dublin.

'What about Banty's wedding?' Damien asked.

Charlie promised to ask Banty if he could leave the reception straight after he had done his best-man duties. They all knew his speech would be short and sincere. He would not be rambling or telling bawdy jokes.

Banty, of course, knew how much Charlie loved boxing. 'Make

your speech,' Banty said, cuffing his brother lightly on the arm. 'And then enjoy the boxing. Leave the dancing to Willie ...'

Charlie was far more nervous standing up to make his wedding speech than he had ever felt when ducking through the ropes to fight. He stroked his thick black moustache anxiously as the room fell silent, apart from a couple of raucous cries from his older brothers to take off his dark glasses. Charlie knew it would be rude to talk about Banty and his new bride while wearing shades and so he slipped them into his suit pocket. His black eye was visible then.

Willie winked at him encouragingly. Charlie managed a smile and tugged at his moustache one last time for luck. It was strange how confident he felt as a boxer when the punches flew with easy grace and he instinctively cut off the corners of a ring. It was a contradiction that Charlie was so eloquent in a dangerous language whereas, in real life, he was neither a smooth nor a garrulous talker. But he had been interviewed often about boxing on television and by newspapermen. It was easier to talk in front of just 60 family members and friends about Banty and Margaret.

He felt his family willing him on – Willie most of all – and he only choked up when mentioning their mother, Bridie, in hospital. She was the only family member missing from the celebrations and Charlie spoke of how seriously ill she had been since suffering a heart attack. But he regained his composure and felt proud to have done a decent job. He felt happy too as he watched his family and friends drinking and dancing once he had sat down in relief. Willie was back on the dance floor and, watching him, Charlie wished his brother could transfer some of those fluid movements to the ring. Stiff Nash would be some fighter then.

Banty shook Charlie's hand, thanked him for everything and reminded him to catch the three o'clock bus to Dublin. 'Away you go, Charlie,' Banty said. 'We'll be fine here.'

*

Damien McDermott and Charlie Nash shared much in common. As well as living close to each other in Creggan, and boxing for St Mary's, they both came from large families. They each had eight sisters and four brothers. Charlie had long since won more boxing titles than he had siblings, and now Damien followed his lead.

In Dublin, on Saturday 29 January 1972, he won his first All-Ireland National title. Supported by Charlie, who made it to ringside in time from Banty's wedding, Damien McDermott became Ireland's Junior bantamweight champion. He also won the best boxer of the night and, even though none of them drank, the St Mary's contingent were giddy with euphoria.

Amid his grief over Mousey Harkin's death, that sweet night made Charlie happy again. That contentment continued into the next day as, on the Sunday afternoon, he and Damien sat in the back of Tommy's car. The trainer was driving and Kevin McCall, the chairman of St Mary's Youth, was in the passenger seat. They chatted happily about Damien's big win and Charlie boxing in the Munich Olympics that summer. Ireland would be coached by Gerry Storey of the Holy Family. They all admired and liked Gerry – whom they agreed, after seeing him again in Dublin, was one of the nicest men they had ever met.

Sitting in the back of that car, they had no idea their home city was about to be engulfed by death.

Derry, Sunday 30 January 1972

A perfect blue sky lit up a cold day. The grey cloud that usually cloaked Derry in winter had retreated and there was excitement as the crowds gathered. The latest march against internment was expected to draw thousands of protesters who would walk from Creggan, where the Nash family lived, to the Guildhall Square in the centre of Derry. Bernadette Devlin, the 24-year-old MP and Republican, would address the crowd.

Willie liked the marches. He enjoyed being in a cheerful throng and his brother Eddie and father, Alexander, would march with him. The Nash family was politically moderate – and the two eldest siblings, Paddy and Eddie, even had links with the army. Paddy had joined the British army and he was based in England as a bandmaster. Eddie had been a part-time member of the army in Enniskillen – and had only left in 1969 when the Troubles began to simmer. He now wanted to walk with Willie and his dad to protest, quietly and calmly, against internment on that beautiful Sunday.

Willie wore his wedding suit again, without a tie, as he liked looking dapper. At Bishop's Field on the Creggan estate, the crowd had swelled to around 15,000 by early afternoon. The mood was buoyant, despite the clatter of a lone army helicopter in the sky, as the march began. They came from all walks of life, driven by a determination to make their voices heard because many men from Derry had been detained, without trial, in internment camps.

The organisers moved through the crowd, urging restraint because they had just learnt the security forces would prevent them entering the city centre. They would be re-routed to Free Derry Corner. People moved down Creggan Street and the mood became defiant and sombre. A truck led the way, a Civil Rights Association banner draped across its top, while community leaders directed the marchers with megaphones. Pale sunshine streamed across Derry.

Members of the 1st Battalion Parachute Regiment were primed outside the Presbyterian Church of Great James Street. They were a third of a mile from the barricades on William Street. This was the army's crack unit, battle-hardened paras who had done tours of Aden on the Arabian Peninsula. They had arrived from Belfast that morning and were stained by their involvement in the Ballymurphy Massacre a few weeks earlier. Their 2nd Battalion had taken charge of internment procedures and ten people had died. Since then the 1st Battalion had been tested by the sustained rioting that had spread across Belfast.

Colonel Derek Wilford, their commanding officer, reminded

them that rioters breaching the barriers on William Street were to be arrested. They were to clamp down on any dissent – just as they had done the previous weekend when using CS gas and rubber bullets on the beach to break up a smaller group of civil rights marchers at Magilligan Strand in Limavady, 25 miles away. Those protesters had stopped outside a new internment camp at Magilligan and the paras were brutal. After a few stones had been thrown at the camp, and some marchers tried to push past the barbed wire, the 1st Battalion fired rubber bullets at close range and also made repeated baton charges. Some of the paras had to be restrained by their senior officers.

John Hume, the SDLP leader who eventually won the Nobel Peace Prize, told Lord Saville and the second Bloody Sunday inquiry in 2002 he had avoided going into Derry that fateful afternoon because he had seen the methods of the paratroopers while he led the meeting at Magilligan Strand.

'If they were firing rubber bullets and gas on a beach,' Hume said, 'I thought, "Good Lord, what would they do on the streets of a town, and what trouble would they cause?"'

Thousands more joined the throng that had left Creggan. A snaking river opened up into a far wider sea of people estimated to be as large as 20,000. They marched until the leading group was brought to a halt on the corner of William and Rossville Streets just over a mile from where they had started. Barrier 14 blocked the entrance to William Street. The protesters were directed down Rossville Street towards Free Derry Corner.

Most people followed the diversion but some younger men peeled away from the crowd. Rather than turning away from the barrier, they moved towards it, their voices growing louder and their faces becoming flushed with excitement. A few bent down to pick up stones and bricks. The first missiles were hurled against a darkening sky at five minutes to four and were deflected by the Perspex shields of the crouching soldiers.

Despite the hiss of tear gas, more joined the push towards the barricades while the vast waves surged on behind them towards the new route past the Rossville Flats. As yet more missiles sailed through the choking air, two soldiers in the 1st Battalion tensed. Their rifles were cocked and trained on two figures.

The soldiers insisted that 15-year-old Damien Donaghy held a black object that resembled a nail bomb as he and John Johnston, aged 55, kept walking towards Barrier 14. Johnston, who was not even on the march, was on his way to visit a friend in Glenfada Park. Soldiers A and B, as they were tagged in the inquest, both fired. Donaghy was hit in the thigh and fell instantly. Johnston was also brought down. Both were alive – but Johnston never recovered and died a few months later. The Saville Inquiry, published 38 years later, in 2010, confirmed that neither Donaghy nor Johnston had been carrying a weapon.

A returning gunshot came from the direction of either the Rossville Flats or Columbcille Court. None of the soldiers were hurt by that single bullet, which instead hit a drainpipe running down the side of the Presbyterian Church. It was then that Wilford sent the 1 Para Support Company into the Bogside, using Saracens – or Sixers, as the large armoured vehicles were also called – while his 1st Battalion moved through the streets on foot. Running soldiers and the Sixers rumbled down Rossville Street, causing the marchers ahead of them to scatter.

The Sixers and the paras bore down ominously on everyone, young and old, angry protesters and peaceful marchers. The faceless sea parted into waves of frightened people. A young man and a woman were knocked to the ground by a Saracen.

Further rioting broke out and soldiers climbed out of the Sixers deep into the Bogside. They hunted down anyone within catching distance. Rubber bullets and batons rained down on innocent people. Others ran away in terror.

Father Edward Daly, a priest from Derry, was among those fleeing the paras. His black coat flew behind him as he headed towards the Rossville Flats in search of cover. His jagged breath fell from him as he tried to escape the car park area where more and more paras peeled out of their Sixers. The car park seemed unending as he ran. His attention was only diverted by the nervous laughter of a teenage boy, amused to see a priest running at full tilt.

John Duddy, or Jackie as everyone called him, was a friend of Charlie and Willie Nash, and of Damien McDermott, too. Jackie was a boxer at the Long Tower gym and he came from a Derry family steeped in boxing. Decades later his nephew John Duddy would become a respected pro fighter in New York. In January 1972, Jackie Duddy was only 17. Despite being a very good amateur boxer, Jackie had a cherubic face. Father Daly would say later that he looked like he was 12 rather than 17. He was laughing and running, looking across at Father Daly, when a bullet caught him in the chest as he entered the courtyard of Rossville Flats.

Jackie went down, as if knocked cold in the ring.

There was a brief hush in the courtyard as the gunfire stopped. Father Daly crouched over Jackie. 'Am I going to die?' Jackie asked softly. The priest could see how badly the boy was bleeding but he shook his head. 'No,' he said.

Father Daly knelt over the prone body of Jackie, squeezing his hand. Another man crouched down to join them and the priest began to pray. It felt important to administer the last rites to an innocent boy.

The courtyard vigil was broken by the eerie whine of more bullets flying over their heads and ricocheting against the opposite wall. Jackie's eyes were now closed. 'Look, son,' Father Daly said desperately, 'we've got to get you out.'

Another two men and a woman came ducking down to help. As they scooped up Jackie's body, Father Daly pulled out a white handkerchief. He wanted it to look like a flag of peace so they would be spared further shooting. A photographer captured an image which would be seen around the world. It represented the innocence and carnage of Bloody Sunday. In this single frame a dead boy was carried by frightened people led by a priest waving a small white hankie as he crouched and weaved against the threat of being shot in cold blood.

They reached Waterloo Street and finally stopped. Coats were laid carefully on the ground so that they could provide a resting place for Jackie Duddy. A local woman, Mrs McCloskey, covered the body with an eiderdown while they waited for an ambulance. There had been more casualties and deaths by then.

Margaret Deery, 38, was shot and injured in the car park – as were Michael Bradley, 22, and Michael Bridge, 25. After he had watched Jackie Duddy being gunned down, Bridge, who had apparently thrown stones at the soldiers manning Barrier 14, picked up half a brick. He held it in his right hand as, approaching the barrier, he screamed: 'Go ahead and shoot me too.' He was shot – in the leg.

Paddy Doherty, a 31-year-old construction worker and a married father of six children, was next. He was shot in the behind as he crawled along the ground, trying to avoid being hit as he aimed to reach safety behind the Rossville Flats. The bullet travelled up into his back and came out through his chest. Doherty, bleeding heavily, knew he was dying. Terrorised people, huddling together out of the line of fire, heard him cry out.

'I don't want to die alone,' he shouted. 'Somebody help me. God help me.'

It was a lonely, terrible sound and, as Geraldine Richmond told the inquest, 'I wanted to help him but I couldn't move. I was too scared.'

Meanwhile Hugh Gilmour, 17 like Jackie Duddy, was shot while running away from soldiers and towards a barricade on Rossville Street. 'I'm hit, I'm hit,' the teenager shouted before he was lifted to the barricade by other ordinary people. They would not be able to save him.

Doherty was near death, and still whimpering. One man could not bear the terrible sound. Barney McGuigan, a 41-year-old husband and former foreman, stood up. 'I'm coming,' he said softly to the dying man. Other people watched in awe as, in the manner of Father Daly, McGuigan held a white handkerchief. He soon raised both hands in surrender, the handkerchief rippling above him. To make himself even more visible, and to show the soldiers he posed no threat as he went to help a dying man, he shouted: 'Don't shoot. Don't shoot.' He took a step forward, and then another.

A 19-year-old member of the ambulance corps watched in horror. At the inquest she remembered how, 'Seconds later Mr McGuigan was shot in the head and landed in my lap at the alley-way at Rossville Street Flats. I could do nothing but weep. He was definitely dead.'

Paddy Doherty was also dead. Soldier F, who killed him, would tell the inquest that he thought Doherty was carrying a pistol. But no weapon was found either on or near his body.

James Wray, 22, Michael Kelly, 17, William McKinney, 27, Gerard McKinney, 35, Kevin McElhinney, 17, and Gerald Donaghey, 17, were all killed by paratroopers in the next ten minutes. Among the 14 people who eventually died on Bloody Sunday, only the youngest, Donaghey, was a member of the IRA. The other 13 boys and men were innocent civilians.

A tribute paid to William McKinney, a printer, in the *Derry Journal* the following week was as typical as it was poignant: 'Willie was not a stone-thrower, a bomber or a gunman. He had gone to the civil rights march in the role of amateur photographer. He was a printer by trade, and an outstanding craftsman. The layout of some of the reports and advertisements in this very issue, which records his untimely death, bear testimony to his professional ability. He was a quiet, pleasant, hard-working young man, helpful to all who were privileged to be associated with him. He was engaged to be married. He had the expectancy of a long and happy life.'

It was proved later that, against a single gunshot, which hit a drainpipe, 21 British paratroopers and soldiers fired 108 rounds of bullets. The British army, and politicians in Westminster, would claim that most of the dead were Republican gunmen and bombers, and that their soldiers had come under fire from nail bombs. All these allegations were shown to be lies decades later at the exhaustive Saville Inquiry.

Three other men died in Derry on Bloody Sunday. They were shot within less than a minute of each other at the rubble barricade on Rossville Street. It was here that 17-year-old Hugh Gilmour lay dying when John Young, also 17, and William Nash, 19, rose up to try to help.

Willie and Eddie Nash and their father had been forced to seek refuge from the gunfire of the 1st Battalion. They seemed safe but Willie and John Young, another St Mary's boy, went to try to help Gilmour and others who lay injured.

John was killed by a single shot to the head. Willie was struck in the chest on Rossville Street.

Eddie, his father Alexander and 20-year-old Michael McDaid all rushed towards Willie. Michael was shot in the face, dying instantly, while Alexander was hit in the arm. He slumped down next to Willie. Alexander was only injured, but the pain was excruciating.

Gunfire and the sound of people crying out echoed around them in the walled city. There were more calls for help but it was too late. Willie Nash was already dead.

The happy mood quietened as Charlie and Damien crossed the border into Northern Ireland in the back of Tommy Donnelly's car. Traffic thickened as army patrols stopped them every 30 minutes. Each time they came closer to home the questions and searches intensified. At least they had their boxing kit in the boot, and Damien's trophies on the back seat, to prove their reasons for being in Dublin.

Tensions were heightened whenever there were civil rights

marches, but this felt different. It seemed ominous and persistent. Tommy switched on the car radio. The news shocked them. If they were unsurprised to hear that there had been rioting, they were chilled when the newsreader reported 'a number of fatalities' in Derry. They listened in silence as that unspecified number grew. Three dead became four, and then five and on until there were reports that 'at least ten people' had been killed.

As they entered Derry they faced another patrol. Army rifles pointed in their direction as soldiers questioned them before finally waving the car through. In the late-afternoon gloom, they slowed at a set of traffic lights. Tommy was in the inside lane and he rolled down his window when he recognised the man waving to him in the adjoining car. Hughie Bell, the butcher, looked agitated.

'Hello, Hughie,' Tommy said. 'What's been happening?'

Hughie looked straight at Tommy, seemingly unaware of Charlie's presence. 'There's been a shooting,' Hughie shouted. 'I think they shot Stiff Nash and wee John Young.'

Damien saw Charlie wince as if he had been struck hard across the face.

'Are you sure?' Tommy shouted.

The butcher nodded, his normally ruddy face looking drawn and grim. They could not talk any longer because the lights had turned green and there was a Saracen across the road, with soldiers watching them.

'Charlie,' Tommy said softly, 'do you want me to get you home first?'

Charlie shook his head. They had to pass Kevin and Damien's streets in Lower Creggan before reaching the Nash family home in Upper Creggan. Kevin and Damien both got out and said goodbye to Charlie. He replied in a daze.

As Tommy turned the corner they saw a small crowd outside Charlie's home. Around 20 people, mostly neighbours, had gathered in the street. Charlie felt cold on the inside and his mouth was dry. But he shook his head when Tommy offered to come in with him. He needed to find out for himself.

'We think Willie and your father have been shot,' someone told Charlie. But no one could answer the 'Where?' and the 'Why?' questions that tumbled through Charlie. There was only confusion.

A neighbour took him aside. 'Charlie, do you want to go to the hospital?'

Charlie nodded. 'I need to see what's happening,' he said. 'And I want to see Mum, too.'

The hospital entrance swarmed with the RUC and soldiers. 'What are you here for?' a soldier asked.

'People are saying my brother and my father were shot today,' Charlie said.

'What are their names?'

'Alexander Nash is my father. My brother is Willie Nash.'

Another squaddie ran his finger down a list. 'Nash, Alexander?' he eventually said.

'Yes,' Charlie said.

'Go into the hospital reception,' the soldier said. 'They'll tell you his ward number.'

'And William Nash?'

The soldier looked down at his paper again and shook his head. He turned the sheet and studied a shorter list. He looked up at Charlie, his expression unchanging. 'Come with me.'

Charlie hesitated. 'Where are we going?'

'You can check at the morgue,' the soldier said, his voice as blank as his face.

Charlie and the soldier walked down into the basement. Terrible thoughts crowded Charlie's mind, but he hoped a mistake had been made. Just 26 hours earlier he and Willie had been at Banty's wedding.

Their footsteps echoed down a corridor. A policeman stood at the entrance to the morgue. The soldier nodded at him and the policeman, reluctantly, moved a few inches so that Charlie could walk past him and into the morgue.

He was shown into a room where lines of bodies were stretched out on the floor. The corpses were covered by sheets.

'Who are you looking for?' an orderly asked him.

'My brother . . . William Nash,' Charlie said.

The first sheet was lifted, and then the second, third, fourth and fifth sheets. Charlie looked down into faces of the dead boys and men. He knew the first five people.

William McKinney, the printer, whose brother Mickey had played in the same football team as Charlie at St Mary's.

Hugh Gilmour, a boy Charlie knew so well. Charlie had played football with Hugh and his brothers. He was friends with all the Gilmour family.

Jackie Duddy, the gentle and amusing boy Charlie had watched box so often. They had been friends and Charlie thought Jackie was a fine, strong boxer.

Michael McDaid was barely recognisable after being shot, but Charlie had known him too.

John Young, another friend, had lived around the corner. Charlie had played football with him.

At each drawing back of a new sheet, the mortuary officer looked at Charlie. The boxer shook his head each time. It was not Willie.

When the sixth sheet was taken away, Charlie made a muffled cry.

Willie lay beneath the sheet. Charlie looked down at the bloody mess of Willie's chest. There was so much blood beneath his shirt and suit.

Charlie knelt down. He gently touched Willie on the arm and then his fingers brushed his brother's face. He rose to his feet, his face wet with tears.

'That's him?' he was asked.

'Yes,' Charlie said. The soldier standing near the door with his gun smiled at him – a cruel, mocking grin.

Charlie walked to the door. The soldier stepped forward and blocked Charlie's path. He kept smiling. Charlie, with a cry, pushed the soldier and made him stagger back.

Two policemen grabbed Charlie, but the boxer had no intention of hitting the soldier. He just wanted to escape, and to find his parents in the hospital.

Slowly, he was led away, leaving the bodies of his brother and their friends in the silence of the morgue. Charlie knew that life would never be the same again. The world had darkened for ever.

CHAPTER 2

Two Bombs

Creggan, Derry, Wednesday 2 February 1972

The weather was desperate that day. Rain fell across Derry all afternoon and the cold seeped into the bones of the thousands watching the slow march of the cortège. Black umbrellas shrouded the funeral of 11 victims of Bloody Sunday while matching black flags fluttered from the upstairs windows of ordinary family homes. The sound of crying could be heard above the wind that bit into the damp, ashen faces of the mourners.

Damien McDermott, who knew nearly all of the victims and had been friends with his fellow boxers William Nash and Jackie Duddy, felt just as desperate on the inside. He should have been celebrating his first Irish title, won four days earlier, but he was reeling like the rest of Derry. Unsettling images lingered in his head.

He had spoken to the sister of John Young, a fellow St Mary's Club boy, dead at the age of 17. She told Damien how, just as Charlie Nash had identified the body of Willie, she had gone to the morgue on Sunday evening to find John.

At first, she just saw sheet-covered bodies. One was unlike the others. Two feet protruded from under the sheet. They wore socks.

But the shoes were gone. Some of the bodies had been dragged through the streets and perhaps the shoes had fallen off. Two hours after the massacre, John's sister could imagine a lonely pair of shoes still lying in the street, on their side, never to be worn again. But she was certain it could not be her brother's shoes.

'That's not him,' she said softly. 'That's not our John.'

'How do you know?' she was asked.

'His socks,' John's sister said. She pointed to the right sock. 'That one has a hole in it. So it can't be John.'

John was a dapper wee boy. He liked to dress well and he even knew a tailor who, as a favour, mended any clothes that were beyond his mother's needlework.

'He wouldn't wear socks with a hole in them,' his sister said defiantly.

Yet, as the orderly persisted and moved to pull back the sheet from the face of the body, she suddenly knew she had been wrong. John must have been unusually careless when he pulled those socks on that morning. He would have seen the hole, but he was in such a rush to join his friends on the march. His sock could be darned another day.

John's sister put a hand to her mouth as she watched the sheet being lifted. She could not look away.

On the morning of the funeral, she looked at Damien and her eyes swam with tears. 'It was John,' she said. The sight of his big toe poking out of the hole in his sock was unbearably sad.

Damien shivered. He was already freezing, having no spare money to buy a heavy overcoat, but a deeper cold ran through him when he saw his friend. Charlie looked haunted as he helped carry Willie's coffin. His 11 brothers and sisters all took turns to act as pallbearers as they walked with the rain-spattered pine coffin on their shoulders, their arms wrapped around each other. Charlie cut a ghostly figure in the swirling drizzle as they left St Mary's Cathedral in Creggan and headed down to the graveyard.

The crowd lining both sides of the street was quiet. Even

hundreds of young men, who had scaled the rooftops to secure a better view of the funeral march, stayed respectfully silent.

There had been no respect, for the dead or the truth, among British politicians in Westminster. Two days earlier Reginald Maudling, the Home Secretary, had made a statement to the House of Commons in response to Bloody Sunday. 'The army returned the fire directed at them with aimed shots and inflicted a number of casualties on those attacking them with firearms and bombs,' Maudling said. 'Of the 13 men killed, four were on the security force's wanted list . . . one man had four nail bombs in his pocket . . . throughout the fighting that ensued, the army fired only at identified targets, at attacking gunmen and bombers. The troops came under indiscriminate firing.'

Maudling announced that an inquiry would be led by Lord Chief Justice John Widgery. Yet any chance of a detailed and balanced investigation had been ruined by the secret memo, uncovered years later, in which Prime Minister Edward Heath reminded Widgery to remember that 'we are in Northern Ireland fighting not only a military war but a propaganda war'.

The truth was less important to the British government than covering up the murderous work of the 1st Battalion. Widgery was instructed to work speedily so that the catastrophe would be consigned to history and rebellion in Northern Ireland could be quashed.

Bernadette Devlin, who had travelled overnight from Derry, having been on the march, was furious when she was denied the chance to address Maudling's deceit as an independent Member of Parliament on the Monday. The speaker of the House, Selwyn Lloyd, refused to acknowledge her persistent requests to be allowed the floor, despite parliamentary convention making it mandatory that any MP who had witnessed an incident under discussion had the right to make a statement. Devlin crossed the floor and slapped Maudling across the face.

Charlie Nash, as a boxer, had no inclination to lift his hand to anyone outside the ring. He had initially wanted to strike the mocking soldier who had blocked him and grinned maliciously in the morgue. But Charlie was a gentle man and, rather than harbouring venom towards the British army, he turned his attention to his parents in hospital. His mother was still seriously ill and his father would need months to recover from his gunshot wound. Charlie knew, however, that they would never get over the loss of their son.

Killing someone else in retribution made no sense – even though the IRA had already paid him a visit. It was done with due solemnity, and the sympathy felt for the Nash family was obvious, but towards the end of their meeting they asked Charlie if he would like to join them. They could do with his fighting spirit, and status in Derry, to intensify their resistance. It was time that they struck back hard while refusing to bow down to the Brits or internment and injustice.

Charlie listened silently and so they asked him directly. Would he join the IRA?

'No,' Charlie said firmly.

They tried again, urging him that fighting back was the only way they would ever get the soldiers off their streets. It was the only way they would ever force through the dream of a united Ireland. It was the only way they would stop more atrocities like Bloody Sunday.

Charlie shook his head. He was a fighter in the ring and nowhere else. How could he condone more bloodshed and carnage? There had to be a different way to bring people together.

He stood up. There was nothing more to say. They could tell he was not for turning and so they left quickly.

Of course the IRA were at the joint funerals. Charlie did not see them but he knew, just as he knew that thousands of young men across Derry, Belfast and all over the North had taken a different approach to him. The paratroopers' killing spree in Derry, and the British government's blatant lying, had provided the IRA with their most powerful weapon of recruitment. The ranks would soon be swollen with new Republican soldiers. War would erupt with devastating consequences for everyone. The British army, and their Loyalist supporters in Northern Ireland, would soon feel the pain of Derry on that funeral day.

Charlie Nash felt numb as he stood at the graveside. The graves had been dug one by one and, at the sound of each new name, another coffin would disappear into the wet earth as prayers were said aloud to the huddled masses. The name of William Nash rang out in the cemetery. Charlie kept his head down, avoiding the tear-streaked faces. Alongside his brothers, with his sisters gathered around them, he helped lift the body of Willie one last time. The coffin hovered above the hole and then, in an almost stately gesture, the Nash boys lowered their brother into the ground.

It was hardest when they watched the grave being filled. The chink of spades and the soft sound of soil being scooped up and sifted on metal would be followed by a thud of fresh earth hitting the pine coffin. It kept raining as they covered Willie, the grave swallowing him up.

The previously obscure name of Derry rang around the world. In Britain, politicians, broadcasters and newspapers insisted on still calling a now-famous town Londonderry, but a more powerful truth was that Bloody Sunday had exposed the darker strains of prejudice and brutality in Northern Ireland. Bernadette Devlin compared Derry to Sharpeville – the South African township where, in 1960, police had opened fire on crowds protesting against one of the central tenets of apartheid and killed 69 people. South Africa was never the same again as the fires of resistance smouldered. Bloody Sunday in Derry would have a similar impact in Northern Ireland.

Simon Winchester, *The Guardian*'s Northern Ireland correspondent, echoed Devlin. 'The tragic and inevitable doomsday situation which has been universally forecast for Northern Ireland arrived in

Londonderry yesterday afternoon when soldiers firing into a large crowd of civil rights demonstrators, shot and killed 13 civilians,' Winchester wrote on 31 January after he had witnessed the mayhem. 'After the shooting, which lasted for about 25 minutes in and around the Rossville Flats of Bogside, the streets had all the appearance of the aftermath of Sharpeville. Where, only moments before, thousands of men and women had been milling around, drifting slowly towards a protest meeting to be held at Free Derry Corner, there was only a handful of bleeding bodies, some lying still, others moving with pain, on the white concrete square. The army's official explanation for the killing was that their troops had fired in response to a number of snipers who had opened up on them from below the flats. But those of us at the meeting heard only one shot before the soldiers opened up with their high-velocity rifles.'

Anger hardened in Dublin. On a rain-sodden evening, not many hours after the Bloody Sunday funerals and for a second night in succession, a large crowd gathered outside the British embassy. All shops, offices, banks, schools and factories had been closed. The day of mourning had been observed across Dublin and, as dusk fell, the rain lashed down. Dozens of people carried black flags and tricolours while a band played the 'Dead March' by Handel. Two thousand people could not be contained by 200 policemen at Merrion Square, where the embassy was located, and the mood turned ugly.

Three coffins draped in black were placed on the embassy steps, two Union Jacks were burnt, and an effigy of a British soldier was set on fire. Petrol bombs were lit and thrown at the embassy. Windows were shattered and, as the flames rose inside the building, a lone woman's song became a communal chant of 'Burn! Burn! Burn!'

There was a shouted warning that a gelignite bomb was about to be launched. The protesters ducked down and then, seconds later, the incendiary device exploded inside the embassy.

The fire brigade eventually arrived but, with their hoses being cut by the protesters, there was little chance of dousing the flames. The British embassy burnt to the ground. It was yet another symbol of the blazing spread of the Troubles.

New Lodge, Belfast, Saturday 5 February 1972

The silence finally broke that night. A few hours before the icy blackness became a murky dawn, a procession of Saracen armoured vehicles rumbled into the New Lodge in north Belfast. In Republican territory, filled with Catholic people living in red-bricked rows of small terraced houses, the British army were back in the dead of night.

Snoring softly in bed next to his wife Belle, Gerry Storey slept peacefully. After a day working at the docks and an evening training boys at the Holy Family Boxing Club, Gerry had slipped into sleep as soon as he kissed Belle and turned over. He slumbered through the army's arrival until the banging of the bin lids woke him. The sound of one woman crouched outside her front door as she crashed the top of a dustbin down on the rain-blackened concrete made him sit up. In that dreamy state between sleep and wakefulness, in a blur of confusion and disquiet, Gerry pictured her in his head.

It was usually one of the youngest wives who ran out first, pulling a dressing gown around her as she brandished the bin lid. Hunched down in her slippers, pale legs bare in the fierce cold, she stared up defiantly at the soldiers jumping down from the green Saracens, their rifles glinting. Her hand pumped the lid up and down, one metallic echo after another as, without a word, she let everyone in their street and beyond know: 'The Brits are here, the Brits are here ...'

Gerry sank back onto his pillow, murmuring a few words to Belle before she checked on the kids. They had three boys – Gerry Jr, Sam and Martin – and a girl, wee Jacqueline, who was still only five. Their first child, Rosanne, had been stillborn. Belle was strong but she and Gerry would never quite get over the loss of their eldest girl. They would think of Rosanne at the strangest times – even amid another raid and the banging of the lids.

The first woman would not be alone for long. Her drumming soon reverberated around the neighbourhood. Four, five, six and then a dozen women on their street and in the surrounding roads kicked up an almighty racket. The whole of New Lodge would be awake and the gunmen among them could find a safer place to stash their weapons.

Gerry respected the women's fiery spark. His years in boxing had honed his instincts and cleared his mind of poison. He dismissed sectarianism and abhorred violence. Gerry believed instead in discipline and courage – and these qualities defined the fighters he admired most. They also shaped these ordinary women as they tried to protect their families.

Operation Demetrius, the name given to the British government's strategy of internment that had begun in August 1971, carried distressing sounds – thrumming Saracens, shouting soldiers, kicked-in doors, screaming people and the clattering dustbins.

At the outset, from the evening of 9 August to the morning of 11 August 1971, ten people had been killed by the British army's Parachute Regiment in Ballymurphy, west Belfast. Soldiers from 2nd Battalion, the Parachute Regiment, had taken 18 Catholic men from their homes and brought them to a community centre, the Henry Taggart Memorial Hall. The men were questioned and beaten and questioned again before being taken to an internment barracks. When hostilities between Republicans in Ballymurphy and Loyalists from neighbouring Springmartin erupted, the paratroopers moved back in. Nine men and one woman were killed.

Nearly six months later, in New Lodge, British soldiers went to work in the wake of the riots that had spread since Bloody Sunday. There was a crackdown on paramilitary activity. But innocent men were also detained because they were under suspicion as Catholics living alongside some militant Republicans.

Gerry had nothing to hide. He could lie in the dark and listen to the warning bins. They reminded him of the wailing sirens and a different war. They also conjured up memories of his mother and how she had taught him to believe they would always be safe.

'We walk with the angels,' his mum had promised him. In December 1971, Gerry retained that same calm certainty that he and his family would be safe.

Thirty years before, on the night of his fourth birthday, the Luftwaffe had bombed Belfast for the first time. On 7 April 1941, 800 bombs fell on an unprepared city, killing 13 people. Twelve of those deaths occurred in the shipyards: the Nazis targeted the docks because 35,000 men worked for Harland and Wolff building destroyers, aircraft carriers and mine sweepers. Miles away, little Gerry's home was rattled to the core as doors flew off their hinges, window frames collapsed and shattered glass blew into the rooms.

His mother, Ellen, or Nelly as everyone called her, rushed the children – Elizabeth, Bobby, Mary and Gerry – to her sister's house. As they moved through the dust and the smoke, Gerry stared at the York Street Mill where his mum worked. The mill looked so tall in the ghostly night, amid the hazy searchlights, and Gerry felt so small. He clutched his mum's hand even tighter. They ran still faster.

One week later, the Luftwaffe returned. Belfast had been given only one extra searchlight and one additional anti-aircraft gun. Two hundred bomb shelters had been built, which was never enough for a city of 500,000. The night echoed again with shrieking sirens. A warden guided Nelly Storey and her children to a small shelter on Vere Street, where they lived. They began to clamber to safety. But then, abruptly, Nelly stopped. She looked into the shelter and shook her head. 'No, Hugh,' she said. 'We are not going here.'

Hugh the warden was agitated. 'Nelly, you have to stay here. All the other shelters are full.'

Nelly Storey refused. She climbed out of the shelter, bringing up the children as the night sky thickened with the drone of approaching bombers. There was such steel in her that the poor warden gave in to Nelly's madness. He pulled them along as he raced to the next shelter. It was packed, but Nelly nodded. This one was all right. They would seek sanctuary here.

Gerry did not understand why his mother was so certain. But early the next morning, when they came out into the smouldering devastation, Gerry saw a sight he would never forget. There was a huge hole in the ground where the shelter his mum had refused to enter had been located. It had been destroyed by a massive bomb. Everyone was dead – including their immediate neighbours Mary-Ann Corr and her son Freddie.

The small boy looked at his mother in wonder. How did she know that one shelter was safe and the other was a deathtrap?

That morning they climbed over the piles of rubble, which was all that was left of their houses. Gerry's hands and knees were whitened by the chalky remnants of brick and concrete blown up by the German bombs. Over 900 people were killed across the city and the bodies were laid out in St George's Market for identification. Others, too badly burnt or blown up to be identified, were buried in mass graves.

Gerry had been transfixed by the only corpse he saw. At the bottom of the New Lodge Road, the body of a soldier was draped across the top of a vehicle used to spread hot tar across pot-holed roads. Gerry's mum turned his head away, but the image would never leave him.

The bombers came again at the next full moon. Two hundred and fifty Luftwaffe planes attacked Belfast at 1am on 5 May 1941. Another 200 people were killed.

Gerry and his family were spared. They had been evacuated across the border to Toomebridge, 30 miles from Belfast in County Antrim, where they lived with his grandmother. They eventually found a white thatched bungalow in Moneyglass, where they stayed until Belfast was safe. Neither the abandonment by their father, who had left for Birmingham when Gerry was only two, nor Hitler's Luftwaffe could break them.

As a 34-year-old man lying in bed early in 1972, while another conflict erupted across Belfast, Gerry remembered his mother coming home in the middle of the day in the mid-1940s. She had an hour-long dinner break from the mill just around the corner. Rather than eating much, she would check on the children and lie on the settee. Her face was colourless and her insides were riddled with ulcers that, as Gerry understood decades later, must have been caused by stress.

Gerry idolised his mother. She was a Catholic and a Republican, supportive of a united Ireland, and different to the Protestants who clung fervently to the Union Jack, and the royal family and Britain. Nelly had lived through the grim days of the 1920s, when Catholic persecution was acute, but she still took people as she found them. Most ordinary Protestants were decent and so Nelly showed them respect rather than animosity. She handed down such equanimity to Gerry and he learnt to treat everyone fairly. They both wanted the country to change, and for Catholics to be given equality, but the IRA and violence were not for them.

Most soldiers carrying out internment swoops knew Gerry was a renowned boxing trainer. His work transcended sectarian strife, but they kept watching him and sometimes raided his house. His brother Bobby and nephews Seamus and Bobby Jr were all detained. Seamus was a member of the IRA and Bobby Sr led the defence of homes in New Lodge when Catholic families were threatened on the interface by Loyalist groups.

Bobby Storey Sr and his wife Peggy had four children – Seamus, Bobby Jr, Geraldine and baby Brian, who had been born with Down's syndrome – and their Annalee Street home was raided repeatedly throughout 1971. After a rifle and pistols were discovered by the army, Bobby Sr and Seamus were taken to Girdwood Barracks and tortured. Bobby Sr was released but Seamus ended up in Crumlin Road Gaol.

On 17 November 1971, Seamus had become a Republican folk hero when, along with eight other prisoners, he had escaped from Crumlin. They had used improvised ladders, made out of rope smuggled into the jail, to scale the high brick walls. Two cars were waiting for them on the other side and their daring escape was celebrated in the New Lodge and across Belfast. They were hailed as the Crumlin Kangaroos and the Belfast folk group, The Wolfhound, wrote a song about them: 'Crumlin Kangaroos (Over the Wall)'.

Bobby Jr was still only 15 and radicalised by everything he saw. He left school that year to work for his dad and help him sell fruit, while Bobby Sr also drove a black cab at night to support the family. Gerry helped where he could because his brother had been made bankrupt by the Belfast City Council. Bobby Sr had owned a small building firm, but the council cancelled all contracts with Catholic-owned companies after the civil rights marches of the late 1960s. Gerry worked on the Catholic side of the docks and his position was safe – but the chances of Bobby Sr and his sons getting work from the Protestant bosses were over.

In the early hours of that Saturday morning, the latest army raid passed Gerry's house. Other men were taken but the boxing trainer could start his day at the Holy Family. As the first light of morning filtered through the curtains, Gerry could sense the new darkness of Belfast.

At the Holy Family, for whom Gerry had boxed as a boy before an eye injury curtailed his amateur career, everyone was welcome as long as they left talk of politics and religion at the door. As the head trainer, Gerry stressed that there could be no mention of the IRA or UVF, of internment or rioting. Swearing was also banned. They were there to improve as boxers.

Such discipline had underpinned the Holy Family's pasting of the paratroopers in the spring of 1969. The paras were Combined Forces boxing champions and looking for competition before they defended their shield. Gerry was asked to supply a team from Belfast to give them a workout. He suggested the Holy Family would put up ten boys against the hardened paras.

'Just your club?' he was asked by the small but loud American sergeant in charge of the paratroopers. 'Are you sure?'

'I'm sure,' Gerry said with a smile.

News of the showdown spread across New Lodge. The entire downstairs area of the Recreation Club was packed for the contest. All the spectators came from the Republican community, but there was no anger towards the paras on a thrilling night – just loud roaring during each one-sided bout. The night ended in a 10-0 landslide win for the Holy Family. It was another testament to Gerry's great skill as a coach. He trained his boys to box scientifically, to hit precisely rather than be hit in return. The Holy Family boxers repelled the raw aggression of the paras with the trademark calm of the best Storey fighters.

The loud American sergeant became more muted with every loss and, a couple of days later, he and his superior officer, Major Field, returned to the Holy Family. Major Field was in charge of the paras' boxing programme, but he had been unable to travel with the team to Belfast because he was carrying out training manoeuvres in Aldershot. He was on crutches.

Major Field saluted Gerry and said: 'Look what you've done to me, Mr Storey.'

Gerry looked down at the crutches quizzically before the major explained what had happened. 'We were getting ready to jump and the results from Belfast started coming in,' he said. 'This one is knocked out by one of your boys, that one is stopped by one of your young fellas. I couldn't believe it and my head was full of it when I jumped. I broke my leg.'

The major swung on his crutches in amusement while the American sergeant pointed at some of the Holy Family boys. 'Look at these mini-marvels training,' he said to Major Field. 'You would think they were in the army.'

Gerry instilled discipline in a non-military way. He never shouted at his boys. Instead, he encouraged and inspired them. Gerry did not share the surprise of the major and the sergeant that the paratroopers had been whitewashed. It seemed logical that his boys, so well schooled under his boxing tutelage, would easily defeat tough paratroopers who were, essentially, ring novices.

He always welcomed boxers from across the sectarian divide. In the context of Belfast's turmoil, it was miraculous that Davy Larmour travelled so often to the Holy Family, in Republican New Lodge, from his home in a Loyalist enclave close to the Shankill Road. Neither he nor Gerry cared that they came from different backgrounds – but it seemed as if the rest of Belfast did. The New Lodge was treacherous to any other person from the Shankill. But to Davy it housed the one gym guaranteed to be open for sparring.

Davy belonged to the Albert Foundry Boxing Club in Paisley Park, near the Shankill Road, just three miles from the Holy Family. The first time Davy visited Gerry's gym he went with his trainer, Steamer Graham. Gerry had assured them they would be safe as his invited guests.

Training began at 10am on that Saturday visit in 1970. Davy was keen, and he and Steamer arrived at 9.30 at the Patrickville Recreation Club that then housed the Holy Family gym alongside a snooker hall. A surprise awaited. There was a blackboard and two rows of benches filled with men wearing trilby hats and overcoats. They glared at Davy and Steamer.

'You're not to be here until ten,' one of the men said curtly.

'Sorry, mister,' Davy said.

Outside the snooker hall, Davy noticed how pale Steamer looked. 'I'm on my way home,' Steamer said. 'That was an IRA meeting . . .'

Before Davy could argue, Steamer bolted back in the direction of the Shankill Road. Davy watched him disappear, feeling a little uncertain as he waited. Ten minutes later he spotted Gerry walking up the New Lodge Road. A relieved Davy went to meet him.

'We made a balls-up, Gerry,' he said. 'Me and Steamer walked into an IRA meeting.'

'They have nothing to do with the Holy Family,' Gerry said. 'You'll be fine with me.'

By the time he and Davy reached the entrance, the last members of the meeting were leaving. 'Hello, Gerry,' one of the IRA men said, tipping his trilby to the trainer.

'Morning, fellas,' Gerry said in his genial way, escorting Davy into the gym as if they had just passed a group of snooker-playing pensioners.

Later that year Davy won a bronze medal at the 1970 Commonwealth Games in Edinburgh. It said much about boxing's unique ability to criss-cross stringent borders that Davy had boxed for Northern Ireland in the Commonwealths but would eventually fight for Ireland, in 1976, with Gerry as his trainer, at the Montreal Olympics. Davy did not care that a Protestant from the Shankill was meant to abhor the green of Ireland and pledge loyalty instead to Britain and the Union Jack. He just wanted to box – which was why he was so welcome at the Holy Family.

Davy probably had more Catholic than Protestant friends because, though an amiable man, he felt happiest in the company of fighters. He ignored religion and just saw good and bad men – and he still believed that there were far more good people than bad in Belfast. Davy only experienced trouble when he got back home to the Shankill Road and a few Loyalist hard men had a pop at him because he'd been training in the New Lodge.

That Saturday morning in early December '71, Gerry had shut the Holy Family gym as soon as training ended. His cousin was getting married and it was a big day for the extended Storey family. The celebrations were typical of an Irish wedding – lasting long into the night. It meant Gerry did not think of him and Belle dropping into McGurk's or the Rocktown or Earl Inn as they often did on a Saturday night.

McGurk's was on North Queen Street, on the corner with Great George's Street. It was an ordinary working-class pub run by an extraordinary man. Patrick McGurk, at 50, was 16 years older than Gerry, but they both exuded a calm and decency that distinguished them in embittered times.

Gerry felt a kinship with McGurk. His bar was pretty much like the Holy Family because Patsy would not tolerate any sectarian talk. He even had a swear jar and anyone who cursed had to pay a penalty. In the Republican heartlands, McGurk's was jammed with local Catholic people. But Patsy McGurk was happy to serve anyone. In the old days, before internment brought the shutters of division down, it was not unknown for policemen from the Royal Ulster Constabulary to drop in for a pint. Patsy poured them a pint and asked how they were doing. Those days were over.

McGurk's policy of excluding sectarianism meant the IRA gunmen drank elsewhere. Working men and women came to McGurk's for peace and company. They did not want to think about the IRA or the Reverend Ian Paisley and the Loyalists. At most they would raise a cackle at the wrath of Paisley who, even in 1959, at a time when Belfast was tranquil, had accused the Queen Mother and Princess Margaret of 'committing spiritual fornication and adultery with the anti-Christ' when meeting the Pope. The ordinary people of McGurk's preferred a happier drink.

Just before nine o'clock that Saturday night, on 4 December 1971, the hiss of car tyres on North Queen Street made an eight-year-old boy, Ian McRory, look up from delivering the *Belfast Telegraph* – the moderate newspaper whose journalists Paisley still castigated as 'the scribbling serpents of Royal Avenue'. The boy watched the solitary car drive slowly past McGurk's. There were four men inside. A Union Jack sticker was plastered to the back window.

The boy, sensing something was amiss, dared not move. He waited in the shadows, hoping the car would drive away. Instead, a man got out of the car. He wore a black balaclava and a long raincoat. He carried a bulky package in his arms. The man used his foot to push open the door to McGurk's.

The light of the heaving pub shone into the black street. The newspaper boy could see more clearly now. Bending over his package, which he had left at the entrance to the bar, the man hunched down. A flame flickered and a long fuse attached to the package began to burn. The door to McGurk's swung shut as the man ran to the car. He clambered into the back seat and the car roared off.

Ian McRory started to run when the huge explosion detonated. The force of the bomb, which weighed between 30 and 50 pounds, threw the running boy into the air. He would survive and live to provide his testimony, but 15 innocent people were blown to pieces, while a further 17 were badly injured.

Gerry had just got back from the wedding when Ray Smith, one of his boxing coaches, called him. It was strange that Ray sounded so relieved to hear his voice.

'You didn't go to McGurk's tonight?' Ray asked.

'No,' Gerry replied. 'I've been at the wedding.'

'It's been bombed,' Ray said. 'They've bombed McGurk's to bits.'

Gerry knew 12 of the 15 people who died – Robert Spotswood, James Smyth, Thomas McLaughlin, Thomas Kane, Edward Kane, David Milligan, Francis Bradley, Philip Garry, Eddie Keenan, Sarah Keenan, James Cromie and Philomena McGurk. He did not know John Colton or Kathleen Irvine and he had not spoken to Marie McGurk, who was Patsy and Philomena's 14-year-old daughter.

He knew some of the men particularly well. Fra Bradley had worked with Gerry at the docks for years – as did his sons Francis Jr and Robert. The two boys were Holy Family boxers. Eddie Keenan and James Smyth were fellow dock workers. He and Bobby Spotswood went to dances together in their twenties. Gerry also remembered how, when he worked as a barman, he had seen Bobby every Friday and Saturday night. Bobby always came over for a yarn. Now he was dead, along with 14 other people who did not have any IRA links.

That fact did not stop the RUC and politicians both in Northern Ireland and London from immediately declaring that the McGurk's bombing has been 'an IRA own goal', claiming that the bomb had been under construction in the bar when it exploded by mistake. It was such a blatant lie that rage spread across Catholic neighbourhoods. The radicalisation of young Republicans, like Bobby Storey, Gerry's 15-year-old nephew, was sealed that terrible night. This would be the deadliest single attack suffered by Belfast throughout the Troubles.

Six years later, when it was finally proved that Loyalist paramilitaries were responsible, Robert Campbell of the UVF was sentenced to life imprisonment for the McGurk's bombing. He would serve 15 years before being released.

Gerry was stricken by the loss of his friends, and so many wasted lives, but he took his lead from Patsy McGurk. Patsy had lost his wife and his daughter but, within hours of the bombing, he was being interviewed on television. 'First of all, I would not like this tragic occasion to embitter relations in the community,' Patsy said quietly. 'After all, we're supposed to be a Christian people, and let's hope this sacrifice might offer up peace in the community. It shouldn't cause friction because I believe what the Good Book says: "Father, forgive them."'

Those words reminded Gerry of his mother. She always told him: 'Times will change for the better. I won't see it and you might not see it, but down the line something good will come.' His mother was Republican-minded but above all else she believed in peace and in people. 'Treat everyone the same,' she always told Gerry, 'no matter what happens.'

His mother, Gerry knew, would have believed that Patsy McGurk was right.

A week later, on 11 December 1971, Patsy McGurk's plea for reconciliation was blown to smithereens on the Shankill Road. At 12.25pm that Saturday afternoon, as the Shankill heaved with Christmas shoppers, a green car pulled up outside the Balmoral Furniture Company. In an echo of the previous week's attack on

McGurk's, a lone man got out of the car and carried a large parcel, which he left on the shop's doorstep. He ran back to the car, which sped off just before the bomb detonated.

Four people were killed instantly – Hugh Bruce and Harold King and two children, two-year-old Tracey Munn and 17-month-old Colin Nichol. With the exception of King, a 29-year-old Catholic, they were Protestant victims of a bomb that had been planted by the Provisional IRA in retaliation for the McGurk's atrocity. The Balmoral bomb destroyed the shop and injured many people. It was such a callous act, intended to cause carnage and death among ordinary people, that the Protestant community was outraged.

Davy Larmour was just 200 yards from the Balmoral showrooms when the bomb went off. He had not been to the Holy Family that Saturday morning. Instead, he had just sauntered down the Shankill Road to pick up some shopping. He was walking home to Woodvale, less than a mile away, when the roar of the bomb made him wheel around.

Davy went to help, but many other people had reached the scene before him. There was so much dust and smoke, and shouting and screaming, that the Shankill Road looked as if it had been transported back to the Second World War and the Blitz. A large silver Granada snaked into view, parking opposite the demolished Balmoral. Davy watched Reverend Ian Paisley climb out of the car. Dressed in black, his dog collar gleaming white in the gloom, he shouted as he walked towards the crowd. 'Listen to me,' Paisley cried out. 'Listen to me!'

The terror of McGurk's, so close to the Holy Family, had now been followed by the terror of the Balmoral. Davy turned away. He could not bear to hear Paisley bark out 'Never surrender' or how the streets of Belfast would flow with blood. Davy wanted to find his family and check they were safe. He tried to hold onto what his strict old father told him so sternly: 'We are all Christians. We all believe in the same God.'

Davy walked down the familiar streets that had become a hotbed for Loyalist paramilitaries who delighted in parading up and down with their weapons in the air. They revelled in the marching season, which reached its crescendo on 12 July when they hailed Prince William of Orange's victory for Protestantism over King James II at the Battle of the Boyne in 1690. Davy was not interested in the distant past. It mattered more that innocent Protestant people suffered horribly at the hands of IRA men who burnt down their houses.

This was his community. These were his people. They were often targeted just because they saw themselves as British rather than Irish. That simple definition caused carnage.

The fighter bunched his hands into fists and thrust them into his pockets. He walked in silence, leaving the desolation, knowing it had only just begun. The worst was still to come.

CHAPTER 3

The Shankill Road Summit

Belfast resembled a ghost town. You could walk from Royal Avenue right up to City Hall and on into New Lodge and barely see a soul. Gerry Storey thought it looked like a set from an old Western. Moving through his home town, he would not have been surprised to see tumbleweed blowing through the empty streets or a creaking barroom door swing open as another gunman loomed into view. There were more guns, bombs and cowboys dressed in sinister black balaclavas than in a Hollywood movie.

It was better to avoid venturing out for all but the most essential tasks. Even when they were doing their grocery shopping, housewives had their bags searched by British soldiers as they passed through security gates. Once work had been done for the day, in offices, shops and factories, most ordinary people knew it was best to get home quickly. There were few after-work pints in the pubs because the streets were not safe, especially as the light ebbed away. Barricades were set up around Belfast, the burnt-out husks of buses and cars a silent reminder of recent rioting and bombings. An unofficial curfew spread across the city most nights after six o'clock.

Gerry searched instead for hope and progress. He loved working

with his young fighters, improving them through disciplined training and thoughtful coaching, watching them bloom between the
ropes. The Holy Family rules remained unchanged. Once you
stepped inside the gym you left the world outside. Before you
reached the heavy bags dangling from steel hooks, and the speed
balls waiting to be pummelled with rhythmic precision, you shed
the Troubles for a while. You trained purely to become a better
boxer and a better person.

When gyms from across the divide, on or near the Shankill
Road, approached him for help, Gerry showed the same magnani-
mous spirit. He was willing to travel into Loyalist territory to pick
up fighters or even to spend time in rival gyms. Most boxing clubs
around Belfast had begun to shut down. It was too dangerous to
operate at night and the few surviving gyms looked to the Holy
Family as a template for the future and an oasis of peace.

Gerry was safe in New Lodge as he came from a well-known
Republican family. The IRA links of his brother Bobby Sr, and
his nephews Seamus and Bobby Jr, were respected. Even some of
his Holy Family boys had become revered IRA figures. Billy Reid,
one of his former boxers, had shot the first British soldier to die in
the Troubles when he killed Gunner Robert Curtis in New Lodge
in February 1971. Three months later, while attempting another
ambush of the army, Reid was shot dead on Academy Street.

'The Ballad of Billy Reid' became a song sung in Republican
circles as the amateur boxer was mythologised. Gerry's abiding
memory of Billy was different. He remembered him as a young
boxer wearing the Holy Family vest as Gerry took a team into
Protestant territory one night. The Troubles had yet to erupt and
Gerry promised everyone's parents that they would be safe. He was
right – even though Billy Reid's opponent was less secure.

It was Billy's first fight and he tore into his rival with nervous
abandon. His arms were windmills and, even if most punches
missed, he landed enough blows to overwhelm the little man
opposite him. Billy's opponent fell through the ropes. He tumbled

out of the ring, with Billy following him. Once they hit the floor, Billy kept throwing punches.

Gerry rushed over to separate them, mortified that he had not taught the rules more clearly to his wee scrapper. Billy never did it again, but a mere mention of his name conjured up that wayward memory: rather than his status as an IRA folk hero, Billy Reid would always be a Holy Family fighter to Gerry.

There was no enduring logic to Gerry's lack of fear outside New Lodge. He worked on the gut instinct that everyone accepted him as a boxing trainer, intent on helping rather than harming, and that his work protected him from the paramilitaries. Belfast had always been a boxing town and Gerry believed the popularity of his sport guaranteed his safety. Most paramilitary leaders were working-class men, just like him, and Gerry could feel their respect for his immersion in boxing. His belief was bolstered by the romantic memory of his mother's insistence that he walked with the angels. Yet he had no hard certainty he would not be attacked or killed for stepping onto Loyalist turf.

Over the years Gerry had always put on boxing shows along the Shankill Road. He adopted the same approach there as he did in New Lodge or the Ardoyne. His boxers would perform in front of anyone and everyone, and Gerry was convinced that they would be admired and protected. He even brought in teams from Canada and Poland, Italy and England to fight in Loyalist and Republican venues.

Overseas teams had been too terrified to travel to Belfast since the onset of the Troubles. But a boxing club from Fort McMurray, in Alberta, Canada, broke the mould when they told Gerry they would fly to Belfast as long as their safety could be assured.

'I guarantee your safety,' Gerry told Rex Clewes, the Canadian coach. 'There will be no trouble.'

It was a statement of breathtaking audacity, based less on Gerry's intimate knowledge of Belfast paramilitary groups than his conviction that people would welcome a night of boxing as a break from the terror and violence of ordinary life. He was right. The Canadians were feted, if pasted inside the ring, in a Loyalist club on the Shankill Road and then, a couple of nights later, in the Crumlin Star in Ardoyne. The Canadians had never received a welcome like it. They did not understand sectarian politics but they loved Belfast.

When Freddie Barr, who ran a respected gym in Kingston, Surrey, received a phone call from Gerry inviting him to bring a team over to Belfast, he was shocked. He had seen all the bombings on the BBC news. Would it really be safe for his English boys to travel to Belfast?

'Absolutely,' Gerry said cheerfully.

'Can you guarantee our safety, Gerry?'

'Certainly, Freddie.'

Gerry even arranged to hire a plane to fly the English team to Belfast, as he knew every show would be a sell-out and cover costs. And so the Surrey team followed the Canadians, and their nights of boxing were successful and peaceful. The English boys had such a good time after their last show that they drank and danced with the local girls until 4am.

There had also been such a demand on the Shankill Road to watch the visitors get outboxed that a black market had sprung up, with cab drivers running most of the trade in tickets.

'The taxi men made a killing,' a Shankill Road hard man complained.

Gerry smiled. It was better making a killing over tickets than with bullets or bombs.

Jimmy Craig, a notorious UDA paramilitary and gangster, revered Gerry as the greatest amateur trainer in the world. Craig also knew that Martin Regan, a leading Republican, was a boxing fan. He asked Gerry to let Regan know he would welcome him as his personal guest, with his safety guaranteed, when they had their next Shankill Road show in a few weeks.

When Gerry told him, Regan hesitated, shocked to have been invited onto the Shankill Road. He then remembered he had a meeting that night, looking relieved to have found a plausible excuse.

'But Gerry,' Regan said, 'why don't you ask Jimmy Craig to come to our next show in the Crumlin Star? I'll make sure there are no problems.'

Craig also had meetings on that particular night, and Gerry accepted their convenient reasons for not visiting enemy territory with wry amusement. He also felt vindicated in his belief that boxing was a force for good in such perilous times. And so he continued to drive across a forsaken Belfast at night, moving from one dangerous neighbourhood to another.

Once the army barriers were erected, he was stopped the first three times he entered the Shankill Road. A soldier shone a torch in his face one bleak night at the security fence separating the communities.

'Who are you?' he was asked.

'Gerry Storey.'

'The boxing trainer?'

'Yes,' Gerry said with a little laugh when hearing the surprise in the soldier's voice.

'Where are you going?' he was asked.

'To the Albert Foundry,' Gerry said. 'Steamer Graham's gym. Just past the Shankill, in Paisley Park.'

'What's going on?' a second soldier asked, even more suspiciously. 'You're on the New Lodge and we saw you last week on both the Shankill and the Falls Road. Now it's Paisley Park. That's not normal.'

'I'm going around the boxing clubs,' Gerry said, 'helping out where I can. It's just a wee bit of boxing,' he reassured them.

His family background was obvious but Gerry was a charmer as well as a man of deep integrity. He was waved through by the soldiers. Eventually they no longer even stopped him. As soon as they saw his bronze Cortina, they lifted the barrier.

Gerry smiled, waved and drove on through the darkness.

*

He knew they could come for him at any time and so Gerry was not surprised when, on a Thursday evening a few months after Bloody Sunday, he received a call from the Loyalist Army Council. The Army Council grouped together paramilitaries from the UDA, UVF and the UFF. These three violent groups were often at odds with each other in how best to win their war against the equally violent IRA while keeping Northern Ireland loyal to the Union Jack, the Queen and the United Kingdom. But the Army Council met regularly to discuss common objectives. The caller referred to them as 'the boys', but he said it with such emphasis that Gerry knew he meant the top brass among the Shankill Road paramilitaries.

'The boys are meeting on Sunday night,' the voice on the phone said. 'And, Gerry, they want to see you.'

Such a call would spread terror through most people in Belfast. The idea of being summoned by the Loyalist Army Council usually sounded like a grim tolling of the bell.

'That's all right,' Gerry said amiably. 'What time do they want me?'

'Eight o'clock,' the voice said. 'We'll send an escort to bring you in.'

'That won't be necessary,' Gerry said firmly. 'I'll drive to the Shankill on my own.'

'All right,' the man said. 'But the boys are expecting you. Do you understand?'

'Yes,' Gerry said, even if he had no idea what they might say to him. He wrote down the address of the Loyalist club where they would meet and wished the caller a good evening.

'Who was that?' Belle asked.

'They want to see me up on the Shankill,' Gerry told his wife.

Belle was so used to Gerry travelling around Belfast that she rarely showed any worry. She trusted Gerry and he knew the streets of Belfast as well as anyone in the city.

'You won't be late?' she said calmly.

'No,' Gerry reassured her. 'Not on a Sunday night. It's just a wee chat.'

On a Sunday night in the spring of 1972, Belfast seemed more deserted than ever as Gerry Storey headed slowly towards the Shankill Road. He felt calm and relieved he had insisted on driving himself. It would not have been wise if he had allowed a Loyalist escort to arrive outside his door and take him away in a strange car. New Lodge did not allow such visits and even Gerry's presence might not have prevented gunplay.

He kept any trepidation about the meeting in check by reasoning he had nothing to hide. The Loyalist Army Council obviously knew what he was doing on the Shankill. If they told him he had to stop his visits, he would simply talk to them and explain his motives. He did not allow himself to consider more sinister possibilities.

Gerry parked his car on a side street just off the Shankill. Apart from three minders standing watch outside the club, there was no one to be seen. Gerry got out of his car, locked it and walked over to the club. The minders were clearly expecting him. One of them, without a word, led Gerry up the narrow stairwell to the first floor. The minder knocked on the door and waited. When the call came, he pushed it open and gestured to Gerry that he should walk inside. This was the moment that would have turned the blood of most men cold. Yet, with just one deep breath to steady himself, Gerry walked into the room. A large group of men, more than a dozen of them, watched him approach the round table where they sat.

'Good evening,' Gerry said, breaking the silence.

'Gerry Storey,' one of the men said, rising to his feet and extending his hand.

Gerry recognised some of the faces. Harry Burgess. Bob Morrison. Tucker Lyttle. He avoided looking too closely at anyone else. It was best he didn't know exactly whom he was meeting. Too much knowledge in Belfast could be a dangerous thing.

'Take a seat, Gerry,' Burgess said, pointing to an empty chair at the table.

Gerry sat down and waited to hear the reason for being summoned. The formality of the setting, and the seriousness of the men, proved he had not been wrong. These boys really were the top paramilitary men in the North.

'We know what you've been doing,' another man said quietly to him. Gerry nodded and waited. 'You've never hid it,' the man said.

There was a long silence and then a different Loyalist leader leant across the table. He was close enough that, if Gerry stretched out his hand, he could ruffle the man's hair. Instead, understanding the intensity of the moment, Gerry simply looked at him.

'We understand what you're trying to do,' the man said. 'We're behind you 100 per cent.'

The tension melted away as approving comments echoed around the table. There was such genuine love and admiration for boxing in this hard-bitten circle of men that Gerry, as the leading amateur trainer in Britain and Ireland, was revered by the Loyalist Army Council. It was incredible – many of the men in that room were used to ordering the murder of a random Catholic or planning targeted attacks on Republican communities. Yet they were embracing a Catholic boxing trainer whose family was linked to the IRA.

'Thank you,' Gerry said, smiling in a way he had not expected to do at the start of the evening.

'Gerry,' Burgess continued, 'we'd love you to run even more of your shows on Rumford Street. Bring the kids over from the Holy Family and box in our club.'

The Rumford Social Club, just off the Shankill Road, was an infamous meeting place for Loyalist paramilitaries. Gerry didn't mind. He was happy to be invited with his wee boxers.

'We know it's a lot to ask,' a heavyset man said. 'But if you're willing to do it, you'll have our protection. And that means the protection of everyone at this table.'

The man spread his arms wide to indicate that the full might of the UDA, the UVF and UFF would protect him. If Gerry had not believed in the power of boxing, he would have thought it was miraculous.

'We mean it,' a new voice said. 'If anybody out there offends you, or anyone with you, they will be dealt with by us.'

'They will be dealt with severely,' another man said gravely, his gruff voice lacing that last word with menace. It was obvious that they would maim or kill anyone who offended him.

'That won't be necessary,' Gerry said. 'My boys will be delighted to box at the Rumford.'

The men rose as one to shake his hand. It was so peaceful and harmonious that Gerry wondered why it could not always be this simple, why only boxing could bring them together.

That same month, underlining the contrasting fearlessness of Gerry Storey and the spirit of reconciliation that defined the Army Council meeting, the Five Nations rugby tournament was not completed. Rugby was similar to boxing as the best players from the North, from clubs in Ulster and elsewhere, became internationals for Ireland. Willie John McBride, a Protestant who worked as a bank manager in Belfast and played for Ballymena, was Ireland's most experienced leader. The imposing and influential lock forward had already played 47 times for Ireland and on 13 occasions for the British Lions. He would go on to captain the greatest Lions team in history, the squad that demolished South Africa on their 1974 tour.

It was striking that McBride and Mike Gibson, another Protestant from the North and Ireland's most gifted player in 1972, pulled on the green shirt and heard the crowd in Dublin serenade them with 'The Soldier's Song'. The Irish anthem, *'Amhrán na bhFiann'*, could not be played in his home town of Ballymena, where 'God Save the Queen' meant so much to the Unionist community, but McBride still played his heart out for Ireland.

He was also convinced that, in 1972, Ireland were the best team in the Five Nations. They won their first two matches away from home – beating France 14–9 in Colombes and then winning 16–12 against England at Twickenham on 12 February. Thirteen days had passed since Bloody Sunday, with the British embassy still a burnt-out ruin in Dublin, and tensions between the two countries were high.

McBride, having been told that he was an assassination target for unknown Republicans, was assigned a bodyguard at the team hotel in London. But the big man, and Ireland, would not be deterred. England were 12–7 ahead with just three minutes left when the inflamed Irish scored a late penalty and a brilliant try to win the match.

Ireland's remaining two matches were at home to Scotland and Wales – with the latter clash set to be a Grand Slam decider. But the Scots and the Welsh refused to travel because they didn't feel safe in Ireland. The Five Nations had to be cancelled and McBride and Gibson were angry that they could not complete a tournament they cherished.

Derry, Thursday 20 April 1972

Charlie Nash turned the newspaper over slowly in his hands. He could not easily absorb the words he read. They seemed so grotesque that he could hardly believe that they had been printed. Everyone he knew in Derry felt the same. People were burning with the deceit and injustice of the Widgery Report into Bloody Sunday. Charlie was consumed, instead, by thoughts of his brother Willie. It felt as if dirt had been rubbed into a raw wound.

Lord Widgery, hand-picked by the British Prime Minister Edward Heath to gloss over the truth of Bloody Sunday, had produced a distorted investigation. The worst lies had been printed in Charlie's newspaper the day after the report was released to the public. Widgery claimed that the carnage had been sparked by shots fired at the British paratroopers. 'To those who seek to apportion responsibility for the events of 30 January the question "Who fired first?" is vital,' Widgery wrote. 'I am entirely satisfied that the first firing in the [Rossville Flats] courtyard was directed at the soldiers.'

Charlie's father and his brother Eddie had both been on the march. They swore that the only shots had come from the guns of the paras. The same view was given to him by friends and independent reporters who had also been witnesses that day.

It felt even worse when Widgery claimed that some of the deceased 'had been firing weapons or handling bombs in the course of the afternoon and that others had been closely supporting them'. He also exonerated the paratroopers and cleared them of any wrongdoing. 'Those accustomed to listening to witnesses could not fail to be impressed by the demeanour of the soldiers of 1 Para,' Widgery concluded. 'They gave their evidence with confidence and without hesitation or prevarication and withstood a rigorous cross-examination without contradicting themselves or each other. With one or two exceptions I accept that they were telling the truth as they remembered it.'

The real truth would only be published officially 38 years later in 2010, when the Saville Inquiry concluded that: 'Despite the contrary evidence given by soldiers, we have concluded that none of them fired in response to attacks or threatened attacks by nail or petrol bombers. No one threw or threatened to throw a nail or petrol bomb at the soldiers on Bloody Sunday.'

Derry was soon ablaze again with rioting as news of the report spread. Charlie saw boys and young men pull black balaclavas over their heads and faces. He saw them running with flaming milk bottles in their hands before hurling them at the RUC and the army. He saw the petrol bombs spinning through the air before exploding into flames. He saw the hate and the anger. He understood. He also wanted to lash out. But Charlie remembered his gentle brother. Willie always wanted to dance more than fight. And so Charlie turned away from the rage and the violence. He walked in the opposite direction – to St Mary's and the haven of boxing.

Rinty Monaghan, the great Belfast flyweight who had been the world champion in 1948, told Davy Larmour that the best way to harden his hands was to soak them in brine. Davy looked up the meaning of brine in the dictionary. It was salt and vinegar. He had taken down a big sweetie jar from his mother's larder and filled it with four bottles of vinegar and three bags of salt. This was his homemade brine.

Every night, after training, Davy watched the small black-and-white television in his parents' front room while soaking his right hand in brine. After half an hour he would swap hands and make sure his left received an equally long soaking. The briny mixture was always freezing. After a week, Davy noticed how the knuckles on both his hands turned hard and white when he bunched them into fists. He believed the brine hardened the bones in his hands.

Davy could not soak his heart in brine. He was relentless in the ring but, outside boxing, he retained his sensitivity. As a small boy at Brown Street Primary School, Davy had been bullied by the bigger kids. There was even worse bullying in class and one of his schoolmasters was brutal. Davy's handwriting was very neat, but it had come at a price. He remembered how the teacher used to creep up behind him and slap his face. 'Your writing looks like a chicken has walked across the page, Larmour,' the teacher sneered. Years later, in 1974, after Davy won the Commonwealth gold medal, with Gerry in his corner, that same teacher wrote to him: 'Davy, we always knew you would do well.'

He had learnt to become a boxer. His mother planted the idea in his head. 'Why don't you go down to Uncle John's gym and learn to defend yourself?' she asked. She had noticed how transfixed he was in front of the television on Saturday afternoons during *America's Fight of the Week* on the BBC. He loved Sugar Ray Robinson and Carmen Basilio.

Little Davy, aged eight in 1960, went down to the local Springmount boxing gym located in an old coal yard. He climbed three flights of a rickety staircase lit by a bare bulb. He was very nervous, even though his dad had bought him six-ounce boxing gloves, and he could not open the door. The trainer, Jimmy Hamilton, let him in. 'What do you want, son?' he growled.

'I want to box,' Davy whispered.

'Where's your vest?' Jimmy asked. 'Where's your trunks and shoes? Where's your towel?'

Davy looked up at him with big eyes. He had no vest, no trunks, no shoes and no towel. He was told to come back when he had the right gear. Running home in tears, Davy burst through the door and threw his new gloves under the stairs. He was finished with boxing, even before he started.

Three weeks later, after his mother had found the money to buy him the proper kit, Davy returned to the gym. Jimmy Hamilton welcomed him back.

Davy liked the smells and sights of the gym right away. He soon discovered he could fight.

He was in secondary school when he realised his achievements in the ring were being noticed. Davy also played the harmonica and the kids always spurred him on to play a new Beatles song. He was caught in the act in 1964 when the crowd around him melted away as soon as their teacher walked into the classroom. The imposing master placed his briefcase on the desk and stared at the suddenly hushed class. He then sat down, took out his newspaper and started reading the sports pages silently.

Everyone looked at him in bemusement. After he had read for a while, he put the newspaper down. 'I'm a creature of habit,' he said, 'and this morning I came down the Malone Road and, like every morning, I bought my newspaper. As soon as I got to school I did the usual and went to the staffroom to read about the dogs and the horses on the back pages.'

The classroom was still hushed while they waited to see where they were being led. 'Now this morning,' the teacher continued, 'I'm reading a story in the back of my paper about how one of my pupils had the distinction of going to Dublin to fight for an Irish boxing title.'

Davy turned very red but, as no one in his class knew that he boxed, the others still looked confused. After a long silence he said: 'Mr Larmour, come up to the front.'

Davy was the smallest in the class and, when he stood up, the kids were all surprised. 'How long have you been boxing, Mr Larmour?' the teacher asked him.

At first Davy's voice was timid, but slowly he gathered confidence as the kids started asking questions. At 12, Davy felt his first flush of renown.

He had won the seven-stone-seven Ulster Boys' championship and, in Dublin, he lifted the All-Ireland title in the same division. On the Friday night after his return, Davy felt elated because he went down to the boxing club and everyone admired the trophy he dared not show to his dad.

'I want to talk to you tonight, boy,' his father had said. His dad was an ex-army man and he was quick to use a strap across Davy's back whenever he felt his son deserved it. That night, not knowing what his dad might say, Davy waited up. He knew that when his dad went to the pub for a pint he would drink alone. It must have been during a solitary session when he heard someone talk about wee Davy's big win in Dublin.

Just before 10.30pm, Davy's father came home. 'Come here, boy,' he said. He always called Davy 'boy' but this time there was an edge to his voice.

'What's wrong, Da?' Davy asked.

'This boxing,' his father said. 'That's you finished.'

The shock hit Davy. 'Why?'

'You've done more than your uncles ever did,' his father said. 'It's enough.'

'I'm not boxing to be better than my uncles,' Davy said quietly.

'You've won an Ulster title and now an Irish title. What more do you want?'

Davy didn't dare say anything about fighting in the Olympic Games one day or maybe turning pro. Those dreams were impossible to express.

'Why do you like boxing?' his father asked.

'I enjoy it,' Davy said. 'And it's good discipline,' he added, trying to appeal to the military man inside his father.

His dad looked at him for a long time. 'What do you feel when you hit someone in the face?'

Davy sat quietly, mulling over his emotions. His eventual answer was simple and true: 'When I hit someone I get electric shocks up my arm.'

His father kept looking at him, as if seeing Davy for the very first time, and then waved him away. 'Go to bed.'

They did not talk about Davy giving up boxing again until his father was on his deathbed years later. Davy only knew how his dad felt because his younger brother John kept asking him: 'Isn't it time you packed it in?' His brother was proud of him being a boxer, but their dad kept pushing John to ask the question.

His mother said nothing about boxing. Davy guessed that, like his father, she worried he might get hurt. Silence settled over the house whenever he went to the gym or returned with his hair matted and his face marked up. It was only later that he learnt how their parents kept up with his boxing. People would say: 'I hear your son won his fight' or, 'I see your son won another title.' They were proud but, deep down, his parents were afraid for Davy.

At the Holy Family, Gerry always worked hard to avoid having any favourites. He was convincingly fair to everyone, but Davy knew the trainer had a special affection for Hugh Russell. With his bright-red hair and freckly face, and being a boy from the New Lodge, Hugh had been a standout fighter at the Holy Family for years.

Gerry joked that Hugh had been 'going on 11 for four years'. He was only meant to spar when he turned 11, but in the last few years before he reached that milestone Hugh would always disappear when the time came to produce evidence of his age. 'I've had the flu, Gerry,' he would tell his trainer when asked why he had not been in the gym on the day they were meant to hand in proof of their birthdate. Gerry knew he was a long way off 11 because when they weighed him the first time, Hugh was only three stone seven. He still wanted to box and Gerry understood. Hugh wanted to do what his big brother Sean did – spar and fight for real at the Holy Family and in competitions across the North and the South.

By the time he finally turned 11 in December 1970, he still weighed under five stone. But all his years of hanging around the Holy Family had rubbed off on him because, in 1971, he won the County Antrim title, as well as the Ulster championships, and even the All-Irelands for the lightest weight category. Hugh was so good, with Gerry in his corner, he was voted the best boxer of the whole National championship for boys aged between 11 and 17. People could hardly believe the little red terrier was such a fine boxer because, between rounds, Hugh had to be lifted on and off the stool by Gerry. His legs would not touch the ground.

Davy Larmour, a flyweight who now weighed eight stone, looked like a heroic figure to wee Hugh as they skipped rope alongside each other on a wintry Saturday morning in February 1972. Davy had not only won the Ulster Senior flyweight title, which was the championship Hugh dreamed of one day winning more than any other, but he had fought in the Commonwealth Games. Even more miraculously, some of Davy's fights had been screened on television. Hugh had watched plenty of John Wayne movies on TV – and Davy Larmour moved in the same exalted territory.

Davy didn't notice Hugh much. He had no idea that a decade later he and the tiny little red-headed kid would fight each other in two of the most memorable and bloodiest fights of the Troubles. The fighter from the Shankill Road and the little boxer from New

Lodge, the Protestant and the Catholic, would show the compelling power of the ring just as their communities seemed hell-bent on destroying each other.

It was enough for Gerry to watch Davy and Hugh, aged 19 and 12, work alongside lines of fighters crammed into the Holy Family sweatbox. Their age, religion and different backgrounds meant nothing. They were two special Holy Family fighters.

National Stadium, Dublin, Friday 28 April 1972

'I'm not going to win,' Davy Larmour said quietly in a corner of the crowded dressing room.

His trainer, Steamer Graham, who had worked with him for years at the Albert Foundry gym close to the Shankill Road, stared at him in disbelief. They were just minutes away from making the long walk to the ring before Davy fought Neil McLaughlin in the flyweight final of the Irish National championships.

'What do you mean, you're not going to win?' Steamer said incredulously.

'They'll never give me the decision here,' Davy replied, looking around a room filled with fighters from the South, as if to remind Steamer that they really were back in Dublin.

'Don't be daft,' Steamer snorted. 'You've beaten McLaughlin before.'

Larmour and McLaughlin had fought four times previously. McLaughlin, a slender but powerful puncher who came from the Bogside in Derry, had lost to Larmour the first time they met. He then avenged that defeat with a bruising victory in Belfast. They had since fought twice more in 1971, with McLaughlin shading the decision at the Ulster championships and then winning the Irish title with a bitterly disputed points victory at the Nationals in Dublin. The pain of those defeats still burnt inside Davy. But the devastation of Bloody Sunday convinced him he had no chance of ever beating McLaughlin in Dublin.

'I'm not going to win this,' he said again.

'Get that thought out of your head,' Steamer instructed him. 'You're going to win it so clearly you'll be the new champ.'

Davy shook his head solemnly.

'What's got into you?' Steamer asked.

'Who is going to vote for a guy from the Shankill over a kid from the Bogside?'

Steamer was just about to answer, but Davy kept on. 'In Dublin? At the National Stadium? Against a Derry man – after Bloody Sunday?'

Davy liked Neil McLaughlin. He was a good boxer, a stand-up fighter who worked behind his rangy jab and carried power in his fists and grit in his heart. Neil, like most boxers, was decent and fair, with few pretensions or affectations. There were rumours that Neil's involvement with the IRA had intensified since Bloody Sunday, but Davy ignored the talk. He took Neil as he found him: a good man who happened to be a testing opponent. It was hard enough to beat Neil, but the thought of fighting him for the Irish title with almost everyone in the hall rooting for a Catholic kid over a brawling wee Prod drained him of hope.

'C'mon,' Steamer urged him. 'You can do it.'

The trainer reminded Davy that a place in Gerry Storey's Ireland team for the Munich Olympics that year could be sealed if he beat McLaughlin in front of his ardent supporters.

It always took courage to step into the ring. But Davy drew on deeper reserves of bravery as he prepared for a fight he was still certain he could not win unless he caught McLaughlin with a peach of a shot and knocked him out. He allowed Steamer to wrap his hands in silence and then pull on his gloves. A white towel was placed around his neck and Gerry came over to wish him luck. Davy was an honorary Holy Family member, but he wore his Albert Foundry vest in honour of his Shankill roots.

Boos cascaded down as Davy made his walk to the ring. All his misgivings about being a Protestant boxer up against the reigning champion from Derry echoed around him. Davy shut out everything. He stopped thinking of injustice and sectarianism, of Derry and Dublin. Everything boiled down to him and McLaughlin in the ring. Nothing else mattered as he bit down on his gumshield and they touched gloves in the centre of the ring.

From the first bell to the last, Larmour dominated. He bullied McLaughlin and sank body shots into his stomach and flanks. Larmour also jolted his head back with sharp jabs. Even two warnings against him in the first round, for ducking too low while McLaughlin tried to spear him with his jab, did not deter the Shankill fighter. Larmour poured on the pressure, winning over the crowd and the fight with each round. At the final bell the arena erupted in appreciation, especially for the Belfast flyweight they had booed on his arrival. Davy embraced Neil. He surely had done enough to bring the title back to Belfast.

Slow handclapping broke out at the announcement of a split decision. The consensus was that Larmour had won the fight clearly. Booing resumed when the winner's name was announced. McLaughlin, usually a Dublin favourite, looked sheepish as he heard the crowd's displeasure.

Davy smiled and shrugged. Another defeat stung but he felt like a winner. Who else from the Shankill Road could have won over a hostile Dublin crowd?

He sat at ringside later, accepting plaudits and commiserations in equal measure as he watched the great Charlie Nash retain his lightweight title with an easy victory over Christy McKenna. Charlie did not celebrate in the ring. He still cut a haunted figure. Less than three months had passed since he lost his brother on Bloody Sunday.

Charlie Nash, somehow, kept fighting on. Davy Larmour would do the same.

Davy's brother John and their father worked in Belfast's Market Quarter. They stood out as Protestants in a Republican area but they had no fear that they would be taken out and shot just because they came from the wrong side of the sectarian divide. Even when other people expressed concerns about their safety, Samuel Larmour brushed aside such fears: 'Them people will do us no harm. We're all right in the markets.'

The markets, everyone said, were run by dangerous Republicans. Davy's father didn't care. He was friendly with some of the top men in the markets, like Joe McCann, a commanding officer of the Official IRA, and so the apprehension of others seemed ridiculous. Joe was always fair and he and Samuel Larmour respected each other. What did it matter that some of the Republicans carried rifles to work? They weren't going to shoot him or John.

Davy worked as an apprentice tiler in Carrickfergus, or Carrick as they called it, 11 miles from Belfast in County Antrim. On a spring evening in May 1972, once work was done for the day, Davy dropped by to see a friend. His pal, Bert Shields, was still not home, but Davy was ushered into the front room. Mrs Shields was nattering to a neighbour so she switched on the television so Davy could watch the news while he waited for Bert.

The news began with a report of a bomb exploding in Ann Street in the centre of Belfast. As Davy watched the black-and-white footage he nearly cried out when he saw his father's lorry on the screen. He would have known his dad's lorry anywhere and now, even with it wrecked on its side and bombed to pieces, he was certain. It was the same lorry his dad and John took to the markets every morning.

Bert's brother rushed in and, glancing at Davy's face, he knew his friend had heard the news. 'That's my da's lorry,' Davy said, his finger trembling as he pointed to the screen.

Bert ran in behind his brother. His voice was hoarse and jagged. 'Davy,' he said, 'you have to get up to the Royal. Your da has been blown up.'

Davy did not move at first. On the television he could hear them talking about an IRA bomb being planted in a yellow Volkswagen.

It had exploded just as a lorry from the markets passed by, near to Musgrave police station and on the way towards Victoria Street.

'That's my da,' Davy said, his gaze fixed on the screen.

A doctor happened to witness the bombing and, seeing the lorry driver bleeding badly from the throat as he stumbled from his vehicle, he moved quickly to help. The driver, fearing another attack, tried to fight him off. 'Lie still, son,' the doctor told him. 'I'm here to help you.' The driver's jugular vein had been cut but the doctor stemmed the flow of blood until an ambulance arrived.

'They're talking about my da,' Davy said, looking up helplessly at Bert and his brother.

'Come on, Davy,' Bert urged. 'Let's go see your daddy in the Royal.'

Bert and his brother drove Davy to the Royal Victoria Hospital. The journey was a blur and Davy was not even sure how he found himself on the third floor just as they wheeled his father out of the operating theatre. Samuel Larmour's face and head were covered in a white balaclava made out of bandages. The balaclava had turned red as blood seeped through the bandages.

'Holy God,' Davy said. He knew his dad was a difficult man. He had felt the back of his hand many times. He also could not escape the disappointment that his father wanted him to give up the glory and pain of boxing for a routine life. They shared no real connection but, still, Davy needed him.

It was hard to believe that the shell of his father, so wounded and traumatised by the bomb, would ever return to ordinary life. He remained in hospital, saying little to anyone as, beneath the bandages and the glazed expression in his eyes, he kept breathing but hardly living. Davy felt no bitterness towards the Republicans who had bombed his father by accident. He was consumed instead by sadness.

Davy had switched his apprentice tiling work to Murray's Tobacco Factory on Sandy Row. It was a Loyalist area, but some Catholics were also employed by the factory. One morning a few weeks after his father had been blown up, he and a Catholic heating engineer worked comfortably together. They swapped small talk as they laid cement on the factory floor. Davy liked the engineer – even though there were rumours that the man was a member of the IRA. When they stopped for a short break, the engineer looked over at him. He spoke quietly and compassionately. 'You all right, wee man?' he asked.

'I'm okay,' Davy said.

After a long pause the man from the IRA said: 'Davy, if it's any consolation to you, there was an explosion in Short Strand last night. It was in a factory where they were making bombs. The four guys who were blown up were the ones who blew up your dad.'

Davy looked steadily at the man as he absorbed the news. 'To tell you the truth,' he said, 'it's no consolation to me because that's four more families who are grieving.'

The Republican nodded his understanding. 'I just thought I'd let you know,' he said softly.

CHAPTER 4

The Darkest Year

It was the darkest year in the history of the Troubles and of Charlie Nash's life. His brother William was one of 497 people who died in 1972 as a direct result of sectarian violence. Charlie's close friends, including Damien McDermott, said he was never the same after Bloody Sunday. He remained a kind and polite man, and a dedicated boxer, but he became even quieter and more introspective after Willie's death.

Decades later, he would look back in wonder at his achievement in boxing for Ireland at the 1972 Olympic Games just seven months after Bloody Sunday. January had been a brute of a month in which he lost his brother and his best friend, Mousey Harkin, his mother suffered a heart attack, his father was shot by the British army, and his home town was devastated.

Despite the fact that punches were thrown at him and he endured physical pain, boxing offered balm for these wounds. Inside a hard and violent sport, Charlie found comfort and peace. The world outside was cruel and malevolent but the ring was ordered and rewarding. Boxing gave Charlie meaning and solace. Men were killing each other senselessly while, inside the ring, boxers were able to find a purity of purpose in improving themselves and respecting their opponents.

There was relief, rather than joy, when Charlie's expected place in Ireland's Olympic squad was confirmed. He had been the National lightweight champion three years in a row and so his selection was a formality. But preparing for the Olympics required a fierce concentration that would divert him from grief and life in Derry. It was made sweeter by the fact that Gerry Storey was his Olympic trainer.

Charlie travelled to Belfast every Friday evening in the summer of '72. He stayed with Gerry and Belle Storey and their four children in New Lodge each Friday and Saturday night. This allowed them to train together at the Holy Family on Friday evening, have two sessions on the Saturday and another on Sunday morning.

Charlie felt at ease with Gerry and his family. The three boys – Gerry Jr, Sam and Martin – were all junior Holy Family fighters and the Storey house was steeped in boxing. Gerry Sr never pushed him to talk about Bloody Sunday. He focused instead on Charlie's boxing skills while Belle was like a second mother on those summer weekends in New Lodge. They settled into a soothing rhythm that helped Charlie recover from all he had been through that year.

Every Friday afternoon, Charlie knocked off early from work at the printing company, where he still manned the guillotine. He could not yet drive so he would catch the bus from Derry to Belfast. It was a long haul – a two-hour journey interrupted by numerous security checkpoints. Gerry would pick him up at the bus station and they were usually at the Holy Family and ready for training within half an hour of Charlie's arrival.

Yet the Troubles were all-consuming in 1972. The militant UDA had 40,000 Loyalist members, and dozens of sectarian murders to its name, while its hated enemy, the Provisional IRA, had taken over Republican militancy. The Provos had a new weapon, the car bomb, which they had begun to test in Belfast. Davy Larmour's dad had been blown up in a trial run for a deadly series of car-bomb attacks planned for Belfast in July. An ordinary car, like the yellow Volkswagen that blew up in front of the Larmours' lorry, could conceal and transport explosives. And once the car was parked and the detonator was ignited at a time designed to cause maximum carnage and death, the exploding metal and glass turned into lethal shrapnel.

Secret talks between the British government and the IRA had been held in London on 7 July – with a young Gerry Adams one of those released from internment to attend the talks – but dialogue broke down. The IRA were emphatic there should be a complete withdrawal of British troops from Northern Ireland. This demand was dismissed by the British government, and hopes of reconciliation had been replaced by increased intransigence on both sides. The Provisional wing of the IRA resolved to unleash an unprecedented campaign of terror.

Charlie reached Belfast on the Friday evening of 21 July 1972 to find mayhem. Twenty-two IRA bombs had been detonated across Belfast in 75 minutes. Nine people had been killed and 130 were injured. Bodies were maimed and mutilated while people scattered in panic and fear – not knowing whether they were running towards or away from another bomb. 'People walking in the streets around 2.30pm seemed to hear a bomb a minute and in the city centre some women became shocked and hysterical and had to be treated,' the *Irish Times* reported. 'Few events in the past awful year have so appalled people.'

Another bleak milestone of terror was enshrined in the history of the Troubles. After Bloody Sunday in Derry, this was Bloody Friday in Belfast.

The aftermath would resonate for years and people in the city remained haunted by all they had seen and heard. Even those who escaped the bombings felt the consequences. Descriptions of body parts being strewn all over the streets echoed around Belfast. People had been murdered or maimed just because they had been unlucky enough to catch a bus on Oxford Street when some of the bombs exploded – or because they stepped out of their homes or offices to do some shopping. Ordinary life had been blown apart.

Gerry wanted to ease off training, but boxing offered salvation amid the madness and misery. The Olympics mattered to them and so, the next morning, they drove to Dublin to resume training in a more tranquil setting.

The drive sparked warm memories for Charlie. He had travelled before with Gerry to Dublin when they had picked up Davy Larmour on the way. Charlie and Davy were good friends and their different religions seemed immaterial on those journeys to Dublin. Neil McLaughlin, however, had been selected ahead of Davy for the Olympics.

Apart from the two Derry fighters, the team included Mick Dowling, Jim Montague, John Rodgers and Christy Elliott. Four of the six boxers were from Northern Ireland, with only Dowling and Elliott being born and raised in the South, and so the Olympic team offered yet more evidence of the special place boxing occupied in the Irish sporting consciousness. Division and strife consumed the rest of society but, in boxing, there was harmony in a united Ireland team. Most other Olympians from Northern Ireland, in contrast, competed for the British team in Munich.

In the last two weeks before they left for Munich, the six Irish boxers trained together in Dublin. Charlie was given two weeks off his printing job to help him prepare to fight the best state-sponsored East European and Cuban boxers, who could train all year round without working in an ordinary job. The odds, as always, were stacked against the Irish.

Munich, at first, provided respite for Charlie Nash. There were no burning barricades, rumbling Saracens, car bombs or violent army raids in the middle of the night. Instead, there was diversity and calm in the Olympic village as the Irish boxers met athletes from around the world and readied themselves for their tilt at glory.

Charlie began to relax away from the relentless tension of Derry and Belfast.

Gerry Storey had his Olympic boxers working on techniques to enhance their fitness and hand–eye co-ordination, which would be emulated later that decade by some great Cuban boxing trainers. He used tennis balls for his boxers to bounce and hit. Most other international coaches laughed at the seeming lunacy, but ten years later, when the Cubans came to box in Ireland, all their coaches used the Storey tennis ball trick to sharpen their fighters. Gerry carried a renown in world boxing that also meant that brilliant professional cornermen like Ray Arcel, the legendary American trainer, would seek him out to discuss fight strategies and psychology.

Gerry was the best-schooled coach Charlie had ever known. His command of the basics of boxing was so rigorous that he passed on such clear advice that even mature Olympic fighters who trained under him improved. He was especially adept in sharpening their combination punching and tactical preparations at this highest level of amateur boxing.

Even Gerry battled for parity against the Communist boxers and trainers who had begun to dominate Olympic competition. Three of his boxers in Munich lost narrowly to fighters who went on to win the gold medal – with Mick Dowling unluckiest of all in losing a split decision to Cuba's Orlando Martinez, the eventual Olympic bantamweight champion.

Charlie Nash won his first two bouts in Munich in style, out-classing Denmark's Erik Madsen before stopping the Mexican Antonio Gin in just over a minute. He needed to beat Poland's Jan Szczepanski in the quarter-finals to guarantee himself at least a bronze medal and, with Gerry guiding him from the corner in the opening two rounds, Charlie opened up a lead. Szczepanski, however, was the European lightweight champion and a hardened professional in comparison to the grieving amateur. The Pole's superior conditioning was plain in the midst of a furious onslaught in the third and final round. Charlie was much more skilled but three bouts in successive days, while struggling to make weight, was too much for him. The referee signalled the fight was over just before the final bell. Szczepanski went on to win gold, but losing to the champion hardly consoled Charlie.

That same evening, on 4 September, the American swimmer Mark Spitz won a record seventh gold medal. But even such a prodigious feat would soon be overshadowed by death.

In the early hours of 5 September 1972, eight members of the Palestinian terrorist group, Black September, broke into the Olympic village and killed two members of the Israeli team and took nine hostages. The noise confused many of the sleeping Olympians, but Charlie knew he was waking up to a sound that reminded him of home.

'That's a rifle,' he said in the dark as his confused teammates asked what was happening. 'Someone's being shot.'

The hostage crisis lasted over 20 hours, with Black September demanding the release of 234 Palestinian prisoners in Israel. Negotiations broke down and German police killed five members of the terrorist group in a failed attempt to rescue the hostages. All the Israeli hostages and a German policeman were shot and the fatalities rose to seventeen.

Charlie, Gerry and the Irish team were safe, but they were numbed by the familiar violence and death. It soon felt closer to home again.

Mary Peters, a 33-year-old secretary from Belfast, had won gold for Great Britain in the pentathlon two days earlier. Within hours of her victory, an anonymous caller phoned the BBC in London to place a death threat: 'Mary Peters is a Protestant and has won a medal for Britain. An attempt will be made on her life and it will be blamed on the IRA. Tell Mary Peters to say something about bringing the people together. I don't want to turn her into a martyr. Her home will be going up in the near future.'

Peters, who was born in England and raised in Ballymena from the age of 11, was a bold and cheery woman. She was thrilled to be an Olympic champion and, while forced to take the death threat seriously, she refused to be intimidated. Armed police kept her away from the crowds when she landed in Belfast, and people resorted to pinning their posters and hanging baskets of gifts for her on the barbed-wire fences that kept them outside the airport. Nevertheless, she travelled down Royal Avenue in the heart of the city and showed her medal to everyone who greeted her. The police were twitchy but Peters told them that, 'If anyone wants to take my life I've achieved what I wanted anyway.'

A few days later she was driven to City Hall on the back of a lorry. Thousands of people lined the streets as Peters waved her gold medal in the air. No shots rang out that day as, briefly, Belfast celebrated its sporting happiness.

Charlie Nash's destiny changed on a different open-topped lorry. After the worst year of his life, he met his future wife on the back of a lorry that paraded through Derry as Charlie, Neil McLaughlin, the swimmer Liam Ball and the judo Olympian Terry Watt were greeted as returning heroes, even without any medals, in their home town. As they reached the Bogside, Charlie's trainer, Tommy Donnelly, lifted a pretty girl onto the back of the lorry. Her name was Betty and she worked in a local shirt factory with Tommy's wife, Josie. Betty shook hands with all four Olympians – as Charlie, despite his fame in Derry, turned very red.

Fate gave the shy boxer a timely nudge ten days later. Charlie was persuaded by some of his friends to cross the border with them on a Saturday night. The small town of Muff was only seven miles away, but it was in County Donegal in the Republic of Ireland rather than in the North. Every Saturday night it hosted a dance in a club called Borderland. Amid daily terror in Derry, the Borderland lit up an escape. It billed itself as the 'Ballroom of Romance' and hundreds of young people from Derry caught the Saturday-night buses that crossed the border, manned by rifle-wielding soldiers, so they could dance and forget everyday life.

Joe Dolan and His Drifters played the Borderland that night and, wearing his best sports jacket, Charlie joined his friends. It was a typical Saturday night in Muff. All the girls, in their favourite dresses, gathered down one side of the hall, chatting among themselves while swaying gently to the music that preceded the arrival of the showband. The boys stood awkwardly opposite them, looking sheepishly at the girls without being brave enough to walk over and ask for a dance.

Charlie was far too embarrassed to wander over, even at the age of 21, to talk to a girl before anyone else did the same. He thought again of Willie and how much his brother had loved to dance. So he slipped outside to the little shop that sold tea and soft drinks to the non-dancers. Charlie felt more comfortable away from the strict separation of the sexes and, after a while, he was bold enough to go back inside.

By now the Drifters were in full swing and Joe Dolan was crooning. Many of the girls had taken to the dance floor and a few boys had joined them, but Charlie preferred to wait. He knew the routine. Three fast songs would be followed by three slow dances. Like almost everyone else, he was waiting for the first slow dance before he would feel ready to take the plunge. Dancing was so much harder than boxing.

He was taken aback when the first slow song, 'Unchained Melody', started. It seemed as if everyone reacted quicker than him and coupled up. Charlie was alone when he saw her.

Betty, the girl from the lorry. She was 19 and very pretty.

She was so close to him it was almost as if they had been flung together. Charlie gulped and then he got the words out: 'Would you like to dance?'

'Yes,' Betty said simply, smiling just as shyly back at him.

As Joe Dolan sang the Righteous Brothers' opening lines – 'Oh, my love, my darling, I've hungered for your touch' – Charlie held Betty. They danced together, close and quiet, throughout the three slow Drifters tunes while Joe warbled about love and magic.

As was customary if you fancied a girl, Charlie asked Betty if she'd like to 'stay on' and keep dancing with him once the trio of foot-shufflers and sweaty hand-holders was over. She said 'Yes' again. They began to bop together to some more upbeat Drifters numbers.

Eventually, Charlie asked Betty, 'Would you like a mineral?'

Betty again said 'Yes' and over their drinks she nodded once more when Charlie wondered if they could catch the bus back to Derry together and he could see her home to Carnhill.

He asked one last question when they reached her front door: 'Can I see you again?'

There was one more clinching 'Yes'. Charlie kissed his new girl goodnight. As the door closed behind him his head and his heart hummed in ways he had not imagined since Bloody Sunday. It was possible, after all, to feel hopeful and happy again.

Carnhill was three miles from Charlie's home in Creggan and it was two in the morning. He knew there would be security check-points and soldiers to pass numerous times on his way home, but Charlie didn't care. These were sombre times – but he felt joyful.

He started the long walk home but, within 30 seconds, he could not stop himself. His walk turned into a jog, which became a run. Charlie Nash ran all the way home, his dancing feet flying beneath him. It was as if he knew that, in less than a year, he and Betty would be married and that, over 45 years later, they'd still be together. He was running to a different future. Charlie would never forget the past but, that night, he could begin again.

Davy Larmour's luck also turned with a new year. On 17 March 1973, St Patrick's Day, Davy married Ellen. He and everyone else they knew called her Ellie. Davy and Ellie had met two years earlier in a Chinese restaurant in Belfast. She walked over to his table, looking concerned. Ellie asked Davy and his friend if she could join them for a few minutes. A fellow upstairs had been giving her a hard time. Davy, who did not give in to bullies, reassured her. She was welcome to stay at their table as long as she liked.

Ellie felt so safe with Davy that her gratitude turned to romance. But their relationship was framed by her acceptance of his dedication to boxing. Seven weeks after their wedding, Davy won his first Irish National title as he beat Brendan Dunne to become bantamweight champion in Dublin on 11 May 1973. His friends from Derry, Damien McDermott and Charlie Nash, also won titles again that year as they moved up, respectively, to lightweight and light-welterweight. Davy's breakthrough win, however, was the talk of the tournament after he had suffered such a contentious decision against Neil McLaughlin twice before in the Republic.

Just before the wedding, his work as an apprentice tiler had resumed in Ballymena at the Michelin tyre factory. Ballymena was conservative and deeply Protestant, a town where the playground swings were tied up on a Sunday. It was also the constituency of Reverend Ian Paisley, who barked out 'Never Surrender to the IRA' and denounced Catholicism whenever he could. 'The dog will return to its vomit, the washed sow will return to its wallowing in the mire,' Paisley roared, 'but by God's grace we will never return to Popery again. No pope here, in Ballymena, in Ulster, in Northern Ireland ever again.'

Davy believed that Paisley's rhetoric, as Ballymena's Member of Parliament for North Antrim, was dangerous and offensive. He preached fire and brimstone that fanned and almost legitimised the murderous paramilitaries of the UDA and UVF. Paisley believed in a separatist ideology, a theological version of apartheid, but Davy refused to accept such segregation and, as a Protestant, abhorred discrimination against Catholics in Northern Ireland. Davy continued training with Gerry at the Holy Family and meeting his Catholic friends and fellow boxers like Paddy Maguire on the Falls Road.

Boxing soon offered Davy another chance to blur the sectarian boundaries. He returned to his job at Michelin as Irish champion and kept his head down. He was not the kind of man to boast about his achievements, so he was taken aback one ordinary Friday at the factory when he was told a priest had arrived at the security gate to see him. Davy knew that not many people from the Shankill Road would ever meet a Catholic priest in Ballymena. He had been tiling the toilets and so he rubbed the grout from his face and hurried to the gate.

His surprise intensified when he saw Father Darragh, who was associated with the All Saints Boxing Club in Ballymena. The priest had astonishing news: Davy had been selected to box his first international for Ireland – against Romania that night in Dublin. There was just enough time for Father Darragh to hand over two train tickets to Davy so that he could travel back to Belfast to pick up his boxing gear and then catch a connection to Dublin.

He arrived in Belfast in a rush and then, realising he had no money as he had forgotten to pick up his pay for the week, he had to run all the way home in his work boots. 'Ma, I need clean boxing gear because I'm fighting in Dublin for Ireland tonight,' he told his bewildered mother as he bounded up the stairs.

His mother hated him being a boxer but, by the time he had filled a bag with his towels, socks, boots, bandages, Vaseline, foul protector and gumshield, she handed over a freshly ironed vest, shirt, shorts and two £5 notes.

'Thanks, Ma,' Davy said with a grin. He caught the bus back to Belfast station and made his train to Dublin. From there a taxi took him to the National Stadium. It was just after 9pm and the turnstiles were closed as the boxing had begun 90 minutes earlier. Davy banged on one of the stadium doors.

'What do ya want?' a man in a peaked cap snarled as he opened the door a crack.

'I'm Davy Larmour and I'm fighting tonight,' the strapping little bantamweight said.

The door opened and a man with a broad Dublin brogue asked his Belfast visitor if he knew the way. Davy nodded and ran to the dressing room, where a tubby former boxer, Benny Carabini, was waiting.

'You made it, wee man,' Benny exclaimed. 'You'd better hurry up and get ready.'

Benny handed him a parcel and Davy tore it open. A pair of white satin boxing shorts with a green belt and stripes running down the side was matched by an emerald-green vest. In the middle of the vest a stitched cotton shield with two stems of green shamrock gleamed beneath the hot lights of the dressing room.

The vest shimmered beneath Davy's gaze. He could barely believe his eyes. His Ireland debut was about to happen. The fact that he was a Protestant from the Loyalist Shankill made him even prouder. He could imagine Reverend Dr Paisley turning purple at the sight of his green Irish vest in place of a Union Jack.

He snapped out of his daze when he heard his name being hollered in the corridor.

'Lar-mour! Davy Lar-mour! You're wanted in the ring!'

Davy stripped off his street clothes and pulled on the National colours and boxing boots. He wrapped his hands hurriedly and carried his gloves to the ring, hoping Gerry Storey would be there to help him. People slapped him on the back and shouted out good luck.

As the two fighters from the previous bout prepared to leave the ring, Davy stood and waited.

'How do you feel?' an Irish official in a green blazer asked him.

'Nervous,' Davy admitted.

'Oh, you'll be okay,' the man promised him airily.

Davy was relieved to see Gerry in the ring. He wanted to ask Gerry why there had been such confusion, but Davy needed to have his gloves pulled on. His squat and swarthy opponent, Aural Mehi, waited in the centre of the ring. There was no time for Gerry to pass on any instructions before they were introduced: 'In the green corner, from the Albert Foundry club in Belfast, and boxing for Ireland, put your hands together for DAVY LARMOURRRRRRR!'

Gerry shoved the gumshield into Davy's mouth while the referee spoke to both fighters. His instructions were lost in the roaring. Davy only heard the last words: 'Shake hands and come out fighting!'

The first round was cagey as Davy and Mehi jabbed at each other warily. They were both trying to gauge each other's ability without taking undue risks. At the bell, Davy returned to the corner and began to understand how deeply stressed he was on the inside. He could see Gerry's mouth moving as he removed the gumshield and handed it down to be cleaned before reaching for a towel. Gerry kept talking while wiping his fighter's face and smearing it again with Vaseline. Davy could not hear a word. He was lost in a vortex of nerves.

He felt cold and stiff as he came out for the second round. Davy felt a shiver as the Romanian moved easily away from his leaden punches and then slipped inside to land some point-scoring jabs. The punches did not hurt enough to snap him out of his numb cocoon. All his usual fighting will drained away.

In the corner, before the last round, Gerry completed the same routine. He calmly removed the gumshield, wiped Davy's sweat away and rubbed Vaseline over his eyebrows. Gerry began talking again, urgently, but the words would not register in Davy's befuddled brain. He wished he could close his exhausted eyes.

Gerry pushed him back out into the ring for the last round. Davy wanted to avoid the indignity of being stopped in his first international. He threw a few decent punches but, for most of the round, Davy clung to his opponent. It was one way of staying on his feet.

At the bell, there was no tension or drama. Davy was only surprised the verdict was not unanimous. 'The winner by majority decision – Mehi!'

As he and Gerry walked back to the dressing room, the disappointment began to bite. Davy resolved to never again enter the ring in such an unprepared state.

Gerry, as always, soothed him in the dressing room. There was even an explanation from an Irish official as to why he had not been informed that he was fighting until just six hours before he stepped into the ring. RTÉ, the Republic's national television broadcaster, had signed a contract with the Irish Amateur Boxing Association to screen 11 international bouts that night. Yet the IABA had only selected their usual team of ten fighters. The call had then gone out that afternoon, when the mistake was highlighted, and Davy was summoned.

Davy wished it could have been different. But he could not help smiling when, coming back from the showers, he saw that his green vest had been folded neatly and placed on top of his bag. It was Gerry's way of reminding Davy that he had done it. He had boxed for Ireland – and he would do so again with much greater success in the coming years. One day, he promised himself, he would win a medal for Ireland in a major tournament.

Damien McDermott, a fellow Irish champion that year, and a friend of both Davy Larmour and Charlie Nash, felt the horror of ordinary violence in Derry. The thrill of winning a National title in Dublin in 1973 turned cold down an alleyway on the Creggan housing estate. There were four gunshots, spaced out evenly enough to suggest that each was aimed at a new target. Damien knew there could be four corpses lying in the alley but, far more likely, one victim had taken all four bullets in different parts of his body. He had lived in Derry long enough to recognise the ricocheting impact of a punishment shooting.

The gunman walked calmly back out into the drizzle of a summer evening. He did not hide his face. Instead he looked straight at the boxer while walking past him. Damien knew the shooter. He was an IRA man whom Damien would talk to often in later years. The man would turn out to be surprisingly pleasant, yet he showed no remorse for the punishments he had meted out as a soldier of the Provisional IRA.

There was nothing pleasant in the alleyway. A young alcoholic from the estate, a lost soul whom Damien knew, lay whimpering and bleeding on the ground. Damien could see the gaping wounds through the man's torn jeans. He had been shot above and below both kneecaps.

'Am I going to die?' the man asked pitifully.

'No, you'll be all right,' Damien said as he used some tape from his boxing bag to tie a tourniquet around each shattered leg.

Another man from the estate had run across the street. He stood at the top of the alley, watching Damien's attempt to staunch the sticky flow of blood from both legs.

'For fuck's sake,' Damien shouted, 'will you get an ambulance?'

'They phoned the ambulance before they shot him,' the man said.

'You smart bastard,' Damien muttered to himself as he tightened the tourniquet.

It had been a trademark punishment shooting. The alcoholic had begun drinking on the estate when he was 17 and had gradually hit the bottle harder and harder. Damien knew the young drinker was spoilt by his granny, who looked after him and tried to ignore his problems, but he was not an evil kid. He was just lost and so, a few days earlier, he had broken into a shop because he needed money for drink. The IRA decided to administer justice – as a way of punishing the drunken thief and a warning to everyone on the Creggan estate that crime would not be tolerated. They were fighting for a higher cause. The cause, however, was not so noble that it precluded kneecappings down a stinking alleyway.

The poor alcoholic whom Damien helped that day would kill himself a few years later. Damien wondered, in later years, how much the man who had shot him in the alley allowed himself to remember of all he had done during the Troubles. He would have been acting under orders, but surely there was a price to pay, inside a man's soul, for such actions?

Damien saw evidence of that cost in a different alcoholic decades later. This desperate drinker is an old woman now, a former member of the IRA, who was infamous for the tarring and feathering of her victims in the 1970s. Men who made mistakes or committed crimes would be shot in the leg, but fallen women were punished differently.

There were terrible scenes from that same summer of 1973. Women accused of sleeping with British soldiers in Derry were dealt with harshly. The future alcoholic would pick out the miscreant and, with three or four other IRA members, she would march her into the centre of the estate. There, they would tie the 'Brit-loving' victim to a lamp post. They had usually shaved the head of the woman before they poured tar over her. Feathers would be scattered on her tarred skin.

The black gunk would take days to wipe away entirely from every painful pore. Sometimes, paint would be used instead of tar and, to complete the grim scene, a placard would be placed around the woman's neck. The words on the sign were crude. They told the whole of Derry that the tarred-and-feathered woman was a 'Soldier Lover' or a 'Whore'. After an hour or two, once the IRA had left the scene, someone from the woman's family would dare to cut her free.

Such images reeled through Damien's mind until, in the serenity of the gym, he would skip rope, work the heavy bag or face the skilful sparring of Charlie Nash. Boxing helped cleanse him of everything he had seen – until the next time.

Wednesday afternoons were always quiet in Belfast in 1973. All the shops shut at 1pm and the rest of the day felt like a Sunday afternoon. Gerry liked Wednesdays because he could knock off early from the Deep Sea Docks, where he drove a forklift truck, and start training his boxers at the Holy Family. He drove down the Antrim Road, enjoying the lack of traffic while planning his gym sessions. He stopped off at home to change and say hello to Belle and the kids. When he got back into his car he heard the familiar noise.

He called it gunplay – as a way of defusing its gravity as the IRA, Loyalist paramilitaries and the army blasted bullets at each other. It sounded as if this latest burst of gunplay was up in west Belfast and so he climbed back into his Cortina. He eased out of Willowbank Gardens and headed east towards the Antrim Road, where he took a right turn. Gerry rolled down his window as it was a warm afternoon. After driving half a mile the gunplay became louder. As he turned left onto the New Lodge Road, the gunshots continued. He wound up his window and, ten seconds later, all was quiet but for the whirr of his Cortina. He felt safe, as always, and rolled into the Patrickville centre where the Holy Family gym was then located.

The gunplay was over. Gerry picked up his bag and locked the car. He had just reached the entrance to the gym when he remembered that he had left some paperwork in the boot. Gerry walked back to the car and had another good look around to see if he could spot any paramilitaries. He saw and heard nothing as he collected the papers and walked to the gym. As soon as he stepped inside, the gunplay resumed. Bullets whirred through the air and smacked into bollards on the road. Little pieces of plastic flew up into the air like meaningless Wednesday afternoon confetti.

Some of his boxers stared at him in surprise. 'Did you come down the New Lodge Road, Gerry?' the heavyweight Patsy Reid asked him.

'I did,' Gerry said. 'I heard the gunplay even before then.'

'It's been going on for 20 minutes,' Reid said. 'It just stopped when you arrived and now it's started again.'

Gerry nodded. He wanted to get the boys back into the ring and away from the shooting. 'Come on, fellas,' he urged them.

Training went well and Gerry forgot all about the bullets whistling past outside – until Patsy and another of his boxers were ready to leave later that afternoon.

'Are you all right going out there now, Patsy?' Gerry asked.

Patsy stuck his head outside and listened. 'It's all over, Gerry,' he said. 'We'll be fine.'

Gerry reminded them to be back in for training the following evening, and turned his attention to the new influx of fighters waiting to work with him.

Patsy and his pal had just reached the bottom of the New Lodge Road when the army intercepted them. Soldiers pressed them against a brick wall, sticking rifles in their backs and kicking their ankles apart to make them spread their legs. They searched the Holy Family boxers and found no weapons. Patsy and his friend were told to turn around.

'Right, who's driving the bronze Cortina?' one of the soldiers asked.

'That's Gerry Storey's car,' Patsy said.

'What is he?' another soldier asked.

'A boxing trainer.'

'Yes,' the soldier snapped. 'We know about Storey and the boxing. But what is he?'

'What do you mean?' Patsy asked.

'He's high-ranking IRA, that's who he is,' the soldier said.

'No,' Patsy insisted, 'he's our trainer at the Holy Family. He's got nothing to do with the 'RA.'

The soldier shoved his face right into Patsy's. 'Listen, when he hit the top of the New Lodge Road to come down here, there was a ceasefire until he got into the club.'

There was a long pause and then the soldier laughed bitterly. 'You really want us to believe he's only a boxing trainer when the IRA won't fire a bullet when he's in eyeshot?'

Patsy shrugged. 'That's Gerry. Everyone knows he's only into the boxing.'

The soldiers stared at Patsy. Then, prodding him and his friend with a rifle, they sent the Holy Family boys out into another quiet afternoon in Belfast.

CHAPTER 5

Crossing Borders

Gerry Storey could not be certain the bomb was meant for him. He knew, however, that it was planted on a foggy Friday afternoon in the Belfast docks with an intent to murder its victims. It would be the first of three bomb attempts that came close to ending his life. An anonymous written threat had already been left for him in late 1972. That scrawled note told him to get out of Belfast if he wanted to stay alive. The trainer threw the warning away. He had a simple retort to anyone who asked why he risked his life: what would happen if all the good people left Belfast?

Nine months later, just before the explosion in the autumn of 1973, boxing consumed Gerry. There was a tournament in Dublin that night and he needed to drive three boys from Belfast so they arrived in time for the first bout. Meanwhile, in the shadowy docks, the bombers considered where they might place their package.

Belfast's divided docks were open to Gerry. He drove his forklift truck across the segregated docklands with the same freedom that allowed him to criss-cross the opposing sectarian quarters of the city in his Cortina. Gerry worked for Deep Sea Docks, a company whose employees were almost exclusively Catholic. He also delivered and collected cargo for Cross Channel Docks, which had a

99 per cent Protestant workforce. Gerry had worked on both sides of the docks for years and he refused to change even when the Troubles escalated. He went wherever he was needed.

At Deep Sea his cross-community work in boxing was well known and accepted, and so it did not seem strange that Gerry should appear so often on the Protestant side. He was also a familiar face on the Cross Channel wharf, and his work was so valuable to the company that the Protestant bosses and dockers just thought of him as 'Gerry' – rather than as a Catholic, a Republican, a 'Taig' or a Fenian bastard.

That afternoon Gerry rode the forklift with Frank McCann, who also worked at the Holy Family and was known as Yank. Gerry and Yank had containers of tobacco to unload at Sinclair Wharf, on the Deep Sea side of the docks, but a call had just come in for them to get to a distant loading berth at Cross Channel to pick up a different cargo. The unexpected call had ruined their plans to finish work early and race off to Dublin.

'Now, Yank,' Gerry asked, 'how are we going to make this work?'

'What about if we get over to Cross Channel and ask them to drop the cargo closer to here?' Yank suggested. 'We can get back here and lift the tobacco while they deliver their cargo.'

Gerry smiled and started the truck. They rattled through the swirling fog and reached the designated spot five minutes later. There was no one else around and the docks looked ghostly. A foghorn on the murky grey water sounded eerie. Gerry soon felt uneasy.

'I'm not sure about this, Yank,' he said quietly. 'I think he's going to come around the other side – from Sinclair Wharf. Let's try and meet him there.'

Yank nodded. Gerry was the boss and he knew the rhythm of the docks better than anyone.

Gerry switched on the engine and swung back in the direction of Sinclair Wharf. They had just reached the gate when the docks shook with a reverberating blast. It was that unmistakable big boom followed by a few moments of stunned silence before the crackle of fire began and the first wisps of black smoke rose from the wreckage.

Yank gripped Gerry's arm after they wheeled around and saw the bomb site. The explosion had happened a few feet from where they had parked while waiting for the cargo to arrive.

'If we hadn't moved ...' Yank said, his voice trailing away as debris from the bomb fluttered up into the gloomy light.

'We would be gone,' Gerry said simply. He knew that they would never have survived the bomb, which had either been planted by the 'RA with the intention of destroying the Cross Channel cargo or had been a Loyalist bomb meant for him.

'Yank,' Gerry said thoughtfully, 'I think we're going to be late for Dublin.'

Boxers were revered in Catholic areas. Davy Larmour was a champion, who trained often at the Holy Family, and so he was accepted. There was unusual aggravation when he returned home to the Shankill Road. A group of taunting Loyalists would mock Davy and, when he ignored them for weeks, they attacked him because of his association with Catholics. He fought back, landing almost as many punches as the blows that tagged him, and people respected him for standing his ground. Yet Davy knew the situation had become serious. He was a candidate for an OBE – one behind the ear, as they said on the Shankill, with that 'one' being a bullet. Davy went to see two senior UVF paramilitaries from his neighbourhood. He explained that he was only going into New Lodge to find better sparring. The UVF leaders, both boxing fans, promised the persecution would stop. A few threatening words must have been said to the men who goaded him because, from then on, they looked away whenever Davy approached them with a training bag slung over his shoulder.

No one could help him in Dublin, however. Instead, in the Republic, he had to endure constant sniping that he was the only Protestant on Ireland's National team. Davy responded pugnaciously when they tried to define him as a Protestant interloper.

'I never put a title on myself,' Davy insisted.

'But you're a Protestant,' his accusers in Dublin said, as if he had committed a crime.

'What's a Protest-ant?' Davy said, accentuating the 'protest' in the name. 'Listen, I'm not protesting against anything. I'm happy the way I am.'

The hounding followed Davy all the way to America in late 1973. Gerry took a small Irish team to fight in Chicago. They were invited to a concert and an imposing representative of NORAID, the Irish-American charity set up to help the IRA with US funding, came over to meet them. He knew Gerry was from a Republican stronghold and so the American turned to Davy and his friend John Rodgers, the Catholic welterweight who had just broken into the Irish team. The man asked John where he came from.

'Lisburn,' John said of his home town, just eight miles from central Belfast.

The man grunted, as if unsure of the significance of Lisburn, and looked down at Davy from his six-foot-six height. 'What about you?' he asked the sturdy little boxer.

'I'm from the Shankill Road,' Davy said as he stretched out his hand in greeting.

The man recoiled as if Davy had stuck a cattle prod up his behind. 'You're joking, I hope?' he said in disgust at the thought that the Irish boxing team might not be filled exclusively with Republicans.

'John, you tell him where I'm from,' Davy said coolly.

Rodgers grinned. 'Wee Davy is definitely from the Shankill Road.'

'In the name of fuck,' the American said in disbelief. He strode over to Gerry to ask for confirmation.

'Of course,' Gerry beamed in his avuncular way. 'This is an Irish boxing team that comes from both sides of the divide.'

Davy, Gerry and John Rodgers cackled in delight as the man stomped off, muttering loudly: 'What the hell are things coming to?'

They were looking to the future and a time when no one in Northern Ireland would be defined by their religion. In the meantime, Davy wanted to find a new definition for himself – as a champion not just of Ireland but the entire Commonwealth of countries. Davy had won bronze for Northern Ireland at the Commonwealth Games in Edinburgh in 1970. In January 1974, he planned to win a gold medal. He knew most of the fighters in the bantamweight division and he thought no one would stop him in Christchurch, New Zealand.

Interviewed on television shortly after returning from Chicago and not long before he flew with Gerry's team to Christchurch, Davy was bullish: 'I've beaten some of them, I've lost to a few, but none scare me. I'm going there to win the gold medal.'

In early February 1974 the black taxi crawled along the Shankill Road. Davy sat in the back seat, bleary and exhausted after the 30-hour journey from New Zealand. He longed to get home so he could fall into bed. Gerry Hamill, his Commonwealth Games teammate, and Jack Monaghan, an Irish boxing official, shared his cab from the airport. Davy would jump out first, once they reached Leopold Street, but they needed to swing off the Shankill and turn right up Cambrai Street. The traffic was unusually heavy, and darkness had fallen.

Leopold Street was the last turning to the left off Cambrai. The long road felt even longer as the taxi slowed. It was only when they turned into Leopold that Davy thought he knew the reason. Crowds thronged the street and a bonfire blazed in the middle of the road.

'Stop the cab,' Davy told the driver. 'They're rioting.'

'No, they're not rioting,' the cabbie insisted as he inched down the road.

'They'll burn your car,' Davy warned him. His father had lost numerous cars that had been burnt out and used on barricades. Davy remembered a little green Morris Minor his dad had loved until it got stolen. It was eventually found on top of a barricade on the New Lodge Road. They had not burnt the Morris Minor but it was perched on top of two other cars and could never be used again. Usually, the rioters doused a car with petrol and lit a match. Davy did not fancy the idea of being caught in a blazing taxi.

'This is not a riot,' the driver said again.

'I want to get out,' Davy replied. He could see his house – fifth from the left-hand corner of Leopold Street. He gave Gerry and Jack some money to pay the driver when he left the cab a few streets further along and went round the back to take his bag out of the boot. People were already running towards him, shouting his name. Davy was confused. If a riot was in full swing would they really be smiling at him?

Before he could even pick up his bag Davy was swept off his feet and hoisted up on the shoulders of a huge man who carried him towards his house. They were calling him champ and so Davy realised that the taxi driver had been right. This was no riot. It was, instead, a celebration of the Commonwealth gold medal he had won in Christchurch.

Davy was taken aback because, four years earlier, his Commonwealth bronze had barely caused a ripple. But his gold medal seemed like a release for people during the bleakest of times on the Shankill Road. All Davy's training in New Lodge, and previously wearing the green vest of Ireland with a team of Catholics, had either been forgiven or forgotten.

Gerry Storey had been like a wise older brother to Davy in Christchurch. He prepared him strategically for every fight, while allowing his boxer the leeway to maintain some of his own training routines. Gerry never believed much in roadwork, but he knew Davy loved to run every morning. Once Davy had completed his run, and recovered, Gerry would revert to the interval training and sprints he believed were far more beneficial to a fighter.

In the flyweight final Davy had faced Chandra Narayanan who was, by some distance, his toughest opponent of the week. The little Indian never stopped punching and Gerry advised Davy to fight on the retreat. He was usually a come-forward fighter but now he became a counter-puncher. The tactical switch worked beautifully and Davy won the decision and the gold medal for Northern Ireland. His years of hard work had finally paid off.

The revellers stormed into Davy's house and he heard a voice cry out from the street below.

'Larmour, Larmour!' Gerry Hamill wailed plaintively.

Davy looked down at his fellow boxer and asked Hamill if he was all right.

Hamill gestured at the crowd behind him. 'Tell them to let us go home,' he pleaded.

Davy could see that the black taxi was hemmed in tight by the swarming crowd. There was no way out of Leopold Road. Boxing fever, and happiness, gripped this corner of Belfast.

Barry McGuigan turned 13 that month, on 28 February 1974, and a gold medal for an Irish fighter at the Commonwealth Games fuelled his boxing fervour. He was already certain his future would be shaped by such glittering moments. Barry wanted to win everything from Junior and Senior Ulster and Irish titles to European – and one day even world – championships.

He had been boxing for only one year in the border town of Clones, located just inside the Republic of Ireland, but he carried a rare power in his fists. Barry had felt it from the moment he first pulled on a boxing glove in a derelict house on Analore Street that led up to the Diamond where his parents ran a grocery store in Clones. He and his friends had climbed into the abandoned house and stumbled across an old pair of boxing gloves. They were genuine eight-ounce gloves from the 1950s, filled with horsehair. They looked full of mystery and beauty.

Barry chose the right glove while one of his friends pulled on the left. They fought each other in a series of one-gloved scraps, and Barry was far better and hit harder than anyone else. He was small and, as an adult, he would turn out to be not much bigger than Davy Larmour when they sparred together in the 1980s. But even then, aged 13, Barry had huge hands.

His fists were like rocks when he and his pals played Hardy Knuckles. On icy winter days in Clones they would test each other. A boy would hold out his fist and someone would smack him hard on the knuckles. It would then be the turn of the boy who had taken the blow to have a crack at his opponent's bunched fist. Barry's knuckles and fists were tougher than anyone else in their group.

He was one of eight children, and the third-eldest, but he was especially close to his older brother Dermot. Barry and Dermot began to spar with each other in the room they shared, and to collect the American boxing magazine *The Ring*, devouring articles about great fighters in Sugar Ray Robinson and Jake LaMotta. But Barry wanted to sample the real thing. He asked his dad, Pat, if he could go to a boxing gym.

The nearest club was in Wattlebridge, on the border with Northern Ireland, accessible only via treacherous roads used regularly by paramilitaries. Beyond that sinister backdrop, Barry was entranced by the gym when he and his dad arrived one afternoon. His dad wrinkled his nose at the stench of sweat mixed with wintergreen oil but Barry savoured it. He loved the roped-off ring at the far end of the rectangular hall and couldn't stop himself popping a few punches at the battered speed ball.

Barry was hooked and, within a few weeks of joining the club, he had his first bout in the Luxor Cinema in Clones. He was very nervous at the prospect of fighting Ronan McManus from St Michael's in Enniskillen. But Barry was also so keen that he tore into his opponent as soon as the referee had given his instructions. The ref had just turned away to speak to the timekeeper – who was Barry's uncle Dennis – but, rather than returning to his corner,

Barry flew at McManus, oblivious to the fact that they needed to wait for the bell. Laughter rang around the cinema as the ref hauled him away and explained boxing protocol.

Barry did not switch tactics when the fight started properly. He ran at McManus and threw a whirlwind of punches without any finesse. But he fought with such fire that his more experienced opponent was overwhelmed. It was surprising such ferocity could be found in a normally polite boy who arranged the fruit and vegetables display so prettily in his parents' shop every morning before school.

Clones was so close to the border that if Barry walked 500 yards down the road from the end of town he would be in the North. The political geography of Clones was complicated by the fact that it was in County Monaghan – one of three Ulster counties, alongside Cavan and Donegal, in the South. It had become a Republican town in the Troubles, but in 1961, when Barry was born as Finbar McGuigan, there had been a fairly even split with around 60 per cent of the population being Catholic and 40 per cent Protestant. By the mid-1970s, amid growing Republicanism, many Protestant families had moved North and the Catholic majority climbed to almost 80 per cent.

Among those Protestants who stayed in Clones, the Mealiff family ran a grocery store and a small hotel across the Diamond in the heart of town. The McGuigans and the Mealiffs were friendly towards each other, without a hint of sectarian animosity. In 1981, when they were both 20, Barry McGuigan and Sandra Mealiff became the most famous mixed-marriage couple in Ireland.

Yet it was difficult to avoid the darkening mood of Clones in the 1970s. There was widespread unemployment and numerous atrocities along the border. Ten years earlier it had been a booming market town at the intersection between the North and the Republic, but the soft border hardened with the Troubles. Army checkpoints emerged and tensions escalated.

Barry's grandfather James, his dad's dad, had been a captain in the IRA in County Tyrone in Northern Ireland. It was soon after the 1916 Easter Uprising and the War of Independence. Even though he was involved only in reconnaissance, utilising his knowledge of the railways, for whom he worked as a porter, James was jailed twice. In late 1922, he was imprisoned for nine months at the infamous camp at Ballykinlar in County Down. Less than a year later he was arrested again during the first wave of internment against Catholics.

At six in the morning, James was woken by soldiers from the notorious Black and Tans regiment, which had been brought to Northern Ireland specifically to quell the IRA. He was cuffed and told to climb into the back of an army lorry. The step was too high and James, being a small man, could not climb up it without using his cuffed hands. A soldier smacked the butt of a rifle into the back of his head and, as blood seeped from his wound, James's wife began to cry. Her sister, Margaret, berated the soldier for his cowardice. Barry's grandmother would tell him years later that the Black and Tan soldier put the bayonet to Margaret's throat and said: 'Shut your mouth or I will put this right through you.'

James McGuigan was imprisoned for 18 months on the prison ship *Argenta* at Larne Dock.

After his release he moved south and found a job on the railways in Clones. He lived a peaceful life as a signalman whose huge hands pulled the massive levers on the tracks.

Barry knew Granddad McGuigan only as a lovely old man who would amuse him with tales of how, to pull up the lever, you had to have brute strength and the knack of snapping the cable at the right time. Hulking beasts of men would fail to lift the levers but little Granddad McGuigan, waving his big meaty hands in front of Barry as if they had magic powers, did it every time. He laughed whenever his grandson said he had hands as big as bunches of bananas.

The warmth of James was handed down to Pat, Barry's dad, who became a singer famous enough to represent Ireland at the

Eurovision Song Contest, held at the Royal Albert Hall, in 1968. Pat McGuigan was a tenor but he could break out into a sweet falsetto without missing a beat. Before he sang professionally Pat had worked as a coaler – shovelling coal into the wagons hitched to the steam engines. After Eurovision, when Barry was only seven, Pat's career took off. He was hugely popular in Dublin and he would travel all over Europe, singing in locations as diverse as Budapest, Copenhagen and Sofia. In Malta, Pat McGuigan and his band, The Big Four, were supported by a young David Bowie.

Pat was too busy for politics, but he performed in front of anyone who invited him. Before Gerry Storey became a revered figure in Loyalist Belfast, Pat would sing in clubs and bars on the Shankill Road. His Catholic background did not matter when he began to croon his ballads. The drinkers on the Shankill always showed their approval.

The Troubles, however, could not be escaped. Barry's mum, Kate, explained the protests in a way that captured the impact on their family shop: 'They're protesting against the British army blowing the roads up and it's crucifying our business,' she said.

Customers who lived ten minutes away in normal circumstances often needed an hour to get to the McGuigans' shop. It was no longer practical for them and they began to visit stores in the North. Business for the McGuigans, as well as the Mealiffs, declined sharply.

Barry didn't understand any of these problems. His mind was occupied by boxing. As his dad travelled so often to concerts, Barry and his friend Noel McGovern cycled on weekday evenings to the boxing gym. It was possible to reach Wattlebridge from Clones without ever crossing the border and venturing into Northern Ireland, but it meant an eight-mile journey. A much quicker alternative was riding down the Cavan Road and then carrying your bike over the blown-up bridges before following the fastest route to Wattlebridge. This meant criss-crossing the border four times on pitch-black roads with only a couple of flashlights to cut through the dark. It was a little scary but halved the length of the journey.

There had been numerous sectarian murders on the border roads, starting early on a Sunday morning in 1972 when three Protestant men were shot at by the IRA. Robin Bell, a British soldier with the Ulster Defence Regiment, was buried with full military honours. The next day, two Catholic farmers, Michael Naan and Andrew Murray, were stabbed to death by soldiers in the British army who had thought they were undercover IRA men. The Pitchfork Murders, as they were called, spread fear along the border.

Barry and Noel never saw any of the paramilitaries, but one night in 1974, as winter approached, they were careering down a hill on the way back from training at Wattlebridge when they almost crashed into an army roadblock. Two men were pinned to the ground by soldiers in camouflage gear and watched over by policemen holding rifles.

'What are you boys doing here?' one of the policemen shouted angrily.

Barry and Noel were too frightened to answer as they stared at the guns. Amid the confusion they thought wrongly that there had been another killing.

'Get the hell out of here,' the policeman yelled.

The boys raced up the hill and back out into the blackness. Barry did not say much on the long ride home, but he kept thinking how lucky they had been that the army had not fired at them. Everything tumbled out of him when he got home and his mum asked why he was so late. Kate McGuigan was decisive: 'You're not going back to Wattlebridge. Find yourself another club – or another sport. All right, Barry?'

'Yes, Mum,' Barry said obediently. He never wanted to criss-cross the border at night again.

His dad helped him join a club in Smithborough, a ten-minute drive away along safer roads. The club was run by Danny McEntee and Frank Mulligan. McEntee was a former Irish Junior champion and a National finalist in the Seniors, who had also fought the great Italian Nino Benvenuti. Already steeped in boxing knowledge from reading *The Ring*, Barry knew he had found the right boxing home if Danny had shared a ring with a former world champion middleweight.

Danny was an old-fashioned purist. He taught Barry how to roll and slip punches, to block and parry, imparting his skills in a calm manner. Under Danny's tutelage, Barry won the Mid-Ulster championships and knocked out almost everyone he fought.

He also came to understand the power of his hitting in a more frightening way. Danny had fallen ill and, in a deserted gym, Frank Mulligan took Barry on the pads. Barry was old enough to realise that Frank was an alcoholic, but he had no idea that the trainer carried an even darker secret. He was sexually abusing young boys and, in 2012, he would be jailed for six years on two counts of raping a 14-year-old in the 1990s. But Frank never touched Barry and, instead, helped him work on his combinations.

Frank was always enthusiastic and that afternoon they moved from pad work to sparring. The trainer pulled on some gloves and a headguard and, as they circled the ring, he snapped out punches at Barry, saying, 'C'mon, c'mon,' as a way of encouraging the teenager to engage.

Barry threw a right, which missed, and followed it with a left hook that caught Frank square on the chin. The trainer went down in a heap. He was clearly unconscious because he did not make a sound even when Barry crouched over him.

'I'm sorry, Frank,' he said. 'I'm sorry. I didn't mean it.'

When Frank didn't respond, Barry thought he might have killed him. He ran out of the gym in a panic and headed for the local priest's house at the bottom of the road. Barry rang the bell and then hammered on the door. There was no answer. The young boxer ran back to the gym and, to his relief, Frank had begun to stir. He managed to prop himself up on an elbow while Barry began apologising again.

'Oh my God,' Frank said slowly. 'I've never been hit like that.'

He looked up at the young fighter and shook his dizzy head again. Barry McGuigan, clearly, was something special.

Pat McGuigan went everywhere. He sang and played with his band in Portadown at the staunch Loyalist social club and he sang and played in west Belfast at fiercely Republican venues. He was a genial man and was close friends with the Miami Showband and their former lead singer Dickie Rock. The Showband were from Dublin rather than Miami and, like Pat McGuigan's The Big Four, they played cover versions of pop songs interspersed with big-band swing, country and western, and occasionally traditional Irish music. They were the most famous group in Ireland and played gigs across the divide in the North. Showband music almost matched boxing's capacity for cross-sectarian popularity.

The Miami Showband were fearless in their willingness to travel anywhere, despite the spate of sectarian killings in 1975. These followed the wave of IRA bombings in England the previous year, when five people were killed and 65 were injured in two Guildford pubs in October 1974. A month later, 21 people died and 182 were wounded when bombs exploded in two Birmingham pubs.

On 31 July 1975, the Miami Showband were ambushed by a gang of UVF gunmen who forced them to pull over on the A1 near Buskhill, seven miles from Newry. They were travelling back from a gig in Banbridge and the UVF men were dressed in British army uniforms.

The Miami Showband were made to line up on the roadside, where they were searched, while two of the UVF men disappeared around the back of the minibus. They planned to fit a time bomb to the vehicle, which would explode once the band were driving back to Dublin. It would look as if they had been smuggling an IRA bomb and, in death, they would be depicted as Republican militants rather than musicians. But the bomb detonated as it was being fitted secretly and both UVF men were killed. The remaining gunmen panicked and started shooting – killing three and injuring two more of the Miami Showband.

Brian McCoy was shot in the back by nine rounds from a 9mm Luger pistol. Fran O'Toole, having tried to drag his badly injured bandmate Stephen Travers to safety, was machine-gunned 22 times. Tony Geraghty was also caught while trying to escape and shot four times in his back and head. His last words were: 'Please don't shoot me. Don't kill me.'

This was the Miami Showband Massacre.

In his parents' front room in Clones, 14-year-old Barry McGuigan watched the incessant coverage on television. He could sense how the fear of God spread through everyone. Murderous lunatics, on both sides of the divide, were on the rampage.

CHAPTER 6

The Clint Eastwood of Belfast

Three years since he had been wounded by an IRA bomb on Ann Street, Samuel Larmour was still a ghost of himself. He was back at work, and driving another of his beloved Morris Minors, but Davy's father had not recovered fully from his terrible physical and emotional injuries. His introspective nature had also deepened. At least he no longer badgered Davy to give up boxing after his boy won a second Irish National title, becoming flyweight champion in Dublin on 25 April 1975.

Samuel understood his middle son was on course to make the Irish team that would travel to the Montreal Olympics with Gerry Storey. He even gave Davy the occasional lift into New Lodge so that he could train with Gerry at the Holy Family.

In the summer of 1975, Davy and his dad slowed at the top of Upper Canning Street. An army checkpoint blocked their path. It was a familiar sight in New Lodge and they were not surprised when a soldier ordered them out of the Morris Minor. Davy watched silently while another soldier turned his training bag upside down so that everything spilled onto the street. He was also quiet as they rummaged through his kit and searched the rest of the car. But he could not contain his anger when the first soldier swore at his father, thinking he was a local Republican rather than an elderly man giving his champion son a lift from the Shankill Road.

Samuel answered him sharply, suggesting he should watch his language. The soldier flipped his rifle around so that the butt was raised at the old man's head. He moved towards Samuel menacingly as if he was about to crack his head open with the gun. Davy grabbed the butt of the rifle and twisted it away from his father.

'Let go,' the soldier said.

'I will,' Davy said, 'once you listen to me. This man fought in the Second World War and he was an army reservist for years. He wore the same uniform as you. He's just giving me a lift to the boxing club.'

Slowly, after Davy released the rifle, the soldier lowered his weapon. He still glared at Davy. 'Get your things,' he said.

As Davy picked up his gear, the soldier turned back to his father. 'You'd better go home.'

'You go on, Dad,' Davy murmured. 'I'll walk from here.'

He watched his father climb shakily into the Morris Minor. Samuel struggled to turn the car on the tight street but, eventually, he was able to find his way out of the blockade.

Davy headed for North Queen Street, where he could see eight soldiers in riot gear beating their big Perspex shields as they marched towards the New Lodge Road, half a mile away. Still seething from the treatment of his father, the little boxer walked quickly past them. They ignored him as they continued to hammer their shields with thick batons. They were steeling themselves for war while sending a warning to their enemy that they were coming.

As he turned into New Lodge Road, Davy nearly bumped into the crouching figure of another of Gerry's boxers from the Holy Family. Both Davy and the other kid had won Junior Ulster boxing titles the previous decade.

'Hello, mate,' Davy said.

His fellow boxer, who had joined the IRA, looked up at him.

'Davy!' he exclaimed. 'How are you?'

'I'm grand,' Davy said. 'You?'

'All good, Davy,' the young fighter said. 'Tell Gerry I'll come see him soon.'

Davy nodded and walked on, allowing his friend to continue making a petrol bomb.

A little further on he waved to yet another of Gerry's boxers, Alex Maskey, who was watching the riots. Alex, who would become the first Republican Lord Mayor of Belfast in the 21st century, smiled and waved back.

As he reached the Holy Family, a platoon of paratroopers appeared from around the back of the building. One of the paras pushed Davy against a wall and made him open his bag.

'Where are you going?' the paratrooper asked.

'To the boxing club,' Davy said, pointing to the Holy Family. 'That's my training gear.'

'Go on,' the para said with a jerk of his head.

As Davy climbed the stairs to the gym he passed another former boxer he had once beaten in the Ulster championships.

'All right?' Davy said.

'Davy,' the man said, offering his hand.

The two former opponents, Holy Family friends from across the divide, shook hands. Davy knew the man had become a commanding officer of the Provisional IRA. He was clearly busy and not in the mood for a chat.

Davy needed the sanctuary of the Holy Family, away from the riot shields and petrol bombs, the paras and the Provos. He swung open the door. The percussive rhythm of speed balls and heavy bags being hit, the whirr of skipping ropes and the thud and grunt of a fierce sparring session inside the ring defined an oasis of peace. Standing at the far side of the ring, watching two fighters at work, Gerry Storey broke into his usual smile.

'Davy!' he shouted in welcome. 'Good man ... bang on time.'

The boxer lifted his hand in greeting and smiled. It felt as if he was home again.

*

Gerry's three sons had begun to blossom in the ring. Gerry Jr, Martin and Sam all showed talent and aptitude for boxing. They were hooked on the business. Boxing at the Ulster Hall was always a sold-out affair and the three boys helped their granddad Sammy Burns – Belle's father – sell programmes outside. The cackling, wisecracking throngs of fans approaching the hall from both sides of Belfast made the boys feel as if boxing carried something magical deep within its blurring art of slipping and hitting, defending and attacking. They knew their dad stood at the very heart of boxing in Belfast. In a seething landscape he gave them certainty that all would be well with the world.

At the Ulster Senior finals on 18 February 1975, Sam Storey did not sell any programmes. He was asked, instead, to feature on the undercard. He was only 12 years old and it was a rare honour for two Junior fights to be showcased before the Senior finals. Sam was asked to fight against Damien Friars from the Holy Trinity club in Turf Lodge, west Belfast, in a repeat of their Ulster Juniors bout a few weeks before. Friars had won that night and Gerry knew why he would lose even before Sam stepped into the ring. Sam had spent the afternoon playing football – for three straight hours.

His dad was not happy. 'Do you know who you're fighting tonight?' Gerry asked him when Sam came in looking muddy and exhausted.

'I'll be all right,' Sam said with a shrug, remembering his dad had warned him that Friars and all the tough wee scrappers from the Holy Trinity were not to be underestimated.

'That's okay, then,' Gerry said quietly, patting his son on the back. He would learn his lesson in the ring.

Sam had lost clearly to Friars that night. He now had the chance to show how good he could be when he was not drained by an afternoon of football. Sam, however, was worried. Friars was a fine boxer and they would be fighting in front of a heaving Ulster Hall.

'You don't need to worry about that,' Gerry said. 'You deserve to be here.'

That reassuring statement gave him conviction. That night Sam Storey showed Belfast he would one day be good enough to fight for a world title. His dad allowed Bobby McAllister to work his corner and Gerry watched impassively from the back of the rocking hall. He could hear Belle shouting out encouragement to wee Sam from the balcony. Belle was classy but, watching her son at work in the ring, she roared him on. Gerry smiled at the end when Sam was announced as the winner by a wide decision.

Gerry was soon back in the ring, working the corner as one of his boys faced the great Charlie Nash. He admired Nash, having trained him in the Olympics, but he was convinced that Gerry Hamill could beat him. Sam had rushed back to ringside, having showered and changed, as Hamill was his favourite fighter. He liked Nash, but Sam thought Hamill was brilliant.

That night, with Gerry Storey guiding him in the corner, Hamill lived up to little Sam's tag for him. He boxed beautifully.

Sam Storey looked up at the ring with wide eyes, watching with awe as his dad steered Hamill to that surprise victory over a renowned Olympian. Following Gerry Storey's tactics perfectly, Hamill dazzled Nash. It looked to Sam as if Charlie Nash was surrounded. He had little chance against an excellent fighter trained by a wizard in the corner.

Charlie Nash had reached the end of the road in June 1975. He was finished with boxing on his return from Katowice, Poland. After he had won his fourth Irish National title at lightweight that April, when he gained revenge and a cut eye forced Hamill to retire on the same night Davy Larmour lifted his flyweight crown, Charlie believed Poland would see him finally become European champion. He took two weeks off work at the printing company in the hope he would win gold in Katowice.

Instead, on 3 June, he lost in the last 16 to Simion Cutov, the Romanian lightweight who would win the title five days later. It was the exact same outcome as the preceding European championships two years earlier when, in Belgrade, Nash also lost to the eventual champion, Cutov, in the same round.

Charlie felt deflated and weary. He had had enough of boxing and could no longer justify taking unpaid leave as he tried to match the full-time athletes from Eastern Europe. He knew the same problems would resurface in Montreal at the 1976 Olympics when, as a mere amateur, it would be difficult for him to beat any of the state-funded fighters from Cuba and the Eastern bloc.

Boxing had given him so much pleasure and pride, amid darkness and despair, but it was over. His wife, Betty, had just had their first baby, Julie, and Charlie needed to live an ordinary life. He needed to earn a solid monthly salary without missing weeks of wages to train in Belfast or Dublin and then travel to another strange city where he might or might not win a medal with a value that was restricted to his self-esteem and public recognition.

Charlie's passion had drained him.

When he had been home for a few days some of the Derry newspaper boys came round to reflect on his latest gallant effort and to establish his aims for the Montreal Olympics. Charlie surprised the reporters, most of Derry and all of Irish boxing when he announced his retirement.

A couple of days passed peacefully and Charlie began to settle into his changed routine. He did not miss the gym and it was a relief to step away from the stringent diet that meant he was always ready to fight at the 135-pound lightweight limit. Charlie had just turned 24 and he felt ready to be a full-time husband, a father and a printer.

Gerry Hassett, in Belfast, had a different plan for Charlie. He was a former professional boxer and a hustler who had lived a full life. During a 19-year career, starting as a welterweight in 1950 and ending up at light-heavyweight, Hassett had 69 fights as a pro. He won 45 of those bouts, but he fought often as a journeyman and, while scrapping for a living in the East End of London, he had been through hundreds more contests in the fairground boxing booths, where he was put up as an Irish hard man against whom anyone could take a crack if they paid their entry fee to the ring. Hassett was too experienced for the fairground bullies, but he never made enough money to carve out a fresh start.

Instead, he worked as a bouncer at some of the roughest night-clubs in Britain and Ireland. Hassett was also Muhammad Ali's bodyguard when the great man came to Ireland in 1972, and he had since set up a security business, but he imagined making big money as a boxing manager and promoter. The professional fight game had disappeared from Northern Ireland.

The Troubles were so grim and frightening that few fighters from the rest of Britain, Europe or abroad would travel to Belfast or Derry. Irish pros hoping to make money in the ring had to move to England. The bombings and shootings drove them out of Northern Ireland.

Davy Larmour's friend Paddy Maguire, an outstanding bantam-weight from near the Falls Road, had made his pro debut at the Ulster Hall in Belfast in March 1969. He won his first eight fights in Belfast but, by early 1971, the Troubles forced him to leave for London. He found work on a building site in Lambeth and, alone in London, tried to rebuild his boxing career. His first fight in London was against the vastly experienced Ghanaian Bob Allotey, a future European champion, who had already had 60 fights.

Maguire lost on points but he won ten of his next 11 bouts and earned himself a chance to fight for the British bantamweight title in December 1974 against Dave Needham at the Nottingham Ice Rink. Only a couple of weeks had passed since two IRA bombs killed 21 people in Birmingham. Maguire was barracked by a hostile crowd who taunted him with cries of 'You've got no bombs now'. Needham won the decision, despite being cut to pieces by Maguire's sharp punching. There would be some measure of jus-tice when Maguire stopped Needham in a rematch at the Royal Albert Hall in London in October 1975, but he would never again fight in Belfast.

Gerry Hassett, however, had an ambitious scheme in mind. Having seen the popularity of Charlie Nash in Derry, Hassett was convinced he had the skill and the following to sustain a career. Together, they could bring pro boxing back to Derry and, eventually, to Belfast.

He was a convincing talker and Charlie agreed to turn pro with Hassett as his promoter. But he insisted he would manage himself. He turned down the first purse Hassett offered him to fight Ray Ross. Charlie had beaten him as an amateur but Ross had been Irish lightweight champion in 1974. Ross also had fought four times as a pro. And so Charlie's purse was pushed up to £200. The ten-round fight would be for the Irish professional lightweight title on 2 October 1975.

Hassett was right. The Templemore Sports Complex in Derry was packed for Charlie's debut. Betty was at ringside for her one and only time as a spectator. She found the experience too distressing, even though Charlie won easily on points, and swore she would never watch another of his fights.

Hassett, meanwhile, could not stop smiling. The sports centre had been rocking with chants of 'Char-lie, Char-lie, Char-lie!' as Derry's favourite son began a journey that would lead him to European and world title fights and help resurrect professional boxing in Northern Ireland. Charlie was simply proud that he had become Irish lightweight champion as both an amateur and a professional in the same year. He had made a small slice of boxing history.

Gerry Storey recognised the power of a postcard. Wherever he found himself in the world on his boxing travels – whether in Munich or Chicago, Christchurch or Havana – Gerry would write a postcard to his nephew Bobby, who was interned for two years at Her Majesty's Prison Maze. Located on an old Royal Air Force base at Long Kesh on the outskirts of Lisburn, the most notorious prison in Northern Ireland was known colloquially as the Maze, the H-blocks or Long Kesh. Gerry just knew that it was a hellhole for Republican prisoners.

A tall and imposing man, Big Bobby Storey had been a target long before he could be interned at the legal age of 17. He was arrested dozens of times, and released, after rioting against the RUC and the British army. But, as soon as they could, the British authorities sent Big Bobby to Long Kesh. He was regarded as a dangerous Republican, even at such a young age, but Gerry knew him only as his nephew who was kind to his younger brother, Brian, who suffered from Down's syndrome and had been abused by Loyalist gangs.

Gerry understood why Big Bobby saw the presence of the British army in Northern Ireland as a cancer that needed to be removed. He had seen the persecution Bobby, Brian, Seamus, Geraldine and their parents suffered over the years. They had been forced to leave the Marrowbone, after coming under Loyalist fire, and find a home on Manor Street, the last Catholic street in one of the most brutal interface areas of north Belfast. The family's attitude towards Loyalists and the British army hardened.

Gerry never forgot the postcards for Bobby when he took Davy Larmour and John Rodgers to box in Chicago, Christchurch and then, in August 1974, at the inaugural world boxing championships in Havana, Cuba. They met Fidel Castro and Kid Chocolate, the great Cuban former world champion, on a memorable trip. Just as he had done in America, and in Christchurch, Gerry picked out three postcards so that he, Davy and John could all write to Big Bobby in prison.

Davy always took his time over the postcards so he could find the right words to lift the spirit of Gerry's nephew. Those postcards helped Bobby Storey. He loved the fact that Uncle Gerry encouraged a Protestant champion in Davy Larmour to write to him, an imprisoned IRA man.

Two months later, in October 1974, Big Bobby was among the IRA prisoners who burnt down the cages at Long Kesh in protest against the inhumane conditions to which they were subjected. Finally, in the summer of 1975, Bobby was released from jail. He came to see Gerry a few days later to thank him for all the boxing postcards. Even in a place as desolate as Long Kesh, boxing had spread some warmth.

Bobby was still beaten up regularly by British soldiers after his release from Long Kesh and they once even took him in a Saracen to an intimidating UDA area just off the Shankill Road. He was thrown out of the Saracen, onto the street, and a soldier shouted: 'He's an IRA man!' Bobby somehow made it home to New Lodge, where his uncle still followed a path away from sectarian violence.

Gerry's biggest challenge was finding enough time in the day to work at the docks, train his boys at the Holy Family and still spend time with Belle and the four kids. Belle was a beautiful woman, and very kind, and Gerry sometimes worried that he did not pay her the attention she deserved. Belle always told him not to worry. She knew how much boxing meant to him and she felt part of the Holy Family – as she showed whether she was washing boxing kit or looking after visiting fighters and being a second mother to them.

Saturday was the one night Gerry tried to keep sacred for Belle. It was their time to be together and he could take Belle out for a few drinks. Towards the end of 1975, another tumultuous year, Gerry broke the news to Belle that he would be in Dublin that weekend with the National team. 'Let's go out on Friday night and have a few drinks at the National club,' he said. Belle nodded and smiled, and Gerry said he would make sure he was back by eight.

On a busy Friday night at the Holy Family, with the new kids flying in the gym, Gerry was happy. He spent more time with the parents, praising their boys, and afterwards he sat around and discussed the prospects for Davy Larmour at the following summer's Olympics in Montreal. When he glanced at his watch he was shocked to see the time. It was 9.45.

Gerry gathered up his gear quickly. 'Poor Belle,' he said, 'I've let her down again.' He did not hang around for a ribbing from the other trainers, and instead he raced home.

'Belle, Belle!' he called out as soon as he opened the door. 'I'm sorry!'

His wife came down the stairs. She looked very pretty in the special dress she had chosen to wear to the National. She gave Gerry a kiss but shook her head when he said they should jump straight in the car and head up to the club.

'Oh, Gerry,' she said, 'it's too late now.'

Gerry, of course, was insistent. He soon had Belle laughing and reaching for her coat as they said goodnight to the kids.

'We won't be long,' she promised.

Belfast shut down early on a Friday night. There were few late nights when the streets were thick with patrols and blockades – and paramilitary gangs were about to unleash another atrocity. And so the National was empty when Gerry and Belle arrived just after 10.15. Jimmy, the barman, was about to roll down the shutters behind the bar when he saw them.

'Come on in, Gerry,' he said. 'You deserve a couple of drinks.'

The National was shut for the night, but Jimmy brought over two pints for Gerry, and a couple of drinks for Belle. 'You enjoy those,' Jimmy said, 'and take as long as you like.'

As always, no matter the circumstances, Gerry and Belle had a great time. They caught up on each other's news for the week and the drinks slipped down easily. Perhaps they could have persuaded Jimmy to let them have one more, but the kids were at home and Gerry needed to be up early for Dublin in the morning.

They climbed into the car and headed back home on the Antrim Road. Their chatter was broken only by the sound of screaming. It was a chilling sound, a screaming that Gerry can still hear in his head more than 40 years later.

At first, a small group of teenagers came racing down the side of the road with the fear of God etched across their faces. 'What's going on here?' Gerry said as he slowed the car.

Belle saw the girl before him. 'Look!' she cried.

A girl stood at the side of the road. Her mouth was open wide as she screamed helplessly: 'He's dead! He's dead!'

A boy lay in the middle of the road and two men stood over him. Gerry knew that they had either just assassinated him or they were about to take his life.

Cars blocked the left-hand kerb, closest to the screaming girl, and so Gerry had to pull over on the opposite side. 'Belle,' he said quietly, 'lock the doors and don't get out of the car.'

Before Belle could protest, Gerry was out of the car and walking towards the men.

'Hey,' he shouted. 'Leave him alone.'

The men turned towards him. Gerry was in the mood to throw a punch or two to send them on their way. He only paused when one of the men put his hand in his pocket and lifted it so Gerry could see the concealed shape of a gun pointing at him.

Gerry never carried a gun, but he was not about to surrender to par-amilitary gangsters. He wore his dark overcoat and so he also plunged his right hand deep into his pocket. With his fingers making the bulging shape of a gun he raised his hand, beneath the coat, at the men.

'If I were you,' Gerry said coolly, 'I would get out of here.'

The men hesitated, and there was a momentary stand-off. Even the screaming girl had fallen silent as she waited to see what would happen next. Gerry kept his gaze fixed on the men.

They took a step backwards and a car came sharking out of the darkness. The two gangsters ran towards it, flung open the doors and the car roared off.

Gerry turned to the girl, who had started to scream again: 'He's dead! He's dead!'

The boy, however, moved and whimpered: 'Thank you, mister, thank you.'

'That's all right, son,' Gerry murmured as he sank onto his haunches. The boy was bleeding from a superficial wound. Gerry looked up at the girl. 'It's all right, love. He's okay.'

The girl kept screaming – wordlessly now – so Gerry slapped her across the face to break the spell.

'He's not dead,' he said gently. 'Look – he's fine.'

Belle had reached the boy and was comforting him. The girl began crying in relief.

Gerry covered the shivering boy with his coat. 'We'll get you into the car and take you to hospital. What's your name, son?'

'Eastwood,' the boy said.

Gerry Storey, the Clint Eastwood of Belfast, calmly picked up the boy in his arms and carried him to the car.

'You saved me, mister,' young Eastwood said as Belle and his girlfriend followed. 'They were going to kill me. But they thought you would shoot them.'

Gerry laughed. 'They didn't know the truth,' he said softly. 'I have no gun.'

Everyone at the Holy Family knew their trainer was a resourceful man. The day he brought a team of his boxers to a tournament in Lisburn had become legendary in the club. The two Russell boys, Sean and Hugh, and a couple of other young fighters were crammed into his old banger, long before he started driving the bronze Cortina, and they were rattling along on the outskirts of Belfast when they hit trouble. The car began to sputter and shudder and within another mile it ground to a halt. Gerry knew little about engines, so there was not much point opening the bonnet. It was a mystery to him how any of his old jalopies got him anywhere.

After standing hopefully at the side of the road, with the four boys staying out of the cold in the car, Gerry raised his arm. An ambulance slowed and the driver rolled down his window.

'Gerry Storey,' he exclaimed. 'What are you doing here?'

He had never met the driver before but Gerry was recognised often in Belfast. 'I'm taking these wee boxers to a tournament in Lisburn,' he explained, 'and my car packed up.'

'Lisburn?' the ambulance driver asked.

'We're not too far,' Gerry said hopefully, wondering if an impossible opportunity was about to open up and rescue him and his boys. 'I don't suppose you're going that way?'

The driver looked across at his assistant in the passenger seat and they laughed together at an outrageous idea. 'Go on, Gerry,' the driver said. 'We'll take you. It looks like an emergency.'

'You're a couple of lifesavers,' Gerry said with a smile of relief.

'We know,' the driver cackled as he watched Gerry tell the boys the incredible news. They opened up the back of the ambulance and the Holy Family team jumped inside.

'I don't suppose you can turn on the siren?' Gerry joked while the boys looked around in wonder at their new team vehicle.

Wee Hugh Russell, who had just turned 11 and was the youngest in the team, could hardly stop laughing when his brother, Sean, asked Gerry a straight-faced question.

'Gerry,' Sean said, 'what do you think they'll make of us in Lisburn ... when we turn up for a boxing tournament in an ambulance?'

Five years later, in December 1975, Hugh turned 16. Gerry was keen to test the wee man. Early the following month Gerry decided his young flyweight terrier was ready to step into a ring with Davy Larmour. There were only six months left before the Montreal Olympics and Davy just needed to retain his Irish National title in Dublin on 1 May 1976 to secure his place in Gerry's squad.

Hugh would join both Gerry and Davy at the docks. Davy had finished his tiling apprenticeship in Ballymena and found a job for himself at Harland and Wolff. Hugh was hopeful he would be able to start working as a tugboat driver as soon as he had finished one more year of school. But boxing bound them even more tightly together. Gerry was convinced Hugh would be good enough to fight in the Olympics in four years and, while Davy prepared for Montreal, the tiny redhead offered him a new warm-up routine.

As fast as he was skilful, Hugh fought as a southpaw. Those

three attributes – speed, skill and boxing with his right fist leading the way in an unorthodox style – were always tricky. Davy knew he might have to fight a slick lefty from Cuba at the Olympics and so he agreed when Gerry suggested they give the ginger kid a chance to spar him.

'Go easy,' Gerry said as he wandered over to Davy's corner at the Holy Family.

'I know,' Davy nodded. 'He's only a kid.'

Hugh Russell, however, was already a proper fighter and intent on making his mark against the Irish champion who was seven years older than him. He landed an early punch and Davy, tasting the blurring leather encasing the teenager's fists, settled down into a more serious rhythm. He began to stalk Hugh in the ring, cutting off the corners. But little Hugh was much faster than expected and he spun out of punching range. Davy came back at him and, with his greater experience, found a way to land a few licks of his own. Hugh took the punches well and let rip with a combination that Davy deflected by rolling his shoulders.

Gerry, standing on the apron of the ring, was surprised by their intensity. It was good for both his boxers, at different stages of their careers, but he wanted to protect his young tyro whom he called Cue rather than Hugh. 'Move, Cue, move,' he instructed. 'You don't want a war with Davy Larmour.'

Hugh got on his bike and for the next three rounds of sparring he let Davy chase him round the ring as they swapped jabs and feints.

'That was very good,' Gerry said at the end of the third. 'What do you think, Cue?'

'Can we spar again soon?' the freckly little redhead asked.

In a beautiful setting in the village of Caherdaniel, on the Ring of Kerry, Gerry Storey pitched his Olympic camp. Sheltered by undulating mountains and overlooking a series of sandy beaches and small islands in a turquoise sea, Caherdaniel was a perfect workplace for Gerry and his boxers – Davy Larmour, Brendan

Dunne, Gerry Hamill, Christy McLoughlin and Brian Byrne. Apart from the secluded and gorgeous backdrop, Gerry brought cutting-edge techniques that had never been used before in an Irish training camp.

It was considered revolutionary in 1976 that Gerry should use video technology to help prepare his Olympic boxers. He filmed them during sparring each day and, at night, he would play back the recordings and explain how they could improve their strategies and execution. Gerry also drilled them with fitness routines that were years ahead of anyone else in Ireland or Britain. He then prepared his mixtures and potions to stem the flow of blood whenever his boys were cut in a fight. Great American trainers like Ray Arcel and Angelo Dundee had already tracked down Gerry when he took his amateur teams to New York and Philadelphia. Even those revered masters of the corner wanted to discover how Gerry could seal a gaping gash in the middle of a fight.

The Irish reporters who visited the camp one afternoon had never seen anything like it. 'Well, Gerry,' one of the star sportswriters from Dublin said, 'you've got your way. You've got your fancy training camp and all your videos and equipment. What results are you expecting?'

'I'm not expecting any results,' Gerry said. 'I'm just getting them ready to be in the best possible shape for competition.'

'What do you mean?' the reporter asked.

'You'll find out. I'm getting them fit enough to be in the ring with these Olympic fighters – but that's not enough to get the results they deserve.'

Gerry knew how amateur boxing worked. It was, for the most part, crooked. At the last European championships in Poland in 1975, at the tournament that sealed Charlie Nash's retirement as an amateur, the Eastern bloc countries had won 36 out of the 42 medals. They had some excellent fighters, and they all trained as professionals, but there was an element of bias in the scoring that skewed the results still further.

In the Olympic Games, at least for boxers, it wasn't always about how good you were but from which country you originated. Among his small team of total amateurs, and up against state-funded fighters who trained like professionals, Gerry believed only wee Davy had a chance of upsetting the odds and winning an Olympic medal.

Gerry's other four fighters all lost early, but Davy had some luck. The Montreal Olympics were boycotted by 28 countries in protest against the IOC decision not to ban New Zealand after the All Blacks played four rugby Tests in South Africa. Davy's first two opponents, Robert Musuku from Sudan and Agustin Martinez from Niger, withdrew from the Olympics.

In the quarter-finals, Davy faced America's Leo Randolph. Gerry had noticed how the North American manager of the tournament would move from one judge to another, smoking his pipe, between rounds. He was a constant reminder to the judges and Davy couldn't help asking himself whether they were being watched closely. Gerry could not prove anything and so he said nothing to deter Davy.

The Belfast flyweight fought beautifully and, if the contest had been anywhere else, Gerry was convinced Davy would have won the decision and an Olympic medal. Davy could even have won gold because, after his fortunate victory in the quarters, Randolph went on to become Olympic champion.

The reporter from Dublin found Gerry at ringside after Davy Larmour's controversial loss. 'You hit the nail on the head a few weeks ago, Gerry,' he said. 'I now know what you mean.'

Sugar Ray Leonard, the star of the 1976 Olympics, was so brilliant he needed no help from the judges to win gold in Montreal. Davy and Gerry met Leonard who, they knew, was heading for a multimillion-dollar career in the professional game, and they were dazzled.

'I'm following Sugar Ray into the pros,' Davy told Gerry. 'I've had enough of the amateurs.'

Gerry Hassett, making a splash with Charlie Nash in Derry, had already told Davy he could help him start a professional career.

'It will be far harder in Belfast,' Gerry warned, knowing he did not need to spell out there was also only one Sugar Ray Leonard.

'Don't worry,' Davy said. 'I'll not be giving up the day job. I know what to expect in Belfast.'

CHAPTER 7

Turning the Shankill Road Green

Danny McAllister was built like a little bull. Strength rippled through his muscled physique, oozing power and menace with every step as he walked into the packed hall. He had a large head and a thickset neck that looked as if it belonged to a middleweight rather than a flyweight. Barry McGuigan, who was about to fight McAllister in the 1977 Ulster Junior final, could hardly believe it. McAllister had somehow scaled seven stone seven. He looked three stone heavier. He also looked as if he was 25, rather than 16, which was McGuigan's age.

McAllister was regarded as the biggest certainty in Irish boxing for years. He was a slugger from the Oliver Plunkett gym on the Falls Road, Republican Belfast's equivalent of the Shankill Road, and he loved knocking out every kid they put in front of him.

Barry had watched all McAllister's fights on the way to the final. McAllister came out swinging – *boom!* – landing big hooks on both wings. Rather than terrifying him, the sight calmed Barry. He only had trouble with slick movers who preferred to back away and avoid combat. Barry preferred his opponents to come at him with mean intent. McAllister, the meanest and strongest of all the Ulster boys in the lighter weights, was made for him.

Gerry Storey was intrigued. He knew all about McAllister, but he had heard the kid from Clones showed real promise. Gerry doubted McGuigan would be able to withstand the furious pressure – but, as Ireland's National coach, Gerry was always keen to assess new talent.

The hall was a fog of smoke as men and women puffed on their cigarettes while roaring on the fighters. McGuigan stepped out first into the swirling haze that settled in a blueish cloud over the ring. The bull followed him and the crowd bellowed.

The heavy smokers nearly choked on their cigarettes when McGuigan dropped McAllister in round one. The Belfast kid was tough, however, and he got up and came back at McGuigan. It was easy for McGuigan to step out of the way – like a nonchalant matador knowing the bull was wounded, but not wanting to end the spectacle too soon and rob the crowd of its bloodthirsty pleasure. Instead, McGuigan bobbed, weaved and speared McAllister with rangy jabs.

McAllister was dropped again in the second round and the crowd whooped in surprise. It was so one-sided that the final bell came as salvation for the beaten-up star of the Falls Road. Barry McGuigan had just won his first Ulster title and Ireland's head coach came over to his corner. It looked as if Gerry Storey's eyes had almost jumped out of his head.

'This kid is exceptional,' Gerry said to Danny McEntee.

'I know,' Danny said with a smile. 'Barry, this is Gerry Storey.'

'Hello, Mr Storey,' Barry said politely, the malevolence of the ring having drained away.

Gerry explained that he would talk to the selectors in Dublin and ask permission for Barry to join them at a training camp – if the young boxer was interested.

It was hard to believe the leading coach in Irish boxing wanted to work with him. Barry turned in surprise to Danny and his trainer nodded encouragingly.

'I'd love that,' Barry said.

'All right,' Gerry said, patting Barry's arm. 'You keep it up and I'll be in touch with Danny.'

Barry's confidence boomed. Two months later he won the All-Ireland National Junior championships at the Parkway Hotel in Limerick. He gave Martin Brereton, an old rival, the mother and father of a beating, knocking him down and hurting him badly. Barry was the fighter of the tournament and he was written about for the first time in the national press. Nearly 200 people from Clones had piled into a convoy of coaches and followed Barry as he won his first National title. There were great celebrations on the three-hour journey home.

Gerry was convinced by the quality of McGuigan and so, a week later, he asked the 16-year-old if he would travel to Dublin to help Phil Sutcliffe prepare for the Senior European championships in East Germany in May 1977. Sutcliffe was a year older and far more experienced. Barry had still beaten him in a tournament in Edenderry, but Sutcliffe was a percussive volume puncher and the new Irish Senior champion.

Barry revelled in the hard interval training, and each afternoon he did well against Sutcliffe in sparring. They worked on his combination punching and the teenager improved noticeably under Gerry's tuition. The trainer made everything seem so obvious it was easy for Barry to follow his advice. In turn, the outstanding technical excellence of Gerry as a coach flourished as his plain words were turned into fluid actions by such a talented fighter. It was riveting to see the trainer and his boxer work in perfect tandem.

An impressed Pat McGuigan asked if Barry could train at the Holy Family. 'Of course,' Gerry said. He invited Barry to join them on weekends in Belfast. Just as Charlie Nash had done, Barry could stay with Gerry and Belle in New Lodge and work on his fighting skills. Barry grinned in delight. He was on his way.

Gerry Hassett gripped Charlie Nash by the throat in the basement of the Grosvenor House Hotel in Mayfair, London, on a Monday night in May 1976. Tension between the promoter and his fighter had escalated and an argument in the dressing room turned violent. Hassett was a much bigger man and he pinned the boxer against the wall. Charlie was easy-going but months of frustration turned to anger. He pushed his promoter away.

'Did you see what just happened?' he said to the hotel bellboy who had delivered a message that his former trainer, Tommy Donnelly, had been barred entry into the hotel.

'Yes, sir,' the bellboy said, as if deciding the unbeaten boxer deserved more respect than his raging promoter.

Hassett snapped: 'Let him in. If that's what he wants so much, let him in.'

Charlie nodded at the bellboy. 'You heard him. Tommy Donnelly is working with me tonight.'

Their increasingly fractious relationship had spilled over into open acrimony when Charlie told Hassett he no longer wanted him in his corner. He needed to be reunited with his amateur trainer. But when Hassett refused to help Tommy get past hotel security, Charlie had refused to fight. The breakdown had been brooding for months.

Seven months earlier Charlie had believed if he worked hard, training every night after work, the rewards would follow. Professional boxing, however, offered unforgiving terrain for a man as straight as Charlie. There were twists and turns, obstacles and pitfalls.

After winning his first five fights in low-key promotions, Charlie needed a more structured approach to his career, which meant bringing Tommy Donnelly back and rethinking Hassett's role as his promoter. It had become obvious that there were more fights for him on offer in London, via Jack Solomons, the most powerful promoter in boxing. Solomons was ready to help, but Charlie needed to compose himself and deal with his opponent. Jimmy Revie was still ranked highly and a convincing win, for a £500 purse, would put Charlie in contention for a British title shot.

Tommy's arrival calmed Charlie. There was just enough time

to confirm his strategy for the fight, and to warm up on the pads, before the knock came on his dressing-room door. Charlie walked through the banquet hall, filled with businessmen in black tie and tuxedos as they enjoyed their dessert before the main event of the evening. He felt a long way from Derry, but the fracas with Hassett had hardened his resolve.

Charlie slipped punches easily and countered with stinging combinations. He dropped Revie in the first and again in the third, at which point the referee stepped in to rescue the veteran. Charlie's victory was more impressive than the eighth-round stoppage the British champion Jim Watt had forced in Revie's previous fight.

After another two victories Charlie had compiled an 8-0 record. His relationship with Hassett, however, was a bitter scrap. Hassett had not travelled to Derry when Charlie headlined a bill at the Templemore Sports Complex, in November 1976, but had sent a boxer-turned-businessman in his place. After the fight Charlie was shocked to see the businessman counting out notes from an envelope containing his purse. The man said he was taking Hassett's cut as Charlie's manager.

'He's not my manager,' Charlie protested. 'I only signed a deal with him to be my promoter.'

The businessman pocketed the money and told Charlie he would have to discuss it with Hassett. There were even more serious discussions because Hassett had signed a contract for Charlie to fight Jim Watt for the British title in Glasgow. Yet there was no television deal and Charlie would earn only '£2,000 all in', which meant he had to pay for all his travel and accommodation expenses in Glasgow.

Solomons advised Charlie that the fight was worth much more than two grand and he should refuse to travel to Glasgow as Hassett had no legal claim on a position as his manager.

Charlie's next lesson in the harsh dealings of professional boxing came with a summons to appear in court. Watt's promoters were suing him. As he had never agreed to the terms of the fight, and

Hassett was not his manager, Charlie was advised by Solomons to fight the case in court. The London promoter said that he would pay the legal bills in the unlikely event Charlie lost the case. Solomons was as canny in his courtroom assessments as he was out of the ring and Charlie was cleared of any wrongdoing. He was also free to cut ties with Hassett and work exclusively with Solomons – who did not claim a cut from any future purse.

Two more routine victories over American opponents in London improved Charlie's record to 11–0 and set up a much harder fight in Derry. Benny Huertas, a grizzled Puerto Rican based in New York, had fought 55 times previously as a professional. Huertas had faced three previous world champions, including Roberto Duran, and he was rough and canny and threw a spiteful jab that broke Charlie's nose. It was still an overwhelming points victory for Charlie, who was rewarded with an even more difficult fight four months later against the world-ranked Larry Stanton. Boxing had become a serious occupation for such a mild man.

Templemore Sports Complex, Derry, Tuesday 26 July 1977

Davy Larmour's mouth felt dry and his hands trembled as they were wrapped on the night of his professional debut. His opponent, Jimmy Bott from Liverpool, had already fought eight times as a pro. Bott was used to the sapping nerves that took hold before the first bell.

These ripples of trepidation were different to fear. Davy was not afraid of being hit and hurt. He had been hit hard many times as an amateur, but he felt numbed rather than hurt by the blows. It might only be an hour after the bout, or the next morning, when he would wince at his bruising. Davy worried instead that Bott might beat him. He could imagine a sea of jeering laughter at his plight.

The pro game carried a profound sense of mystery. It was a step into the deep unknown, and the strangeness was accentuated by the fact that he warmed up without his familiar vest from the Albert Foundry gym or even the green singlet of Ireland. Pro boxing left its new fighters feeling naked and vulnerable as they went into battle bare-chested.

It helped that familiar faces from Derry were preparing for their own fights. Charlie Nash headlined the bill, against Larry Stanton, while Davy's old amateur rival Neil McLaughlin was about to have his ninth fight. Neil had beaten Davy more times than he had lost in the amateurs, but he had already suffered five defeats as a pro. That sobering statistic was balanced by the appearance of Damien McDermott, who came into the dressing room to say hello. Damien was not fighting but he had won his first two professional bouts at the same venue. Davy was determined to make an equally positive start to his paid career.

He was already working in two other jobs. His main occupation was as a stager for Harland and Wolff in the Belfast docks. This meant he did hard physical labour in those sections of the dry docks where damaged ships were lifted by the massive Samson and Goliath cranes and settled into place, with the help of the stagers, so repairs could be carried out. Davy had also begun to drive a taxi on the evenings when he was not training in the gym. Most weekend nights he drove his private-hire cab through the smouldering streets of Belfast, skirting the riots and barricades, the army checkpoints and stray gunmen. He would drive anywhere in the city, from the Shankill to the Falls, from the Ardoyne to Ballybeen. There was more reason to feel fear in his cab than in a boxing ring.

When he was called to the ring he felt ready. Boxers were usually accorded respect but, in such a perilous time, he heard a smattering of boos. Once again, he was a Protestant fighting in the Catholic heartlands of Derry. Davy had lost many decisions on the referee's scorecard in Derry and Dublin, when it often seemed as if his religion counted more against him than the skill of his opponent. He resolved to leave no room for argument.

At the bell, Davy moved quickly to the centre of the ring. He hit Bott with jabs and heavy combinations and felt surprised at the ease with which he seemed to be hurting a pro fighter. He poured on yet more pressure and then, with brutal suddenness, Bott was drilled to the canvas by a right cross and left hook. Davy knew it was all over. Jimmy Bott had defeat etched across his dazed features as he made little attempt to beat the count. A first-round knockout in less than 30 seconds was a thrilling start to Davy's pro career.

'No one will want to fight you after that performance,' Damien McDermott said.

Davy grinned and headed for the showers. He wanted to be back at ringside in time to see Charlie Nash in the biggest fight of his career. Maybe, Davy hoped, he would be a headline fighter himself one day, like Charlie, and able to give up his dangerous taxi-driving job.

There was no early finish for Charlie Nash against Larry Stanton – an ambitious American rated number 11 in the world. Stanton could box as well as fight on the inside and he pushed Nash hard over ten tightly contested rounds. Nash won the decision but it had been his hardest fight. The quiet boy from Derry was ready for even more brutal examinations.

Barry McGuigan had suffered a dip but he came back with a bold plan. In late 1977, he had lost in the semi-finals of the Irish Juniors. It had been a shock defeat to a chunky kid called Mick Holmes. When they fought again he would knock out Holmes with a devastating punch but, in the Juniors, McGuigan was sloppy and he deserved to lose. Amid the disappointment he decided to try to win the Ulster Senior title at his very first attempt.

There was an Irish logic to his audacity. Losing in the Juniors and winning a prestigious Senior title six weeks later sounded like redemption to a 16-year-old boy. The teenage McGuigan might have spoken in a high-pitched squeak, but he carried dynamite in his fists and iron in his soul.

The Ulster Seniors were a prominent feature in the Irish boxing calendar at the end of every January and, in 1978, Barry's older brother, Dermot, helped him plot his fight strategy. Dermot knew Barry had the skill to outwit most senior Irish boxers in his weight division, but also that fully grown men would absorb the power of his punches more readily than the kids he had been knocking out. They hit much harder too and so it was time for Barry to show he could box as well as fight. He needed to master the boxer's purest aim: to hit his opponent without being hit much himself.

Sean Russell – the older brother of Hugh, and a Holy Family star – was the overwhelming favourite for the bantamweight title. He had won many Junior titles and he looked to be on course to become National champion later that year. Trained by Gerry, Russell was quick and confident and he settled down at ringside to see who he would face in the final. Barry's semi-final was against Noel Reynolds from Lisburn. Reynolds was a rough brawler, in his early twenties, who wanted to expose the Clones novice.

Instead, McGuigan outclassed Reynolds from the opening bell, moving in and out of range and landing spiteful punches. As Reynolds wilted, McGuigan ripped in a body blow that dropped him. Somehow Reynolds got up and clung on for three rounds. He made it to the final bell, but he had been knocked down a second time and he was hurt whenever McGuigan connected with a heavy blow.

'How old are you?' Reynolds asked Barry in the dressing room.

'Sixteen.'

'*Sixteen*?' Reynolds exclaimed in disbelief.

'I turn 17 next month.'

Reynolds wrapped an arm around his conqueror's shoulders. 'I've never been hit like that in my life. You know you've got Sean Russell in the final?'

Barry nodded, waiting for Reynolds to warn him about the difficulties he would endure.

'You're going to knock him out,' Reynolds promised.

Barry was startled by such a brazen prediction. He continued to unwrap his hands.

Sean Russell arrived. He introduced himself, offered his hand and congratulated Barry on his performance. The teenager was unsure how to react. None of his previous opponents had ever been so complimentary and Russell was meant to be better than anyone he had ever faced.

'I'm sorry, Sean,' Reynolds said, 'but this kid is going to knock you out.'

Russell laughed. 'He's just a wee kid. He's not going to knock me out.'

As Russell walked over to his brother Hugh, Reynolds whispered to Barry: 'You will . . .'

Hugh Russell, like Barry, was in his first Ulster Senior final. His opponent, Jimmy Carson, also fought for the Holy Family. Hugh had often sparred Carson and he was sure he had the measure of the older fighter, who had made the final of the Irish National championships the two previous years.

Having just turned 19, Hugh's confidence was boosted by the fact Gerry would work Carson's corner. Hugh had noticed that whenever two Holy Family fighters met each other in a major tournament, Gerry tended to look after the fighter he thought would lose and need him more.

Bobby McAllister, another Holy Family coach, helped Hugh. He did not need to say much to the little redhead as Hugh knew exactly what to expect from Carson: a very good amateur who fell slightly short of international standards. Hugh was looking to force his way into the National team and an Ulster title would be the first step. The outcome followed predictions. Hugh won a wide decision over Carson and he was soon back at ringside to watch his big brother fight McGuigan.

Gerry knew McGuigan was special. He tried to warn Russell, but his words were not enough. Early in the first round, McGuigan backed Russell against the ropes and unleashed a barrage of blows as he switched from the body to the head. He dropped Russell in the corner and the Belfast fighter only just beat the count.

McGuigan's shots in the second round had a real whip to them and Russell winced often when he was caught. There was purpose and clarity to McGuigan's work and, when the inevitable openings emerged, he nailed Russell. Two heavy punches knocked down Russell twice more in the round. The partisan Belfast crowd, most of whom were backing the Holy Family fighter, had been stunned. There were only a few muted cries when the fight was stopped.

There was ecstasy among the Clones contingent who had travelled the 80 miles to Belfast. After Barry had received his medal and showered, everyone from Clones climbed into their cars so that they could get back in time for the 10pm screening on Ulster TV. It was usually a 90-minute drive but, on that cold January night, it took them two hours to reach Monaghan, which was still 13 miles from Clones. An army checkpoint at Middletown had delayed them as the soldiers made everyone get out while they searched the cars.

It was just after ten when they turned into Monaghan's Four Seasons Hotel, a familiar music venue to Pat McGuigan, and they raced into the lounge. Pat knew the manager and so they could switch on the TV and settle down to watch. Just a few minutes later, Barry saw himself.

'Oh, son,' Pat said, 'look at that beautiful mop of hair!'

Barry blushed as Dermot cackled. But the room quietened briefly while they waited for the first bell – as if they were suddenly not quite sure what they might see next. Other guests had crowded round the television. A woman turned to Barry, who was sitting on the floor, watching himself on television, and said: 'Is that you?'

'Yes,' Barry said proudly, 'that's me.'

It was a surreal experience. As everyone around him roared and yelped, Barry watched himself fight for the first time. He thought he looked reckless, but there was no doubting the way he broke down Russell and made him surrender. He looked up at the screen in wonder as the commentator, Harry Thompson, nailed his conclusion as the television pictures showed Barry with his hands raised at the end of the fight: 'McGuigan is a bit rough, still a bit raw, but this fellow has got *serious* potential.'

Dermot looked at his younger brother. His eyes glistened with pride. 'This is only the start,' he predicted.

Barry smiled. 'I know,' he said, sounding honest rather than arrogant.

'It's too dangerous,' Felix Jones, the president of the Irish Amateur Boxing Association, told Gerry Storey in Dublin. 'We'll have to cancel Belfast.'

'Felix, you can't,' Gerry said with a firm shake of his head. 'The East Germans are coming.'

'Are you crazy?' Jones asked. 'After everything that has happened?'

A week earlier, on 17 February 1978, the IRA had attached a large bomb to petrol-filled canisters hanging from meat hooks just out of sight beneath the window of the main restaurant at the La Mon Hotel in Gransha, six miles from Belfast's city centre. The IRA had planned to telephone through a warning about the imminent bomb blast, as they said they always aimed to do when not targeting the army or the police, but their mission went awry.

The closest public phone booth had been vandalised so they had to drive to find another one. Their journey was interrupted by a checkpoint and, by the time they were allowed to drive on and find a working telephone, only a few minutes remained before the explosion. There was not enough time to clear the hotel and 12 people were burnt to death, with a further 30 injured by the bomb. The La Mon attack had been the worst atrocity since Bloody Sunday and the McGurk's Bar bombing in December 1971.

The death toll since the start of the Troubles climbed past the 2,000 mark. After the La Mon bomb, official records confirmed that exactly 2,003 people had died in sectarian violence up until then.

The idea of Gerry Storey pressing on with his scheme against such a murderous backdrop seemed madness to Jones. He had been alarmed the first time Gerry suggested that an Irish selection should box East Germany on the Shankill Road. It was difficult to envisage the Loyalist paramilitaries of the UDA and the UVF allowing the green-vested Irish into the red-white-and-blue enclave of Protestantism and loyalty to the Union Jack.

'The Irish vest will be worn by boxers,' Gerry said simply. 'That makes it different.'

He detailed all the meetings he had held with the highest-ranking officials in the UDA, the UFF and the UVF on one side and the Provisional IRA on the opposing side. Gerry had received personal guarantees from all the leaders that an international between Ireland and East Germany could be held at the Rumford Social Club – a Loyalist working men's club just off the Shankill Road – without any fear of attacks. It would be a peaceful night of boxing.

The La Mon bomb seemed to have changed everything. But Gerry remained adamant. Over the previous few days he had spoken again to all the leaders, including Tommy 'Tucker' Lyttle, the brigadier of the vitriolic UDA. He had received the same promises of safety. After a long silence, Jones asked a pointed question. 'Gerry,' he said, 'can you guarantee the safety of the East German team in Belfast?'

'Yes,' Gerry said intently. 'I guarantee the safety of everyone. I guarantee there will be no trouble.'

Jones looked at his head coach for ten long seconds. 'All right,' he eventually said. 'It's on your shoulders.'

Rumford Social Club, Shankill Road, Belfast,
Monday 6 March 1978

The paramilitaries were out in force that night. They manned the doors to a rammed club and made sure that every spectator handed over any guns they might be carrying. Their weapons could be collected on the way out.

Inside the club the atmosphere was electric but good humoured.

There was no obvious animosity towards the green vests worn by the local boxers, or even the white shamrock on the front of each singlet. Everyone wanted to see the international debuts of the two new teenage Ulster Senior champions, Hugh Russell and Barry McGuigan. The fact that they were Catholic kids from the New Lodge and Clones mattered less than their fighting skills.

There was only trouble during the fourth contest, when Gerry Hamill knocked down his German opponent. Fans close to the ring heard the referee tell the German to stay down and he would disqualify Hamill. There was immediate bedlam as the referee waved the contest over and went across to the stricken German, who was pawing sadly at his head to indicate he had been butted.

So many bets had been placed on the outcome that, rather than sectarian animosity, the loss of money looked like causing a full-scale riot. Tucker Lyttle, who was a bookmaker as well as a UDA hard man, jumped into the ring. After consulting with Gerry in Hamill's corner, Lyttle called for calm. He praised the courage of both fighters and then yelled: 'We're paying out Hamill as the winner.'

There was a roar and, sheepishly, the referee raised Hamill's arm. It had been a clear punch that won him the fight and the social club stomped their approval of another legitimate Irish victory. Peace and jubilation were assured.

Barry McGuigan was the headline fight – partly because his opponent, Torsten Koch, had been devastating a few nights earlier. Koch had fought Gussie Farrell, the reigning Irish Senior bantamweight champion, in Dublin and totally dominated him. The German was also freakishly tall, at six foot, for a bantamweight.

The Shankill club lit up when McGuigan and Koch walked to the ring. Both fighters were cheered – but the support was intense for McGuigan, the grandson of a former IRA captain, who lived across the border in the Republic. On the Shankill Road that night, however, he was just a brilliant wee boxer with the great Gerry Storey in his corner.

In a fierce battle, McGuigan tried to negate the greater reach of the taller German by staying on top of Koch. He had tasted the rangy power of Koch's long-distance hitting, as a whippy southpaw, and so he poured on the pressure. He fought the German on the inside, hurting him with body punches and jolting uppercuts. Koch could not cope with McGuigan's ferocity and he was well beaten. There was boisterous appreciation for McGuigan, whose green vest had turned dark with sweat. He and the rest of his teammates waved to the crowd, feeling utterly at home on the Shankill Road.

As the boxers went back to the dressing rooms to change into their street clothes, a popular showband called Club Sound began to thump out some familiar songs, and the hall erupted with delight when Pat McGuigan joined them to belt out a few ditties on vocals. He was well known from past Shankill Road performances and the crowd joined in when he began to sing 'I Got a Tiger by the Tail'. Gerry Storey, bringing his boys out into the singing throng, smiled. Boxing had done it again.

Later that night, after Gerry had got all his boxers safely off the Shankill Road, a bemused Felix Jones sat down for a meal with some high-ranking army officers. He asked them what they made of Gerry fulfilling his guarantee that there would be no trouble that night.

'Mr Jones,' the senior commander said, 'our squaddies and snipers wish Storey brought a team onto the Shankill every night. They said this is the only time they've felt safe from trouble.'

CHAPTER 8

A Second Warning

Gerry Storey's peaceful work prompted secret plans to eliminate him – but he was oblivious to the sinister plotting. He was caught up in developing his fighters at the Holy Family and in the Irish National squad. He also tried hard to be a good husband to Belle and a good father. Boxing often got in the way. One day he came home from work and spent an hour on the phone on fight business before Belle tapped her watch. He was due to drop her off at hospital for a routine check. Gerry held up his hand in a plea for five more minutes.

'I'll get a taxi,' Belle said softly.

'Hold on,' Gerry said down the phone to his caller before he turned to Belle.

'Come down to the docks with me,' he suggested. 'It'll take me 20 minutes to load the trailers and then I'll take you up to the hospital and wait with you.'

Belle had never been to the docks before and, in curious surprise, she nodded.

Ten minutes later he was ready to drive Belle to the docks. 'This will be fun,' he promised, before joking: 'You'll see how important I am.'

Belle knew her husband had a special job at Belfast docks – as one of the few forklift drivers allowed to work in both the Catholic and the Protestant quarters. When he was away with a boxing team, there would often be days when goods could not be moved from the Catholic to the Protestant side, or the reverse. Gerry was always welcome right across the docklands.

Sunshine streamed across Sinclair Wharf as Gerry rolled down his window so that Belle could hear the squawks of the dirty-white seagulls. He showed her the big tankers docked in the bay and the giant cranes looming over them. Gerry then parked near his forklift and the containers of tobacco he would load.

'Come in for a cup of tea,' he said, gesturing to the hut where the workmen took their breaks. 'I'll be 20 minutes.'

Belle was happier waiting in the car. She would enjoy the peace and quiet without the kids in tow. Gerry had just got out of the car and turned towards the forklift when a man yelped.

'Gerry! Gerry Storey! Don't go near your truck!' Billy O'Neill ran towards his friend. 'There's a bomb under your wheel!' he shouted.

Gerry stared at his forklift truck. A dark shape nestled against the back wheel.

'It's a bomb,' Billy confirmed. 'A big one.'

They had discovered it by chance. A driver called Alfie, who worked closely with Gerry, had arrived to pick up a load of tobacco from the forklift. As Alfie strolled towards the forklift to check the contents, he saw the dark shape. At first he thought it was the container of water Gerry always carried for the radiator. He bent down and saw wires curling out of the package.

If Alfie had not walked over, he would not have checked underneath the forklift. And if Belle hadn't been so curious about the docks on her first visit, Gerry would have started up the forklift before Billy had seen him.

Once the bomb had been exploded in a safe location, a senior policeman confirmed the news. If Gerry had turned the ignition the bomb would have detonated. The policeman looked at him. 'You would have been blown to smithereens, Mr Storey.'

Belle asked him if the bomb was meant for Gerry. 'Yes. It was a targeted attack.'

Belle was so shaken that, rather than taking her to hospital, Gerry drove her home. He made her a cup of tea and told her he needed some clarity. When he called Harry Burgess, the Loyalist leader was surprised. He reassured Gerry it could not have been any of his men. Both the UDA and the UVF had instructed their soldiers that Gerry and his boxers should never be attacked on their patch of Belfast. No one would dare break that order. The IRA had given a similar message to cover Republican turf. The docks, however, occupied neutral territory.

The Special Branch suggested that he might have been targeted by a rogue dissident who fell outside the paramilitary orbit. Maybe someone within boxing was jealous of his success? Gerry had too much faith in boxing men. But he agreed to go down with the Special Branch to meet his manager at the Belfast docks.

When he heard that the bomb had been aimed at Gerry, his boss chuckled. 'You don't have to tell me that,' he said before pointing at Gerry. 'No one will get into a car with that man!'

When the laughter died, the Special Branch had serious advice for Gerry. He needed to be very careful and check every time beneath his car and his truck for another dark shape. Someone, clearly, wanted to kill him.

Charlie Nash had read about the rise of Barry McGuigan. When the young amateur called to ask if they might spar, there was no hesitation from the new British champion. He invited McGuigan to come down to St Mary's in Derry that Sunday afternoon in the spring of 1978. They would have 'a wee session'.

A few months earlier, on Tuesday 28 February 1978, six nights before Gerry Storey took McGuigan and Ireland to the Shankill Road, Nash had become the British lightweight champion. It was a fevered night in Derry and a moment of poignant symbolism. Derry, and the Nash family, had been torn apart by the British army on Bloody Sunday and six years later the Westminster government continued to insist the killings had been provoked by Republican gunmen and rioters.

Despite the wish of the vast majority of people in Derry to join a united Ireland, the city remained part of the United Kingdom. Charlie carried a British passport even if his heart was forever Irish. But he knew, as a boxer, that if he won the British title he would be a step closer to European and world championship contests in the next few years. So he accepted the offer to fight Johnny Claydon from London for the vacant British lightweight belt.

Claydon was a decent opponent, having won 14 of his 20 fights, and the contest was held at the Templemore Sports Complex in Derry. The only doubt in Charlie's head was that, in his previous fight in October 1977, he had lost for the first time. In the Ulster Hall in Belfast, a clash of heads opened a nasty gash over Charlie's right eye and the fight had to be stopped in the fifth round with the verdict given to Adolfo Osses, a veteran from Panama. The fact that his perfect 13–0 record was ruined by a freak cut and a mediocre opponent hurt Charlie deeply.

The faith of Derry in their champion was undented, however, and the Templemore was sold out. White banners, stitched in black with the simple name of Charlie, were held above the crowd of 2,000 – with the chant of 'Char-lie, Char-lie, Char-lie!' resounding throughout the fight. Charlie was so far ahead, having won every round, that the referee took pity on Claydon and stopped the fight in the 12th of a 15-round bout.

Charlie Nash was the new British champion. His fans swamped the ring, chanting and holding up V for Victory signs. Charlie had conquered the British for the whole of Derry.

Later that night they held a riotous reception at St Mary's. When Charlie finally arrived the band began to play 'Congratulations', which turned into communal singing of 'The Town I Loved So Well'. Derry was the town, and Charlie was their champion.

Barry McGuigan had been in the crowd that February night at the Templemore. But he was oblivious to the emotion that had surged through St Mary's when, weeks later, he and his father turned up at the club on a hushed Sunday afternoon. Charlie was friendly but businesslike. He had just finished three rounds of sparring with Damien McDermott when Barry completed his warm-up.

'Are you ready?' Charlie asked.

Barry nodded, looking suddenly nervous. He was ten years younger than Charlie.

'How many rounds do you want?' Charlie asked.

'Three,' Barry said softly.

'Okay. Let's go.'

Barry's reputation as a big puncher had reached Derry, and Charlie knew he was not to be taken lightly. He decided to box the amateur as if facing a hardened pro. Charlie was too gentle a man to set about his work with malice, but he was out to show McGuigan how it felt to face a man who made money as a fighter. He was quicker and more skilful, which was unsurprising considering the decade of experience that separated him from the 17-year-old. In the second and third rounds Charlie moved easily around the ring, picking off Barry whenever he tried to close the distance. His jabs were sharp and rarely missed. The gulf between the pro and the amateur were more hurtful to Barry than the actual punches.

As soon as sparring ended, Barry headed for a storeroom at the back of the gym. Charlie, meanwhile, began to hit the heavy bag. He barely noticed when, five minutes later, Pat McGuigan called over Charlie's trainer, Tommy Donnelly. Sweat flew from Charlie as he pummelled the bag with clubbing punches that sounded very different to routine sparring.

Tommy disappeared into the storeroom. Charlie kept working the bag, making it dance and sag as the metal chain attaching it to the rafters spun beneath his punches. Eventually, Tommy came back, looking concerned. 'Charlie, can you talk to young Barry?'

'Is he okay?'

Tommy nodded to the storeroom so that Charlie could find out for himself.

After he had towelled himself dry and removed his gloves, Charlie headed for the storeroom.

Barry sat in the corner on a wooden chair. He looked desperately sad. 'What's the matter?' Charlie asked him gently. He could see that Barry had been crying.

Barry shrugged silently. 'Come on,' Charlie said. 'What's up?'

It all came out in a flood then, with tears to sharpen the pain of his words. Barry explained that he had done plenty of quality sparring. He had even been to London and worked with Charlie Magri, who had just become the British flyweight champion. Barry had cracked Magri so hard with a couple of punches he had broken his nose. Magri's trainer, Terry Lawless, had to stop the session to remind the teenager that 'we spar light here'.

Barry looked up, his eyes filling again. 'I did that, but I couldn't hit you out there.'

Charlie explained how styles made sparring sessions, as well as fights. He also pointed out he had had 14 pro fights while Barry still had years left in the amateurs. Charlie was almost 27, Barry was 17. He was a big lightweight while Barry was a bantamweight. The natural differences between them explained why Barry should not take their session so badly.

'Why don't you come back next Sunday for another few rounds?' Charlie suggested.

Barry nearly smiled. 'Okay,' he said.

A week later, the contrast was marked. There were, of course, two versions of the same spar. Charlie would say years later that young Barry had been so down in the dumps that he decided to go easy on him. He allowed Barry to dictate the pace and bang away at his body. They did a lot of in-fighting, which suited Barry more than him, and Charlie was simply reactive as he took some heavy punches and only landed a few of his own. He was happy that, after three rounds, Barry smiled again.

'See,' Charlie said, 'you were far better today. You'll make a good pro one day.'

Barry wrote a few years later that he gave Charlie 'a good pasting' in their second spar to make up for the humiliation he had felt a week earlier. In a different century, when McGuigan was in his late fifties and Nash in his late sixties, there was no needle between the two old fighters. McGuigan said 'gym stories' were always muddled and contradictory while Nash was glad he had helped boost a young fighter's confidence. They agreed to disagree over what had really happened the last time they shared a ring in Derry.

Davy Larmour still worked at the docks but money was scarce and so, on weekend nights, he continued to drive a taxi around the burning streets of Belfast. He needed the money – his boxing career had stuttered after his crushing knockout of Jimmy Bott in his first paid fight.

It was hard to find beatable opposition from whom he could learn and, instead, he waited seven months before he next stepped into the ring. The only fight he could secure was with an excellent unbeaten prospect, John Feeney, who had compiled a flawless 6-0 record. Davy lost to him, and to George Sutton in his next fight, and by May 1978 his record was a modest 2–2.

Many taxi drivers were too frightened to cross the sectarian divide, but Davy was ready to drive into the Republican heartlands because he was familiar with the streets as a boxer and, of course, he came from the Shankill Road. He had just driven down Durham Street, turned left on Glengall Street and was heading for Wellington Place with three passengers when they hit an army roadblock.

There were two cars ahead of them and one of the men in the

back said, 'We'll get out now.' Davy pulled in and the three of them slipped out into the night. The army were all over Davy's car then. They searched it inside and out before waving him on his way. It was only the next day that Davy, when cleaning the car, pulled up the back-seat cover and discovered a weapon the army had missed. It was a dagger with a foot-long saw blade attached to a black rubber handle. The word Typhoon was stencilled into the handle and it resembled a diver's knife. Davy shuddered to think of the damage his passengers planned on doing with that brute of a knife.

A taxi-driving friend of Davy's was far unluckier. He picked up two men near the Europa Hotel – the most bombed hotel in Europe – and they asked him to take them to Glencairn, a Protestant area near the Shankill. The taxi driver was a Protestant but, married to a Catholic woman, he carried no sectarian prejudice. An open-minded attitude could not save him. His passengers were Republican paramilitaries in the mood for killing a Protestant. On the outskirts of Glencairn they shot the driver in the head.

Life seemed far safer in a boxing ring and, with money so tight, Davy accepted his fifth fight with just 48 hours' notice. On Tuesday 27 June 1978, he was asked to travel to Caerphilly in Wales to fight Johnny Owen, who was unbeaten after 14 fights, that Thursday night. The previous November, Owen had become British bantamweight champion after stopping Davy's close friend Paddy Maguire.

Paddy's toughness was renowned and so it was a forbidding prospect for Davy to fight Owen in his Welsh backyard without any training. Davy also knew that, to shift the 12 pounds he needed to lose to make bantamweight, he would have to take laxatives. It was hopeless preparation but the purse was decent and, on the night he was offered the fight, Charlie Nash had another big win in Derry. He knocked out Adolfo Osses in the third round and so avenged his only loss. Charlie was climbing high again, and Davy wanted to do the same.

The risk of fighting a boxer as good as Johnny Owen, however, ended badly. Weight-drained and ill-prepared, Davy was stopped in round seven. But no one could have known then that Davy would hit a winning streak in the ring that would lead him to some epic cross-sectarian battles in Belfast. By contrast, two years later, poor Johnny Owen would lose his life after fighting for the world bantamweight title against Luis Pintor in Los Angeles. Boxing was a salvation for some fighters and a graveyard for others.

Barry McGuigan spent most weekends at work at the Holy Family with Gerry Storey. He would spar often with Davy Larmour. It was good for him to keep working with pro fighters and, to mix it up, Gerry would sometimes take Barry to the Albert Foundry, Davy's home gym just off the Shankill. A running track and an old shed stood outside the gym but, most of all, Barry remembered the perishing cold. Even when they turned up a couple of gas heaters the gym was still freezing. Only the ferocity of sparring with Davy warmed him up.

His dad would drive him back to Clones late at night. It was terrifying whenever they were stopped by the army on a country road. Their hearts would feel like they were jumping out of their chests when Pat rolled down the window. 'You were driving a bit fast there,' a soldier might say and both Barry and his father wanted to say: 'We're from the South and we're petrified. What do you expect us to do?' But Pat remained courteous as it made no sense to provoke the army.

It became easier as Barry's boxing reputation grew and he was recognised. There was still a burning disappointment that would change the course of his life for ever. It would also alter the direction of boxing history and spread new hope in the Troubles.

Barry became Irish Senior bantamweight champion when he beat Michael Holmes in Dublin in April 1978. He dropped Holmes and his easy victory should have made him an automatic pick for the European under-19 championships. Instead, the selectors chose

Holmes ahead of him. Barry only discovered the news when reading the Sunday papers. Irish officials claimed he was 'too young', but Barry could not believe they had picked a fighter he had beaten comfortably to become National champion.

Gerry consoled him. 'Don't worry about it,' he said, 'something else will come round for you.' The trainer had already tipped off the Northern Ireland Sports Council that McGuigan had been jettisoned by the Irish boxing selectors in Dublin. A call was placed to McGuigan and he was asked if, despite living in the Republic of Ireland, he had any Northern Irish roots. Barry told them about his paternal grandfather, James, who had been born and raised in the North. He did not mention that James McGuigan had also been a captain in the IRA.

When Northern Ireland made overtures to select him for the Commonwealth Games, a silent 'Fuck you' towards the South echoed in Barry's head. Ireland would not compete in the Commonwealths, but if Barry boxed for the North he knew he would turn away from Dublin for ever. He also knew he would have Gerry in his corner for the North, and so it was an easy decision to spurn the Republic.

His decision to box for Northern Ireland in the Commonwealth Games would make his reputation – both as a champion boxer and a young man willing to cross borders between two countries and two communities. McGuigan's move to the North won him the kind of attention he would never have enjoyed had he remained a purely Irish fighter from Clones. The daring nature of his career had been established in that bold choice.

There were also more serious ramifications because Republicans in Clones expected him to represent Ireland. But he agreed to join Gerry's squad alongside Hugh Russell, Jimmy Carson, Kenny Webb, Gerry Hamill, Kenny Beattie and Tony McAvoy.

McGuigan bloomed under Storey's tutelage. He had always had a sharp jab, a hard right and a big left hook. Gerry showed him how to put them together. Confidence surged through him. When they reached Edmonton, Canada, for the Commonwealths in August 1978, Barry was happy to share a room with Hugh Russell.

They trained with the New Zealand and Australia teams in an ice hockey arena and were ferried to and from their accommodation in old yellow school buses. After sparring and working the heavy bags during training they sometimes did pad sessions in the wide hallways of their living quarters which they shared, bizarrely, with the older men who played lawn bowls. The *'bom, bom, bom, bom, bang'* sound of fists smacking into leather would reverberate against the bare walls.

'Jesus Christ, you boys are frightening,' one of the bowlers exclaimed to Barry.

The adopted Northern Irish sensation simply grinned before he went back to work with Gerry, who concentrated on sharpening his combination punching and movement. One *bom, bom, bom, bom, bang* flurry of shots would be followed by a little roll of the shoulders and a move to the side before, under Gerry's instructions, Barry would step back inside and pummel the pads with another blurring combination. As his force and fluidity improved, Barry marvelled at the impact Gerry's training had on him.

He won his first two fights before facing the local favourite, Bill Ranelli, in the semi-final. The Canadian was aggressive, but McGuigan knocked him out with a ten-punch combination. Ranelli crumpled on the canvas and the crowd was silenced. The final awaited.

Gerry Hamill won gold at lightweight, Kenny Beattie lost to the future great professional Mike McCallum in the welterweight final, and Hugh Russell picked up a bronze medal at flyweight. Barry had the hardest test, but Gerry spared him an early sight of his opponent – Tumat Sogolik from Papua New Guinea.

All the finalists warmed up together, with fighters of different weights loosening up alongside each other. Barry's eye was caught by a very black and imposing lightweight. He was relieved his own opponent would be much smaller. When his name was called out, alongside Sogolik, Barry was shocked when the big black guy began walking ahead of him.

'He's heard the wrong name,' Barry said.

'No,' Gerry said quietly. 'That's your guy.'

'Holy fuck!'

Gerry hustled him along to the ring. 'You'll be fine, Barry, you can outbox him.'

A few minutes later, the bell rang and the monster from Papua New Guinea walked towards him. Wearing number 133 on his green Northern Ireland vest, with his legs and arms moving in a blur, Barry boxed well and for the first round he kept Sogolik at the end of his jab. And then, midway through the second, Sogolik landed a huge punch. It felt as if a house had caved in on Barry. He somehow stayed on his feet, but he was so shaken that the referee gave him a standing count.

In the third he outboxed Sogolik again and scored with his fast jab and combinations. He had just begun to open up when Sogolik forced another standing count. McGuigan shook his head but the right uppercut had landed. He recovered and, heeding Storey's urge to finish strongly, he came back at Sogolik with some point-scoring punches. 'The young man is boxing a tremendously courageous battle under heavy pressure – even though he's quite frail compared to Sogolik,' said Harry Carpenter, the BBC's venerable television commentator.

At the bell, as the pictures cut away to the Queen's applauding husband, Carpenter said: 'Clearly, Prince Philip enjoyed that.'

Des Lynam, commentating for BBC radio, thought McGuigan had shaded it while Carpenter believed the two standing counts had been decisive in favour of Sogolik.

The fighters were brought back to the centre of the ring to hear the decision. Barry wore a white satin gown, trimmed with green, while Sogolik remained in his vest and trunks. The teenager flung back his head, in a mix of delight and disbelief, when his full name, Finbar Barry McGuigan, was called out as the winner. Barry raised his arms. As soon as he opened his eyes again they filled with tears. Barry was crying as he embraced his opponent. The big man was no monster. Sogolik lifted little Barry off his feet in a bear hug and swung him round in the air.

The moment came for him to step onto the Commonwealth Games podium. As they began to play 'Danny Boy' as the Northern Irish anthem, Barry thought of his parents and of how often his father had sung this song, which seemed so apt back home in Clones where there was so much happiness yet grief. When he heard the famous line – 'I'll be here in sunshine or in shadow' – the tears slid down his face.

The power of boxing during the Troubles moved the 17-year-old champion when he and his team flew into Belfast. Three thousand people were at the airport to welcome them. Later that day, when he finally got to Monaghan, in the South, another thousand Irish locals celebrated with him. They didn't care that he had won gold for Northern Ireland.

And so the course of Barry McGuigan's life, and the rise of boxing in the Troubles, shifted in these seismic moments. The fateful decision of some anonymous amateur boxing administrators in Dublin, to leave him out of their team to contest the European championships, had driven McGuigan into the welcoming arms of the Northern Ireland squad. Gerry Storey's training helped him win Commonwealth gold and the uplifting impact resonated in the North and the South. The raw power of boxing, combined with the beguiling appeal of McGuigan's innocent character, set a template that would inspire him to follow this same cross-border and cross-sectarian path throughout his later professional career. He could now see a way to make Gerry's philosophy his own.

Barry McGuigan and Sandra Mealiff had met on the Diamond in Clones when they were both three years old and their families ran businesses alongside each other, with no one minding that the Mealiffs were Protestant and the McGuigans were Catholic. The

Mealiffs were much more affluent – partly because they had only five children compared to the McGuigans' brood of eight. There were other economic reasons. The Mealiff income from their grocery shop, which ran in friendly competition with the McGuigans', was supplemented by the hotel Sandra's dad owned and ran on the Diamond. They also kept pigs, calves and hundreds of chickens in their backyard – so not only were they self-sufficient but the chickens gave them additional revenue.

Sandra's father was much more conventional than Barry's dad. He was the chairman of the local council while Pat McGuigan was a professional singer who travelled all over the world. Sandra thought the McGuigans were wonderfully bohemian and daring. Even when it came to ice cream the difference was obvious. The McGuigans ran the trendy store while the Mealiffs were more conservative. Pat would come back from New York and say to Kate, his wife, who ran the shop, 'We need a Mr Whippy machine – they're all the rage in America.' Sandra's dad would shrug. He had no intention of investing in Mr Whippy. Most of the kids urged their parents to shop at the McGuigans' and Sandra understood. She wanted to spend as much with them as she could.

The Troubles loomed over their lives. Sandra went to school across the border, in the North, in Newtownbutler and Fermanagh, while Barry was educated in Clones. Sandra's senior school was next door to the British army barracks.

Years earlier her cousin Kathryn Eakin was killed by an IRA bomb in Claudy, not far from Derry, on 31 July 1972. Kathryn, aged 8, was the youngest of nine victims. The force of the bomb blew Kathryn against the window and fractured her skull. Sandra, who was only 11 then, felt she would never quite get over what had happened to her little cousin. For the next year her aunt, Kathryn's mum, kept cooking food for her lost daughter at every meal.

There was a more peaceful routine in Clones. Sandra's brothers Sam and David were great friends with Dermot and Barry and she hung out with Sharon, Barry's sister. At first Sandra was not attracted to Barry. She warmed to the softer side of Dermot. When Sandra would be too scared to climb down from the top of the chicken cages because she had no head for heights, Barry and her brothers would run off while Dermot fetched a ladder for her.

There was a contrasting intensity in Barry that she found, in her teenage phrase, 'a little weird'. He was incredibly driven, even as a child, and Sandra and everyone else thought it was odd. Barry had plenty of friends and he was engaging. But he was also insular and fiercely concentrated. He wanted to be the best and he was willing to work as hard as it took. Once he found boxing, he refused to go out because he would be training every evening. And at school he was the model student. He worked hard and he was always ready to help his teachers. Sandra and Sharon would roll their eyes when they heard stories about Barry. If a teacher said, 'I need to go out and get a sandwich,' Barry would pipe up: 'Don't you worry. I'll run and get it for you. I'm doing a training run anyway.' He was the dreaded goody-two-shoes.

Even Sandra's dad thought Barry was unusual. When he heard Barry say, 'I'm off to the gym,' Mr Mealiff looked at him in dis-belief. 'Are you off your trolley?' he asked, seriously. No one else went to the gym in Clones in those days.

Barry knew boxers needed to be compelled. The boxing gym became his life. As he began to succeed, so surprise at his seeming strangeness turned to admiration. Sandra was in the packed crowd for Barry's first amateur bout at the Luxor Cinema – and she ended up arguing with his defeated opponent in her dad's hotel. The kid claimed that Barry had only beaten him because he had started throwing punches before the bell had even rung. Sandra and her friends defended Barry because they had begun to appreciate how much he poured into boxing. He was no ordinary boy. He was a special fighter who made them all proud.

When Barry won Commonwealth gold, Sandra's father was among a group of local businessmen who clubbed together to buy him a gold bracelet in honour of all he had done for Clones.

Everyone had watched him win in Edmonton but, even then, Sandra did not feel any romantic longing for Barry.

They only started going out together, almost by chance, a month after Barry got back to Clones. Sandra and Sharon were off to a Saturday-night disco in Monaghan in late September 1978. Barry was the only one of their gang who could drive and so he offered the girls a lift. But soon all their friends wanted to join them and the girls had to hitch there. But Barry made up for it by driving them home.

As they pulled up at the Diamond, Barry turned to Sandra and asked her if she would like to listen to a song that had just started on the radio. One of the others in the back seat piped up: 'It's brilliant. Let's all listen to it.' McGuigan's intensity rose to the surface and the young boxer conveyed his message with a single stare. Everyone else, besides him and Sandra, got out.

The Protestant girl and the Catholic boy kissed for the first time, oblivious to the Troubles around them. Sandra Mealiff and Barry McGuigan were together – as they still are over 40 years later.

Charlie Nash's mother, Bridie, died on his wife's birthday, on 16 May 1979. She had been ill for eight years with heart problems, since even before they lost Willie on Bloody Sunday, but her death still came as a shock. Charlie remembered how, on the night he won the British title in February 1978, his mother had been unable to stay at ringside to watch him. She was too frightened of him being hurt and so she had walked out of the Templemore Sports Complex soon after the fight started. She had maintained a quiet vigil outside, pacing in front of the entrance, clutching a pair of rosary beads and praying for Charlie.

He could not draw on her support six weeks later, on 27 June 1979, when he fought the French champion Andre Holyk for the vacant European lightweight title – again at the Templemore in Derry. Charlie thought about withdrawing from the bout, but his promoter Jack Solomons stressed that he might not get another crack at becoming the champion of Europe. He also knew his mother would have wanted him to win the title for Derry.

Charlie still worked at the print company. As always before a fight, he took two weeks off to prepare himself. Holyk had lost only three of his 40 bouts and he had even beaten Jim Watt, the world lightweight champion, the first time they had met.

A European title fight in Derry, featuring Charlie Nash, was described by Harry Thompson on BBC Northern Ireland 'as the biggest night in recent Irish boxing history'. The Templemore was packed again, and the chanting for Charlie could be heard during the preliminary bouts.

Charlie Nash came out to sustained roaring. When he stepped inside the ring he removed his robe and, after he had touched gloves with his French opponent, he retreated to his corner where he knelt down on one knee and said a brief prayer.

As they waited for the opening bell, both fighters danced on the spot. Nash, with his trademark moustache drooping round the corners of his mouth, looked calm. He chose to box Holyk at distance, using his southpaw stance and plenty of movement to avoid the biggest punches while landing crisp combinations of his own. Every Nash punch that connected was accompanied by a bellow from the crowd.

'Char-lie, Char-lie, Char-lie . . . ' soon turned into chants of 'Easy, easy, easy . . .' as the crowd told the judges how they were scoring the fight.

His points victory was decisive. Charlie Nash, the king of Derry, was the new lightweight champion of Europe. He held his arms aloft but he did not really smile as his head swam with memories of his mother and of Willie, cut down seven and a half years earlier.

Interviewed the following evening on the BBC, Charlie wore a dark pinstripe suit and a black tie with flashes of white running down the middle. He was bruised around the left eye and he looked very shy. But when he was told that Watt, the Scottish world champion, had dismissed him as a possible opponent because he faded after eight rounds, Charlie sounded unusually assertive.

'I've just gone 12 rounds with a man who outpointed Jim Watt three years ago,' he said. 'Watt was three years younger and stronger than he is now. That speaks for itself.'

The European champion was soon prompted into being more garrulous. A new Charlie Nash had stepped forward as he said of the world champion: 'Jim Watt, as far as I'm concerned, is overrated. He's a good professional but, at the same time, he is too slow. He hasn't really got a knockout punch even though he's stopped a lot of opponents. With my ability and speed, I can beat him any day.'

'Jim Watt says it's Glasgow or nowhere,' Harry Thompson pointed out.

'I am prepared to fight Jim Watt anywhere,' Charlie Nash said with the intent of a man who had been to dark places and survived. 'I know I can beat him.'

Samuel Larmour lay on his deathbed. In November 1979, a week before he was due to fight Dave Smith, Davy went home to see his father. There was such sadness in the house, with everyone knowing death was imminent.

Emotional words were not shared easily in a Protestant home in Belfast in the 1970s. Davy found it hard to tell his dad how he loved him, because he knew such raw intimacy would make the old man uncomfortable. Even when he had been blown up by an IRA bomb, he preferred to suffer in silence. The wall around him made it difficult for anyone else to show how much they cared.

Davy moved slowly and softly as he climbed the stairs to see his father for one of the last times in his life. The family was gathered around the bed. Davy sat with them for almost an hour as he and his two brothers broke the silence with talk of their lives at work. They weren't sure how much their father heard because he already looked ghostly.

Eventually, Davy stood up. 'Dad,' he said, 'I must go.'

His father turned his head to look at him. Davy felt a pang of guilt in leaving and so he explained why he had to say goodbye. 'I have to go to training. I'm fighting in a week.'

The dying old man looked at his son, whom he loved, a long time. He licked his lips, swallowed and found the strength to say one line: 'Make this your last.'

Davy nodded. 'Okay, Dad,' he said. His father stared at him, his eyes looking sunken and pleading in his head. Davy felt the need to stretch the lie. 'I'll make this my last fight.'

He knew he wanted to keep fighting, for he was a boxer above all else, but it felt right to offer comfort. Davy squeezed his father's hand. He felt no pressure in return and so he let go. Davy looked down at his own hands and remembered how he once had soaked them in brine to harden his skin. He could still see how white his knuckles had turned when he removed a hand from the freezing liquid and bunched it into a fist. It was cold outside and so he thrust his briny hands into his pockets, instinctively turning them into fists, as he walked down the stairs, out the front door and into the winter night.

A week later, on 26 November 1979, Davy Larmour won again, easily outpointing the London bantamweight Dave Smith in the main fight of the night at a full Ulster Hall. It was Davy's third win in a row and he felt proud to be fighting in his home town. He would have liked to dedicate the victory to his dying father but, knowing he had lied to him, it felt wrong.

Davy mourned his dad a few days later. But he did not consider keeping the promise made on his father's deathbed. Boxing meant too much to him. He needed to keep fighting.

CHAPTER 9

The Camera

Brondby Hallen, Brondby, Denmark, Thursday 6 December 1979

Eighteen years of grinding work had led Charlie Nash to a curious location in Denmark and the defining night of his career. Ken Buchanan was the best British fighter in decades. A measure of his brilliance was marked by the fact that the great Roberto Duran described him as his hardest opponent. A young and dangerous Duran took the world lightweight title away from Buchanan at Madison Square Garden in 1972 when he finally overwhelmed the Scot.

Seven years on, aged 34, Buchanan approached the end. But in his 17 fights since Duran he had won 16. His only loss had been in Japan, against Guts Ishimatsu who retained the WBC world light-weight title in 1975. Buchanan retired but he had returned to the ring in 1979 with a new promoter, Mogens Palle from Denmark.

Charlie Nash was the European champion and an outsider in front of a sold-out crowd of 8,000. At 28 he felt fitter than ever. In between working at the printers, he had trained hard four nights a week and on Saturday and Sunday afternoons. Charlie ran along the lovely Lisfannon Beach, close to Buncrana, before his trainer

Tommy Donnelly took him to the tortuous sand dunes. He sprinted up and down 20 times and then did 15 rounds of shadow-boxing. Each day he felt stronger.

Sparring at St Mary's was concentrated and four boxers, including Damien McDermott, each fought Charlie for one round at a time, meaning he faced a fresh sparring partner who came at him with new vigour in every round. He would do 12 rounds most nights while his sparring partners stepped into the ring with him for only three rounds each. The intensity helped his style, which featured so much lateral movement.

As an amateur he had loved the way Buchanan fought with such skill and accuracy. Over the years, Charlie had also become a high-quality lightweight. There was one clear difference: Buchanan's punches carried more spite than Charlie's lighter hitting. The lack of explosive power in Charlie's fists made his life as a pro much harder as he had to outbox most of his rivals rather than earning some respite with a few quick knockouts.

He felt very nervous in Brondby when he stepped into the ring against his boxing hero. There were just over a hundred of his own supporters in the arena and the essential loneliness of boxing ran through him again. The ring canvas was a strange colour, the green of a tennis court, and Charlie bounced anxiously in his corner. Buchanan was a contrasting study in stillness.

Before the first bell, Charlie crossed himself and said a little prayer. It was the most testing fight of his career.

In a highly technical contest, Buchanan kept drawing Nash in and clipping him with the jab. The Irishman's strategy – to wait for Buchanan to come at him and then counter-punch with exquisite timing – went awry. He was slightly behind on the scorecards after five rounds when he returned to the corner. A swelling had begun to show under his right eye.

'Get stuck in, Charlie,' his trainer Tommy Donnelly urged. 'Try to back him up.'

He started to throw more combinations and pour pressure on

Buchanan. Nash won the next three rounds, but he eased off in the ninth to give himself a breather. Buchanan was so experienced he immediately took advantage. There was no option but to guts it out for the rest of the fight and, being younger and fitter, Nash edged ahead. But they were both firing punches at the bell.

The two fighters embraced and Charlie lifted Buchanan's hand before quickly raising his own right arm as a reminder to the judges that he thought he had beaten the old master. Charlie looked exhausted, his hair matted with sweat, while Buchanan appeared equally drained.

They waited for the verdict, separated by the referee, who held each man by the hand. It was close but decisive. The three neutral judges were unanimous that it had been tight with scores of 116–115 and 118–116, twice, in favour of Charlie Nash, who retained his European title. A giant wreath was placed around his neck. Charlie turned to the shouting photographers as Buchanan walked around the ring, blowing kisses to the crowd. They responded with applause but, generously, Buchanan came back to Nash. He pointed to the champion, in a gesture that suggested he deserved the credit, and again embraced the man from Derry.

Charlie Nash was still the lightweight king of European boxing. A chance to become world champion now awaited.

Bobby Storey, Gerry's nephew, was arrested again in December 1979 in London. He was charged with conspiring to help Brian Keenan, a leading IRA figure, escape from Brixton Prison. A second charge centred on his part in a conspiracy to hijack a helicopter. Keenan's importance to Republican militancy was underlined by the fact that a four-man rescue team had been instructed to bust him out of Brixton. Big Bobby Storey, Bobby Campbell, Gerard Tuite and Dickie Glenholmes tried and failed to complete the dramatic prison break. Keenan was sentenced to 21 years while Storey was jailed for two years.

It continued the pattern that marked the life of Gerry's nephew. After he had been released from Long Kesh in 1975, having burnt down the cages the previous year, Bobby was arrested again in 1976 and charged with blowing up the Skyways Hotel. He was held on remand for 13 months but never convicted. On the day of his release, Storey was rearrested and charged with a shooting. The case against him coul`d not be proved and he was released – only to be charged five months later with shooting two soldiers in Turf Lodge. The charges were dropped in December 1977. He was accused again of shooting a different soldier in 1978 but released in May 1979.

Big Bobby ended the year as he had begun it: back in prison and looking forward to the next postcards from Uncle Gerry and his boxers.

The relationship between Gerry and his nephew was typical of many families in Northern Ireland during the Troubles. They differed radically in their perceptions of how best to bring hope to people, and so Gerry and Bobby never discussed their contrasting outlooks. There was loyalty to each other, for they were blood relatives, but each man understood the conviction of the other. Bobby never attempted to persuade Gerry to support the IRA; in turn, the boxing trainer did not try to wean his nephew away from his path as a militant Republican. There was mutual respect but, more piercingly, silence around their opposing methods. It was enough to know that Gerry believed in his commitment to reconciliation and peace and that he loved his nephew, whether Big Bobby was in or out of jail.

Gerry's life changed after he was offered a new job with the Ulster Sports Council. The pay was better than the docks and the work more in keeping with his training at the Holy Family and with Ireland. He clinched the move when he managed to persuade the Deep Sea Docks, his former employer, to let his eldest son, Gerry Jr, take over his position.

In late 1979, in his first week with the Sports Council, he drove Gerry Jr down to the docks on his way to work. 'Dad, come on in for a bit of craic,' Gerry Jr said.

Gerry looked at his watch. He had a good half-hour before he was needed at the council and so he smiled and said how much he would enjoy seeing everyone again. He also wanted to thank them for making Gerry Jr so welcome. They pulled into the docks and Gerry was soon surrounded by old workmates, who began their usual wisecracking. After they had each had a cup of tea, Gerry Jr said goodbye to his father and walked down to the old forklift. Gerry watched his son with a mixture of pride and poignance. He was sad to have given up his old job, but it lifted him to see his boy do the same work he had done for so many years.

Gerry walked over to see the tallyman – the worker at the docks who discharged the cargo and recorded it in his log book. They had worked together for a long time, and the tallyman pumped Gerry's hand and asked him about his new job. Soon, they both turned their gaze back to Gerry Jr. Gerry watched as his son moved the forklift adroitly and scooped up the cargo. It was then he drew in a sharp breath. Gerry squinted to make sure his eyes had not tricked him.

There was no doubt. One of the tobacco bags was a different colour. It was a much darker shade, and Gerry felt the familiar shiver of dread.

He had to think quickly. If he shouted out to Gerry Jr that he wanted to check the bags, his son would just drive off. Gerry Jr was his own man and he would not want his old fella meddling in a job that belonged to him now. So, as calmly as he could, Gerry ran over to the forklift.

'Gerry,' he said, 'the tallyman wants you to start at bay number six.'

Junior nodded and reversed the forklift back to bay six. The watching tallyman had moved across. He glanced at his old workmate. 'Have you got that feeling again?' he asked.

Gerry nodded. The tallyman immediately sensed the serious-ness of the moment. 'Switch it off, son,' he said quietly to Gerry Jr.

'Look,' Gerry said once his boy was safely off the forklift. 'This bag's a different shade.'

The tallyman nodded. 'You're right. I never noticed it until now.'

Carefully, they peered under the dark bag. The wires of a bomb were visible.

'They didn't know you had left us,' the tallyman said to Gerry. 'This was meant for you.'

'It's the third one,' Gerry said grimly. He asked the tallyman to call the bomb disposal boys. 'I need to go see someone about this.'

All his warmth and quips had gone as Gerry said goodbye to Junior and the tallyman. He knew he had to put a stop to it or, one day, he and his family would not be so lucky. Gerry drove to the UDA headquarters on Rumford Street. He walked in and asked for Harry Burgess.

'Everything all right, Gerry?' Burgess asked in his office.

'No, Harry. The bomb this morning wouldn't have got me. It would have got my son.'

'What are you talking about?' Burgess said in surprise.

Gerry told him about the discoloured bag of tobacco and the bomb beneath it.

'Jesus, don't be telling me that,' Burgess said.

'Harry, it's the third bomb attempt on me.'

'It's not coming from our side.'

'Well, I know it's not coming from the Republican side,' Gerry said.

Burgess pointed out that the docks were difficult to monitor with so many people coming in and out.

'I don't care,' Gerry said. 'You need to put a stop to it.'

Burgess nodded. He offered his hand and gave Gerry his word. He would make sure that everyone knew to lay off Gerry Storey, his family and friends.

'And my boxers,' Gerry added.

'I'll see to it,' Burgess promised.

Gerry never found out how Harry Burgess did it, but that third attempt on his life would be the last. He would be left alone from then on to keep working in his own way. He had survived three assassination attempts with his principles of peace and harmony intact.

Nineteen seventy-nine had been another bloody year in the Troubles. There were 125 deaths and some high-profile fatalities. Lord Louis Mountbatten, Prince Philip's uncle and a distant cousin of the Queen, was assassinated by the IRA in August 1979. Five months earlier, they also killed Richard Sykes, the British ambassador in Holland, and Airey Neave, the Conservative spokesman on Northern Ireland, as he left the House of Commons. Margaret Thatcher was elected as British Prime Minister in May 1979 and her hard-line stance against the IRA deepened tensions. The battle lines became more entrenched and even the February 1979 jailing of the Shankill Butchers gang, who had killed 19 Catholics, failed to diminish the waves of terrorism being unleashed from both sectarian camps.

On 23 December 1979, an RUC reservist was murdered by the IRA as he crossed the border and reached Glaslough, 20 miles from Barry McGuigan's home in Clones. The 48-year-old Protestant, Stanley Hazelton, had been ambushed on his way to collect the family's Christmas turkey. Described as a 'good neighbour' by a Catholic priest in Tyrone, Hazelton had survived a previous attempt on his life when his workplace was bombed three years earlier. This time he was not so lucky.

On the last day of a violent year, a 19-year-old Catholic machinist, Sean Cairns, was shot in the head while watching television at his parents' home in west Belfast. A hooded Loyalist paramilitary burst into the house, 400 yards from the interface with a Protestant community, and killed the teenager. The coroner summed up the latest murder with stark accuracy: 'This is another of those sad, insane, motiveless, random assassinations which occur all too frequently in Northern Ireland.'

Kelvin Hall, Glasgow, Friday 14 March 1980

The night Charlie had been striving towards for years had finally arrived. He would fight Jim Watt for the WBC world lightweight title in Glasgow. His £15,000 purse mattered less than a world title victory that would help heal both Charlie and the people of Derry.

Sectarianism scarred Glasgow. The rancorous history of the city's football rivals, Celtic and Rangers, was rooted in opposing religious affiliations. Celtic's fans were predominantly Catholic and they were ridiculed as 'Fenian bastards' by their hated counterparts at Rangers. They, in turn, mocked Rangers' supporters as 'Orange bastards'. Rangers were an overwhelmingly Protestant club and run along such rigid lines that it would be another nine years before they signed Mo Johnston, their first openly Catholic player since the First World War. The fact that Johnston was a former Celtic player mattered less than his religion to some Rangers supporters.

David Miller, the general secretary of the Rangers Supporters Association, said of Johnston's signing in 1989: 'It is a sad day for Rangers. There will be a lot of people handing in their season tickets. I don't want to see a Roman Catholic at Ibrox. It really sticks in my throat.'

Nine years earlier, at the height of the Troubles across the sea, the mood in Glasgow was even more vociferous. Charlie Nash just wanted to be a boxer, closing in on a world title, and yet he was asked over and over again how he felt about the fact that Jim Watt was such a passionate Rangers fan.

It doesn't matter, Charlie kept saying, Jim Watt is a good man and a fine world champion.

Watt himself had already answered the bigots who tried to stoke up the sectarian rivalry. He pointed out that he was married to a Catholic. He loved Rangers, and his boxing trunks were the same royal blue as his team, but he didn't hate anyone. Watt was quiet and polite, but Charlie was not sure how much the Scot respected him. He thought Watt dismissed him as a light hitter with questionable stamina. Charlie resolved to show him a different perspective.

In his dressing room, and even on the long walk to the ring through a boisterous crowd, Charlie had felt eerily calm. After the trauma of Bloody Sunday, nothing could spook him. He was ready to make a statement – for Derry, for his brother Willie and for himself.

Charlie and Tommy Donnelly had decided on a new strategy. They knew Watt expected him to rely on his usual style of slipping, moving and counter-punching. But Watt was such a strong fighter, who seemed at his best towards the end of a 15-round contest, that they needed to try to cut him down earlier.

'You can hurt him, Charlie,' Donnelly kept telling him, 'and it's best to do it early.'

Rather than boxing at a circumspect distance, Charlie would risk getting a taste of Watt's power and attempt to dominate from the outset. To become a world champion, he had to take a chance and look to hurt Watt. It was better than allowing the Scot to grind him down.

From the opening bell, as the two southpaws moved towards each other, Nash was quicker. He landed the first jabs, spearing them through the crackling atmosphere of the Kelvin Hall. Nash used his right hand too, and went to the body, as he tried to impose his will on the champion. Both fighters were a blur of movement, skipping and turning lightly on their feet, like sombre dancers, their upper bodies bobbing and weaving with a rhythm of their own as they tried to evade punches while looking for an opening. They watched each other like two twitching snakes, wary yet venomous.

After Watt clipped him with a right lead, Nash responded with a jab of his own. They each took a step back and kept moving, swaying with intent. It was then that Nash unleashed a right uppercut and a left cross that stopped Watt in his tracks and left him open for a short, sweet right hand. Watt went down hard, on the seat of his Rangers trunks, at the impact of that perfect three-punch combination.

It happened unexpectedly but Nash wheeled away to a neutral corner. The bespectacled referee, who wore large tortoiseshell glasses, looked as if he could not believe what he had just seen. He grabbed Nash by the right arm and pulled him back. It was an act of pure surprise because the knockdown had been so clear he should have started counting instead.

Watt, lifted by the sight of the referee preventing Nash from going to a neutral corner, rose to his feet. He had been knocked down hard, but he was keen to prove that it had been a fluke. Yet there had been skill rather than luck in Nash's crisp hitting. The referee, Sid Nathan, waved them together with a flourish of his arms, like a conductor steering his orchestra through a rocky start, and barked, 'Box on . . .'

Nash waded in, swinging with both hands, but his shock at the lack of a count and his urgent desire to finish Watt meant it was easy for the champion to wrap him in a clinch. Watt had a few precious seconds to clear his head before the referee broke them apart.

Watt backed away with a grimace. Nash missed with a big right uppercut as Watt swayed out of the way, but he then caught the Scot with two hard punches. Watt's gaunt face was flushed but he hit Nash with a right hand. The challenger dabbed at his left eye. He could feel a trickle of blood just before the bell sounded. Sid Nathan jumped between the fighters with another flourish. It had been a startling round and both sat down on their stools with relief. Watt needed respite. Nash needed to gather himself while his corner worked on his eye.

Harry Carpenter, commentating for the BBC, delighted in the 'astonishing' first round but noted the 'vivid red smear' above Nash's eye. Donnelly pressed a swab and a cotton bud against the cut to stem the flow of blood. It was not an especially bad cut and Donnelly could wipe the sweat from Nash's face, tell him how well he had done and to stick to their plan.

Watt was a determined champion and the minute-long break helped him. He came out looking much more purposeful and started using his right jab as a way of trying to widen the cut and wrest back control. At 31, and after 42 fights, Watt's age was balanced by his vast experience. Nash kept coming forward, throwing jabs and combinations with accuracy and force. But Watt fought for his life as champion. He was much more aggressive and fierce because he knew that, to dent the ambition of Nash, he needed to hurt him. Watt caught Nash flush on the jaw and the man from Derry was forced to take a step back. Up against the ropes, Nash fought back. Watt retreated but the Scottish fans spurred him on in song, their voices filling the arena.

It had been a close round and the cut above Nash's left eye had begun to bleed again. As Donnelly pressed a cotton bud hard into the wound, Nash tilted back his head so he could drink some water. He then spat into the steel bucket next to his feet. Donnelly did not dare lift the reddening bud from the cut so he used his other hand to smear Vaseline over his fighter's cheeks. Eventually, he sealed the cut shut and sent Nash back into battle.

The third was more decisive. Watt had shaken off his disastrous opening and he hit Nash consistently with his right jab and a hard left cross. Nash lacked the same accuracy and his punches often fell short. It was another hard round, won by Watt, and the champion took some deep breaths as he was sponged down on his stool. Nash's cut was no worse and Donnelly urged him to be more assertive.

As if he was still conducting a symphony, the referee waved them back into the fray with an ostentatious little twirl of his hands. Nash went to work first, his right jab snaking out repeatedly as he sought to regain the ascendancy. 'There is a good portion of the city of Derry in this arena tonight, right behind Charlie Nash,'

Carpenter suggested as the chant of 'Char-lie, Char-lie, Char-lie!' rose above the raucous Scottish support. 'He said before this fight that he wanted to bring the title back for the whole of Derry.'

Nash rocked Watt with another three-punch combination, driving him back towards the ropes and attacking the body. Carpenter noted how Watt's defences 'have been scattered by three good punches' and how 'when Nash takes it to Watt he does look dangerous'. Another decent right from Nash landed before Watt responded with a big left of his own. They clinched and tumbled over as Watt's right boot pressed against Nash's left foot. A combination of the punch and their tangled feet brought them both down. It looked less of a clean knockdown than that endured by Watt in the opening round, but the referee began counting as soon as Watt was back on his feet. Nash pulled himself up via the ropes, looking just a little groggy, and at the count of eight his fists were back in position.

Watt came steaming in, punches flying as Nash retreated to the ropes. The Scot stalked him, backing Nash up, as he searched for the conclusive blow. A crunching left cross dropped Nash to his knees. He looked in desperate trouble.

'Mary Peters is sitting right beside me,' Carpenter said of the 1972 Olympic gold medallist from Belfast, 'and she's shouting "Charlie, Charlie!"'

Nash tried to hold off the marauding Watt with pawing punches. It looked as if he was fighting underwater, his arms struggling to move with any speed or precision. They clinched but Nash could not delay the inevitable. A left cross nailed him. 'Charlie's gone again,' Carpenter yelled. 'The legs have completely gone.'

The counting Nathan had reached 'six ... seven ... eight ...' when he waved his arms.

Nash looked vacantly at him, trying to keep his gumshield in place with his left glove as Nathan's hands scissored in front of him. The referee then spread his arms wide as if the final notes of a percussive symphony could fade away.

Charlie Nash had been stopped with under a minute left of round four. The dream was over.

Barry McGuigan had been dreaming of Olympic glory for six years. Ever since he was 13, and he had fallen for boxing in Clones, the teenager knew what he wanted. At school, in woodwork, he made a little T-square and wrote on the back: 'Please God, let me win the gold medal in 1980.'

The momentous Olympic year, however, started badly for McGuigan after he was chosen to box for Ulster against Leinster in the National Stadium in Dublin. Barry walked to the ring for his fight against Richie Foster with his hand wraps held down by sticky tape. An official intervened, just as he began to pull on his gloves, and insisted that Barry use proper tape.

'This is all I've got,' Barry said. The official was adamant and said Barry would have to go back to the dressing room to find the correct tape.

In a rage, Barry simply tore the bandages off his hands and, even though they were unprotected, slipped them inside his gloves. He battered Foster, his anger fuelling him, and dropped his opponent three times. Yet he did as much long-term damage to his Olympic prospects, chipping a knuckle bone in his left hand.

At first he seemed to recover after an orthopaedic surgeon injected the knuckle with cortisone. Barry missed the Ulster Seniors, but he was back in time for the Irish National championship – only for the same bone to be chipped during his easy semi-final victory. He had to withdraw from the final. More cortisone and rest helped and he assured his place in the Olympic team after boxing well in Italy and East Germany.

Trouble returned in a different form during Gerry Storey's Olympic training camp. Barry, who had been named captain of the boxing team, was too big and hit too hard for the smaller fighters. They put him in the ring with Tommy Davitt, a hard-hitting professional welterweight. Sparring was fiercely competitive until, in the fifth of six planned rounds, Davitt threw a left hook that cracked McGuigan's ribs. His pre-Olympic sparring was over and, to add to his woes, his injured hand throbbed again.

In Moscow, in the Olympic village, Barry's room-mate was Hugh Russell. They represented the best medal hopes in an Ireland team that also included Gerry Hawkins, Phil Sutcliffe, Sean Doyle, Martin Brereton and the rib-cracking Davitt's younger brother, PJ. Hugh's problems had been different in the build-up to Moscow. He had worked as a tugman at the docks but his bosses would not allow him to take time off work for the training camp and the Olympics. Gerry did his best to help, but his influence was limited after he had left the docks to work for the Sports Council. Hugh, at the age of 20, had been a tugman for only a couple of years and so he was given a stark choice: keep your job or go to the Olympics.

His parents persuaded him that a chance to box in the Olympic Games could not be missed. They promised to support him once he came back from Moscow. It was still a difficult decision because he made decent money on the tugboats and he was bringing his parents a wage packet comparable to his father's. The Olympics, however, seemed a magical escape from the Troubles.

Barry thought Moscow was sterile but it looked to wee Hugh as if he had arrived in heaven. The women in the Olympic village seemed impossibly beautiful and he thrived among the camaraderie and a sense that they were living among the best athletes in the world. But, when they looked closer, it was plain that these were no ordinary Olympics. Images of Lenin and the hammer and sickle were made by the crowd holding up cards as a way of showing that the Soviet Union was intent on using the Games as a propaganda tool. This was in reaction to the fact that only 80 countries took part in Moscow – the smallest entry since the 1956 Olympics – as 66 nations were boycotting the Games in protest against the Soviet Union's invasion of Afghanistan. These were the most controversial Olympic Games since Hitler had used the event as a showcase for Nazi propaganda in Berlin in 1936.

The boxing competition began on the first day of Olympic competition on 20 July 1980 and, feeling galvanised, Hugh won every round of his opening bout against Samir Khiniab of Iraq. Two days later, he defeated Emmanuel Mlundwa of Tanzania in a similar 5-0 whitewash.

There was more expectation on McGuigan and he started well, also fighting against a Tanzanian in Issack Mabushi. He knocked down Mabushi in the second round, and forced two standing counts before the bout was stopped in the third. But he winced when, watching the bout on a video recording later that afternoon, he heard Harry Carpenter suggest that, 'It looks like McGuigan's hand problems are over.' His hand ached. He remembered the dejection he felt when he returned to his corner and told Gerry his hand had gone again.

Gerry swore softly. There was nothing they could do, with the next fight 48 hours away.

McGuigan's injured hand was numbed with anaesthetic and, against Zambia's Winfred Kabunda, he felt he had boxed well and done enough to win. But the judges gave the decision to Kabunda. The Olympic hopes for the kid from Clones were ruined and he did not feel any better when Kabunda was robbed in his next fight against the eventual gold medal winner – Rudi Fink of East Germany. McGuigan had had his fill of amateur boxing.

Everyone else on the Irish team was also eliminated in the first few days – with the exception of Hugh Russell. He had reached the quarter-finals, where he faced the very tall North Korean flyweight Yo Ryon-sik in a battle that would decide which of them would be awarded at least a bronze medal. Hugh was seven inches shorter than the Korean and he struggled.

Gerry kept him calm, just as he had ensured that Hugh stayed concentrated after his first two emphatic wins, and the fight ebbed and flowed. It was a hard contest to score and they had almost resigned themselves to another victory for a Communist boxer – when, for once, the luck of the Irish prevailed. Hugh won the fight

3–2 on the scorecards. He became only the sixth Irish boxer in history to make the Olympic podium.

The semi-final was on the second-last day of the Olympics, 1 August, and Hugh was beaten by the eventual champion Petar Lesov of Bulgaria. Lesov looked too hulking to be a flyweight but, somehow, he made the weight. His victory reduced Hugh to tears in the dressing room.

'Don't cry, Cue,' Gerry said, saying Hugh's name in his usual way. 'You should feel proud.'

The following day the little red-headed terrier had recovered and he felt surging pride when the medal was draped around his neck.

It was difficult to speak to his parents from Moscow – both because of the logistics of calling from the Soviet Union and the fact that his parents did not have a phone in New Lodge. At least his Uncle Dan had a shared phone line and so Hugh managed to speak to his mum and dad after his medal had been engraved. His mother surprised him by saying the heavy rioting in New Lodge only seemed to stop when one of his fights was screened on television. The petrol bombs were put down and people went inside to watch Wee Hugh fight in Moscow.

For 15 minutes at a time, the streets of New Lodge would be strangely deserted. The Olympic bronze medallist could hardly believe that boxing could bring a fleeting peace. But his Holy Family trainer smiled sagely. 'Of course,' Gerry Storey said.

They counted all the money they had made from exchanging currency on the black market and marvelled at how little they had spent as everything was free in the Olympic village. Barry was still hurting, but he felt better knowing he could finally afford to buy Sandra an engagement ring. At each training session back home, she would record every set of exercise drills, every round he sparred and even every punch he threw. Barry asked Sandra to count each blow so it could be jotted down in the book that was similar to the log her dad used to record every transaction in the shop.

At the end of training he would ask Sandra, 'How many punches did I throw today?' She would reply, '430.' He'd say, 'No, actually it was 432.'

'So you've been counting, too?' Sandra exclaimed.

'Yeah,' Barry said.

Sandra knew how good he was in the ring and she was just as driven to help him succeed. They had no money and so their evenings out were going to the gym or, occasionally, they would go window-shopping to dream of the items they might buy one day. At least, after the Olympics, Barry could finally buy her engagement ring.

Hugh, without a girlfriend back home, was unsure how best to spend his Olympic money. He just knew he had to get rid of all his roubles as they would be useless back in Belfast. Gerry went out with him on their final afternoon in Moscow and it was then that Hugh saw the camera. Big was beautiful in 1980, and the Zenith camera was a gorgeous monster. It had a huge lens and it was bayoneted onto its frame as if it was a rifle.

'What would they make of that in Belfast?' Gerry said wryly.

'Should I buy it?' Hugh said uncertainly. He had never taken a photograph before in his life.

Gerry nodded. 'I think it suits you,' he said, as if he knew that Hugh Russell was destined to become one of the great news photographers of the Troubles. His giant Zenith camera from Moscow would change his life for ever.

Hugh's home street in New Lodge was decorated with a massive banner that read 'Welcome Home, Bronzy'. The bronze medal around his neck was the happiest symbol New Lodge had seen in years and the curly redhead was hoisted onto the shoulders of two burly men. They walked behind a band playing music and in front of a huge crowd who looked up at the banner in wonder.

It had been made out of coffin lining by Artie Osborne, a local undertaker. He had also made all the bunting out of different coloured coffin linings. In Belfast, life could be found even in a place of death.

There was no rioting in New Lodge on that cloudy summer afternoon in August 1980 and the 'I Shot J. R.' T-shirts were the only visible signs of gunplay. J. R. Ewing, the sleazy oil tycoon, had been shot earlier that year in the television series *Dallas* and even the people of Northern Ireland had been caught up in a global phenomenon. But Hugh Russell was now far more famous than J. R. Ewing in Belfast.

A few weeks later, the celebrated photographer Brendan Murphy arrived at Hugh's house. His vivid and compassionate portraits of violence and grief, shot on the streets of Belfast, often made the front page of the *Irish News* look as beautiful as it was haunting. Murphy had been commissioned to photograph the mighty Bronzy, and he and Hugh forged an immediate bond. A recovering alcoholic, Murphy felt an instinctive empathy with fighters, and he understood the fierce intimacy of their struggles in the ring. He had photographed Hugh before, but this was a portrait that needed him to spend time around the fighter.

'What's that?' Murphy asked after they had been together for 20 minutes. He pointed at the Zenith lurking in a corner of the front room of the family's maisonette.

'It's a camera from Moscow,' Hugh said.

Murphy held the Zenith camera with great care. 'Have you used it?'

Hugh nodded shyly. 'I've joined the wee camera club down the road.'

Murphy asked if he could see some of his photographs. Hugh hesitated as he knew that the black-and-white photographs he had started taking of life in New Lodge were not very good. But, at the same time, he wanted to share them with Murphy, a great photographer. They sat in silence as Murphy sifted through a dozen photographs. He gave each one attention and care as he studied it. Eventually he looked up. 'Would you like to become a photographer?'

The boxer surprised himself by nodding. 'Yes,' Hugh said simply.

'Good,' Murphy said thoughtfully. 'I think I can help you.'

CHAPTER 10

Hunger

B arney Eastwood, a millionaire bookmaker, had an eye for an opening. He had amassed his fortune shrewdly from the moment he used a £3,000 bank loan to buy a pub in Carrickfergus on the Antrim coast. Eastwood and his wife managed the pub well and began taking small bets over the bar counter. As the years passed, his amateur bookmaking turned into a booming enterprise. By 1980, he ran a betting chain with almost 20 shops and an annual turnover in the multimillions. He also expanded into property, but it was the complicated business of boxing that held a thrilling attraction for him.

Eastwood had dabbled in boxing promotion in the late 1950s, but the Troubles had made it impossible to sustain the professional fight game in Belfast. Yet Eastwood saw chinks of hope, and profit, in the modest success of small-time promoters like Gerry Hassett who tried to revive boxing in Belfast. Hassett lacked the financial muscle and promotional knowledge to make a lasting impact, but a real appetite for professional boxing remained.

Charlie Nash had passionate support in Derry but Eastwood sensed that canny promotion of much younger fighters could bring boxing back to Belfast on a regular basis and make a considerable profit. He just needed to find the right new boxers.

No one knew more about boxing in Belfast than Gerry Storey. Eastwood approached Storey when he saw him walking down Castle Lane in late 1979. He had met him many times before and so he led the trainer into a small church. In an empty pew on a weekday afternoon, Eastwood explained that he was considering a return to boxing. His ambition was to promote a local boxer to a world title.

'I'm thinking of Danny McAllister,' he said in a hushed tone as if not wanting to be overheard by anyone else in a holy setting.

'Danny's a good kid,' Gerry said of the talented lightweight who boxed at the Oliver Plunkett gym on the Falls Road. 'But he's not the one.'

Eastwood rubbed his nose doubtfully. Gerry had often seen Eastwood rub his nose when he was troubled or confused. 'Who would you recommend?' Eastwood asked, as if seeking help in a confessional booth.

'Only one fighter fits the bill. This kid will go on to become a world champion.'

'Who would that be?' Eastwood asked, still tweaking and stroking his nose.

'Barry McGuigan.'

'The wee fellow from Clones?'

'That's your man. He boxed the head off Danny McAllister.'

Gerry patted Eastwood on the arm and said it was time he got back to the Holy Family. Eastwood shook Gerry's hand thoughtfully and said goodbye.

Gerry had just reached the bottom step of the church when he heard Eastwood running after him. The millionaire clutched at his coat. 'Gerry Storey,' he said, 'in all the years I've known you, I've never heard you make a statement like that. What makes you so sure of this kid?'

Gerry spoke about some of the great old Belfast fighters, like

Freddie Gilroy and Johnny Caldwell, whom Eastwood had revered. They were among the best boxers Gerry had seen but McGuigan would be better.

'This kid is special,' he said. Gerry explained that McGuigan could punch hard. He was tough and dedicated. He didn't smoke or drink and he absolutely loved boxing. Gerry said one more sentence: 'He's the best I've seen and he'll go all the way to a world title.'

'You're that sure?' Eastwood asked. He had stopped rubbing his nose.

'It's only my opinion,' Gerry said with an amused shrug. 'But I'll be amazed if I'm wrong.'

Gerry Storey was not the only boxing insider to expect greatness from Barry McGuigan. Mickey Duff, already the most powerful promoter in Britain, wrote personally to the teenager to ask him to join his stable – while stressing that he had never written a letter of invitation to any fighter before. Terry Lawless, who had warned Barry not to punch so hard during sparring at his East London gym, wanted to become his trainer and manager, a role he soon filled for Frank Bruno. Eddie Thomas, the Welshman who had managed Howard Winstone and Ken Buchanan to world titles, urged McGuigan to join his team. Irish-Americans also put themselves forward as managerial wizards. They promised to make McGuigan rich.

Pat McGuigan, who had met more impresarios, agents and managers than he cared to remember in the music business, turned to a man he could trust. Gerry Storey had acted as a go-between when introducing Barney Eastwood to the McGuigans, without pressuring them to link up with the bookmaker. Pat knew Gerry would offer balanced advice.

Gerry emphasised the need for Barry, who would turn 20 in February 1981, to concentrate on boxing. That concentration would be enhanced if he felt comfortable in his surroundings.

Gerry could not imagine a raw young fighter from Clones adapting to life far from home in London or Wales. Eastwood offered the advantage of Barry training in Belfast, close to Clones, while Gerry highlighted how his Holy Family boxers were supported across the sectarian divide.

'It will be the same for Barry,' Gerry said prophetically. 'He will have supporters' clubs on the Shankill Road and supporters' clubs on the Falls Road.'

The prospect of his son boxing in Northern Ireland appealed to Pat. But his hopes that Gerry would confirm himself as Barry's professional trainer remained unfulfilled. Gerry was a friend of Eastwood's, but that did not mean he would be the kind of trainer whom the promoter could control. Eastwood realised that, for all his easy charm, Gerry was fiercely independent. Gerry was also devoted to his amateur boxers and he had his work with the Ulster Sports Council. It would be difficult for him to give up a steady council job. There were arguments and disputes in professional boxing, and so Gerry preferred to pour all his energies into helping his Holy Family boys become better boxers and better people.

Gerry's advice that Barry should join Eastwood carried no personal gain. He simply offered clear-cut insights that made it easy for Eastwood to seal an agreement with the McGuigans. The promoter said he expected to fill beautiful venues in Belfast, like the Ulster Hall and the King's Hall, while appealing to both warring communities. Eastwood charmed the McGuigans. But the real power soon tilted in favour of the promoter.

'What would you prefer me to call you?' Barry asked. 'Barney, BJ or Mr Eastwood?'

'I'd prefer Mr Eastwood,' the promoter said quietly yet firmly.

Eighty-six people died as a result of sectarian violence in 1980. It was the lowest number of fatalities since 1970. Yet any idea that this might be progress was blunted by the interconnected nature of many of these murders. The loop of retaliation seemed endless.

On 12 January 1980, a 46-year-old taxi driver, Thomas Montgomery, was killed in cold blood on the junction of Crumlin and Woodvale Roads. He was less than a mile from the Shankill Road when he was intercepted in the early hours by six young men who had slipped into Loyalist territory from the Republican neighbourhood of Ardoyne. He had been driving slowly through heavy fog when the mob set about stoning his cab. They had been drinking and decided to hunt down a victim as they were bent on avenging the death of their friend, Alexander Reid, who had been dragged from a taxi on the Shankill Road on 3 January.

Reid had been killed by the UDA, who had planned on 'getting a Roman Catholic' in retaliation for the murder of a Protestant. After he had been arrested, the murderer admitted: 'I took hold of the Catholic [the 20-year-old Reid, a labourer] and set myself up as judge, jury and executioner. I beat him to death with a breeze block in an alleyway off the Shankill.'

Nine days later, as the young men from Ardoyne stoned the Protestant cab, a lump of concrete shattered the windscreen and struck Montgomery's head. His taxi smashed into a wall and Montgomery died as one of the mob yelled: 'We've got the bastard.'

In court, it was established that none of the boys from Ardoyne belonged to the IRA. 'You have been described as sectarian hoodlums,' the judge said, 'because you attacked and killed this man for no other reason than he was a Protestant taxi driver. A lot of people have been killed in Northern Ireland – but there is no justification for going out and killing again. A friend is killed and you go out and kill somebody else. So the wheel goes round.'

There was foreboding that far worse turmoil was about to be unleashed. Tensions had escalated in October when seven Republican prisoners at Long Kesh began a hunger strike to intensify their protest against the conditions of their incarceration. The battle between the prisoners and their captors had started in 1976 when the British government withdrew Special Category Status

On 30 January 1972, Father Edward Daly waved a white handkerchief as he led a small group carrying the body of Jackie Duddy on Bloody Sunday. A 17-year-old boxer from Derry, Duddy was one of 14 people killed by British paratroopers. (© Mirrorpix)

Just under three months after losing his brother, Willie, on Bloody Sunday, Charlie Nash (right) retained his Irish lightweight title at the national amateur championships in Dublin. (© Getty Images)

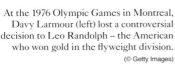

At the 1976 Olympic Games in Montreal, Davy Larmour (left) lost a controversial decision to Leo Randolph – the American who won gold in the flyweight division.
(© Getty Images)

Barry McGuigan (left) knocked out the local favourite, Bill Ranelli, in the semi-finals of the Commonwealth Games in Edmonton in August 1978. McGuigan boxed for Northern Ireland and became Commonwealth featherweight champion. (© Getty Images)

In August 1980 Hugh Russell was carried through the streets of Belfast after winning a bronze medal at the Moscow Olympics. There was no rioting in New Lodge that day and the 'I Shot J. R.' T-shirts were the only visible signs of gunplay.

Hugh Russell leans over the ropes to kiss his mother, Eileen, after winning his bloody first fight against Davy Larmour in October 1982. Russell, a Catholic, and Larmour, a Protestant, went to hospital together to be stitched up. (© Brendan Murphy)

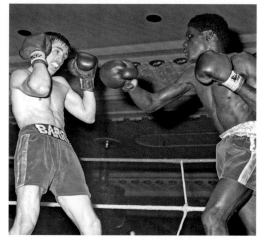

Barry McGuigan (left) covers up against Nigeria's Young Ali in London on 14 June 1982. McGuigan won by KO and, tragically, Young Ali died after being in a coma for five months following the fight. (© Press Association)

Barry and Sandra McGuigan outside his father's shop in Clones. Barry holds his son, Blain, with whom Sandra had been pregnant when Young Ali fell into a coma. (© Getty Images)

Bobby Sands led the Republican hunger strikes in the Maze prison in 1981. He was 27 when he died on 5 May 1981 – after his hunger strike lasted for 66 days. (© Press Association)

The bleak setting of the Maze prison where, in the immediate aftermath of the hunger strikes, Gerry Storey was asked by both the Republican and Loyalist prisoners to help them find fresh hope through boxing lessons. (© Press Association)

Pat McGuigan sings 'Danny Boy' just before Barry's successful world title fight against Eusebio Pedroza in London, on 8 June 1985. The crowd joined in and sang the famous line: '*I'll be here in sunshine or in shadow*.'
(© Getty Images)

Barry McGuigan knocks down Pedroza in Round 7. He won a unanimous decision in front of a live BBC television audience of 20 million. (© Getty Images)

Hugh Russell's photograph of a little girl opening her front door in Belfast. The three bullet holes are clearly visible. (© Hugh Russell)

Edgar Graham, the Unionist politician, was shot dead by the IRA on 7 December 1983. Hugh Russell, who was still a professional fighter, took this photograph, which was on the front page of the *Irish News* the following morning. (© Hugh Russell)

Gerry Conlon spent 15 years in prison after being convicted wrongly of the Guildford pub bombings in October 1974. Here, on 19 October 1989, Hugh Russell took this famous first photograph of Conlon's liberty. (© Hugh Russell)

arry McGuigan today, at his gym
Wandsworth, south-west London.
Tom Jenkins)

Hugh Russell and Davy Larmour, who fought two savage
battles against each other in the early 1980s, enjoy a joke
together outside the Holy Family gym in New Lodge,
Belfast, in early 2019. (© Tom Jenkins)

Charlie Nash, in front
of a mural of himself
as a young boxer in
Derry, in late 2018.
(© Margaret McLaughlin)

Gerry Storey is in his element, surrounded by some of his past and current boxers at the Holy Family gym. (© Hugh Russell)

Gerry Storey's nephew, Bobby Storey, is a leading Republican figure in Belfast. Here, Bobby is flanked by Michelle O'Neill, vice-president of Sinn Féin, and Gerry Adams, the former president of Sinn Féin. This photograph was taken in July 2018, shortly after explosive devices had been thrown at the homes of Storey and Adams in west Belfast. (© Getty Images)

Gerry Storey in the ring at his beloved Holy Family. This photograph was taken by Hugh Russell – one of Gerry's 'favourite wee boxers'. (© Hugh Russell)

for paramilitary inmates. They were no longer regarded as political prisoners but as dangerous criminals.

It was vital to the identity of the IRA, in regard to its prisoners and how the organisation was perceived publicly, that their violence and murder should be seen in a political context. Morale would be dented if they were reduced to criminals rather than political dissidents. In September 1976, members of the IRA and the Irish National Liberation Army (INLA) began their blanket protest against their changed status. They refused to wear new prison uniforms and remained naked or wrapped blankets around their pale bodies in the Maze. They made five demands: the right not to wear a prison uniform; the right not to do prison work; the right to associate with other prisoners and organise educational and recreational pursuits; the right to one visit, one letter and one parcel a week; and for remission of their sentences to be restored.

The prison authorities and the British government were never going to make these concessions just because prisoners were wrapped in blankets and so, in 1978, a more distressing protest was introduced. The prisoners in the Republican quarter of the Maze also complained of being attacked by wardens when they left their cells to empty their chamber pots. So they refused to 'slop out' and, instead, their waste remained in the corners of their cells. The stench became unbearable, attracting flies and maggots to each stinking pot. As they filled the containers so the prisoners went further. They covered their cell walls in shit.

After the initial stomach-heaving trauma, the smell lessened as they smeared their excrement and turned the walls brown. Seamus Walsh, an IRA prisoner who participated in the Dirty Protest, admitted it was 'unbelievably horrendous'. Even after the inmates had been forcibly hosed down and attempts had been made to clean the cells, they resumed their protest.

Pat McGeown, a Republican prisoner, also described a typical day in the filthy Maze. 'There were times when you would vomit. There were times when you were so run-down that you would lie for days and not do anything. The rain would be coming in the window and you would be lying there with the maggots crawling all over you.'

Archbishop Tomás Ó Fiaich, however, noted the defiance of the prisoners in the Maze: 'They intend to continue their protest indefinitely and it seems they prefer to face death rather than submit to being classed as criminals. Anyone with the least knowledge of Irish history knows how deeply this attitude runs in our country's past.'

The prisoners began to resemble haunted figures from the Soviet gulags with their emaciated, dirty and naked bodies, matted hair and long beards. Depression settled over them and many of the men lay quietly in their filthy cells. The IRA leaders in the Maze knew they could not sustain this upsetting ritual indefinitely.

Margaret Thatcher, as the new British Prime Minister, also raised the stakes of an ancient conflict. Apart from the fact that her understanding of sectarian politics was limited, Thatcher favoured an intransigent approach. Her political ethos, whether dealing with unemployment, the Falklands conflict, the miners' strike or Northern Ireland, was etched in stone. She could be praised as being strong and clear or damned for being inflexible and cruel. Thatcher did not care about being perceived as caring or compassionate. Instead, she was driven to divide and dominate. When it came to Northern Ireland, her 'us or them' outlook fitted the embittered mood of sectarian politics. It was also underpinned by popular support in England, after a spate of IRA atrocities against innocent people, and also by her own personal hurt after she had lost her close ally Airey Neave on 30 March 1979.

Thirty-four days before her election as Prime Minister, Neave, who was then Thatcher's Shadow Secretary of State for Northern Ireland, was killed by a car bomb as he left the House of Commons. The INLA and the IRA both claimed responsibility for the killing. It emerged eventually that INLA operatives had carried out the murder and the organisation tried to justify the killing by saying

Neave had made 'rabid militarist calls for more repression against the Irish people'. Thatcher, in response, described Neave as 'one of freedom's warriors. Courageous, staunch, true. He lived for his beliefs and now he has died for them.' He had also led Thatcher's campaign to become the Conservative Party leader and headed her private office. His death meant that the conflict in Northern Ireland, and the war against militant Republicans, had become personal to Thatcher.

She saw none of the history nor past persecution of Catholics, none of the legitimate grievances nor any of the inequities that persisted in Northern Ireland. There was no room for nuance or subtlety, for forgiveness or reconciliation. Thatcher saw stark black-and-white certainties. The British were good; Irish terrorists were evil. There was no political argument to be debated – just terrorism, which needed to be crushed.

The Republican prisoners in the Maze resolved to test the limits of Thatcher's obstinacy. They were ready to die if their long-standing demands were not met.

Hunger strikes, as a protest against people in power, had been part of Irish history for hundreds of years. In 1917, prisoners in Dublin's Mountjoy Prison revived the hunger strike. In the wake of the previous year's Easter Rising, Irish prisoners refused to eat after they had been beaten for removing their prison uniforms and rejecting all forms of work in jail. Their leader Thomas Ashe died and over 30,000 mourners attended his funeral.

In 1920, Terence MacSwiney, the Lord Mayor of Cork and an IRA commanding officer, began a hunger strike against British involvement in Irish politics. MacSwiney described a hunger strike in poetic language meant to stir the masses: 'Tis the bravest test, the noblest test that offers the surest and greatest victory.'

MacSwiney and two of his colleagues starved to death. It took 74 agonising days for MacSwiney to die, while Joseph Murray survived two days longer to record the longest fast in history. There was an outpouring of Republican conviction, fuelled by

MacSwiney's words: 'The contest on our side is not one of rivalry or vengeance, but of endurance. It is not those who can inflict the most, but those that can suffer the most who will conquer.'

In June 1972, Billy McKee led 40 IRA prisoners on a starvation protest that lasted 37 days. The British government finally granted 'prisoner of war' status to Republican inmates as part of an agreement for a temporary ceasefire. There were more hunger strikes in 1974 and 1976. Some were interrupted by force-feeding whereas Seán Mac Stíofáin, a former IRA Chief of Staff, abandoned his strike after 57 days. His influence within the IRA waned and he was eventually sidelined.

The hunger strike became a battleground within the Republican movement. Prisoners regarded it as a potent strategy that often forced concessions from the authorities. The selflessness and the suffering seemed to echo the Bible more than the rattle of an Armalite rifle or Semtex bomb. It was a graphic attempt to legitimise and sanctify the violence framing the hunger strike.

Yet, for Republican leaders, a failed hunger strike carried disastrous consequences. The organisation would look weak and foolish. Even more damagingly, morale within the Republican movement would be shattered by the lack of concessions.

Inside the Maze there was utter certainty. Brendan Hughes, a charismatic commanding officer of the IRA in the cages and H-blocks of the Maze, was nicknamed '*Dorcha*' or 'The Dark' because of his swarthy skin. The Dark was emphatic in his smuggled communications with the leadership outside. Conditions in prison had become intolerable and four years of protests with blankets and dirt had changed nothing. Drastic action was needed.

The IRA wanted to concentrate on a campaign of terror in the belief that armed struggle would be the only way to force Britain to relinquish control of Irish affairs. If the war could be won, the prisoners would become free men. A hunger strike, with careful attention needed for publicity, was all-consuming and distracting.

The Dark was adamant. There were more IRA leaders inside

the Maze than out, and they needed to act on behalf of ordinary prisoners. Hughes would lead the hunger strike. His deputy officer in the Maze, Bobby Sands, also planned to starve but was persuaded to keep eating and replace Hughes as leader while the strike unfolded.

Hughes convinced the IRA's Army Council to support a joint seven-man strike to force change in the prison. Six IRA members – Hughes, Raymond McCartney, Tommy McKearney, Sean McKenna, Leon Green and Tom McFeely – and John Nixon of the INLA began their hunger strike in the Maze on 27 October 1980.

As predicted by The Dark, the action forced the British government into secret negotiations with the IRA. Thatcher's public claim that 'we will not talk to terrorists' was ignored in private as Foreign Office officials and the IRA Army Council used a Catholic businessman, nicknamed 'The Mountain Climber', to discuss ways to broker a settlement. On 1 December, further pressure was heaped on the government when three new hunger strikers emerged at the Armagh women's prison. There was genuine hope that progress was being made, but the hunger strikers were undermined by the decision of all seven men in the Maze to start the strike simultaneously. As soon as one of them began to slip away they would be dented. They could only be as strong as their weakest link. A staggered strike would have been more effective as they each reached the furthest point of starvation at different times.

In the eighth week, the resolve of the strikers wavered as Sean McKenna fell seriously ill. Negotiations became more fevered when McKenna was transferred to the Royal Victoria Hospital. Knowing that McKenna's fate rested with him, Hughes clung to the hope he had been given the previous day when he was told the Foreign Office had agreed to send a document containing significant concessions.

McKenna was close to death and so The Dark decided to end the strike. There was initial euphoria among Bobby Sands and the other prisoners. They were relieved that their comrades would not die and that their painful efforts had made a major difference.

Yet, when the document arrived from London, it was a bitter disappointment and did little to change anything for the prisoners. It seemed as if the British had reneged on their promises. The Republicans had blinked first in a deadly battle of poker – and they had folded and lost.

Sands was so incensed that he wanted to start a new hunger strike, which he would lead, immediately. He knew that the only way to beat the Brits was to go still harder, with more men, and die, one after the other. Sands was persuaded to wait and give the prisoners time to organise themselves properly, but the decision had been made.

On 4 February 1981, a formal public statement was issued by the Republican prisoners in the Maze. As the British government had failed to make any significant concessions, a second hunger strike would start on 1 March – marking the fifth anniversary of the date when the Republican inmates had lost their Special Category Status as political prisoners. Margaret Thatcher was adamant. 'There is no such thing as political murder, political bombing or political violence,' she said. 'There is only criminal murder, criminal bombing or criminal violence. We will not compromise. Crime is crime is crime. It is not political. There can be no question of granting political status.'

Sinn Féin, the political wing of the IRA, confirmed the prisoners would undertake a hunger strike one at a time. On Sunday 1 March Bobby Sands would be the first to stop eating. He would not waver until the political status of all Republican prisoners was recognised.

Just before he began his lonely descent into starvation, Sands sent for the Maze chaplain, Denis Faul. The priest tried to change Sands' mind, telling him the strike would cause untold misery and violence. Sands shook his head. He loved poetry and he admired the poetic strain of some biblical passages. He quoted these lines:

'Greater love hath no man than this, that a man lay down his life for his friends.'

Faul knew the words came from John 15:13. 'Bobby, I'm not going to bother you any more,' he said. 'You're obviously in good conscience.'

The priest knew then that the young man, who would turn 27 just eight days after his hunger strike began, was ready to die.

Barry McGuigan met Eddie Shaw every morning in the National Foresters club in north-west Belfast. The Catholic pub on Stanley Street was a third of a mile from the Immaculata Boxing Club tucked away on Ardmoulin Place. Close to the interface separating the Falls Road from the Shankill Road, the Immaculata gym was dwarfed by the giant shadow of Divis Tower. The tower rose out of the battered heart of the Divis Flats complex and soared 200 feet into the Belfast sky. It had been built in 1966, as a slab of brutalist architecture, and named after the Divis mountain in nearby County Antrim.

Inside the 20-storey building, 850 flats housed around 2,400 residents. The tower was surrounded by 12 smaller blocks of flats, each being eight storeys high, and it dominated a landscape scarred by barbed wire, IRA slogans, burnt-out cars and gangs of scrawny kids. A new name had been daubed on the walls of the flats topped by black IRA flags: 'Bobby Sands. Hero. Saviour.'

The hunger strikes had begun just as Barry McGuigan started training for his professional debut. Any hope of fighting first in Belfast had been set aside. The city felt like a tinderbox. To escape the conflict, Barney Eastwood arranged for Barry to appear on a Charlie Nash bill in Dublin on 10 May. He had two months to prepare with Shaw, whom Eastwood had appointed as his trainer. Eddie was a decent trainer, but he was not of the same calibre as Gerry Storey. He was competent and compliant and there was no friction between the promoter, trainer and fighter. Conflict and hostility, however, surrounded them.

The Divis Flats carried a fearsome reputation. Their troubling presence was accentuated by the fact that the British army had taken over the top two floors of the tower. As they could not easily get in or out of the Divis Flats by foot, the army used the top of the tower as a lookout point and a landing pad for their helicopters. The remaining 18 storeys and all the flats housed a community that included some vociferous supporters of the IRA.

Barry was less afraid of the paramilitaries than of the kids who watched his and Eddie's zigzagging dash most mornings from the Foresters to the Immaculata. Barry had learnt in his first week that walking in a straight line meant certain trouble when the kids treated all pedestrians as amusing targets for their dangerous missiles. They threw an assortment of heavy objects from the highest flats and aimed to maim any stray soul walking past.

As the hunger strikes began, with the rest of Belfast as taut as a tightrope, it made for a chaotic madhouse around the Divis Flats. The kids were nutcases whether they were launching their weapons from eight or 18 storeys. Above them the army choppers and British soldiers would be watching and waiting, but the kids didn't care. They just whooped whenever they came close to crushing anyone below. A chair or a stool spiralling down would have cracked his head open and Barry shuddered when the wood splintered on the concrete pavement a few feet from his and Eddie's weaving run.

He knew that they looked like a comedy duo – a pasty little featherweight with a wispy moustache and his trainer, whose beer belly had him wobbling and wheezing. Barry and Eddie zigged and zagged, nearly tripping over each other as they looked up to check if anything was hurtling towards them. It felt deadly serious when the kids flung a fridge at them from the top floor of a flat. Barry had to yank Eddie to safety as the fridge crashed into the pavement close to where they had ducked away.

Some days, Barry and Eddie were surprised by the absolute quiet of the Divis Flats. The stillness was unnerving. The next day would be the same but then, as if out of nowhere, the kids would be back, roaring and throwing another deadly object down at them.

Barry soon got used to Eddie's wayward timekeeping. He would wait for 15 minutes some days before Ned McCormick, who trained fighters at Immaculata, arrived to meet him. Ned had heard that Eddie was running late and so he came over to the Foresters to find Barry.

Steeped in Republican politics, and a respected figure in the community, even Ned was not granted immunity from the madhouse. He was just another target for the crazy Divis Flats kids. A few weeks after the fridge nearly got him and Eddie, Barry was shocked by an even more surreal attack. He and Ned were doing a 100-yard zigzag through the most dangerous stretch of the tower blocks when they just missed a flying chunk.

'What the fuck was that?' Ned yelled.

Barry looked on as, beneath the thunderous delight of the Divis kids, Ned turned the splattered meat and bone over with his foot. It was the back leg of a cow.

Ned and Barry sprinted for the gym. They made it inside safely. 'I can't fucking believe it,' Ned said. 'We could have had our necks broken by a cow leg.'

'How did they even get a leg up there?' Barry asked.

'Anything goes around here, wee man,' Ned said.

The Immaculata gym was in the basement. It was a square concrete block, stark in character and with the stink of boxing sweat at its centre. Barry loved its authenticity. It felt to him just like a boxing gym should feel. A big blue ring was in the corner, heavy bags hung from the ceiling, paint peeled from the walls and, even though it was always freezing cold, the big old pillars soon became wet as if they were sweating as much as the fighters.

A driveway leading into the Divis Flats ran right alongside the gym. When the door to the gym was left open they could see the cars careering into the tower block area, which was forbidden territory to outsiders. Some of the kids would go into the city centre and nick a car. They were skilled at breaking in, wiring the car so it would start or simply sticking a little screwdriver into the ignition and turning it until the engine fired into life. The kids knew they had just a brief time to go for a joyride before the police spotted them. So they would tear along the alleyway next to the gym and then do a handbrake turn and flip round and come back in the opposite direction.

One tearaway lost control of his joyride and the car smashed through the front door of the Immaculata. Francie McCullagh was hitting the punch bag when the car crashed into the gym. He was so angry he began screaming 'You fucking little bastards!' at the driver and his joyriding partner. Francie was older, and much bigger as a light-heavyweight, and Barry had heard that he had done time inside. He and his father were rumoured to have IRA links, but Barry asked no questions. It was enough to know that, on international trips for Ireland, Francie was one of his funniest teammates. But he had a temper and that afternoon he was intent on hitting the joyriders.

'Francie, Francie!' Ned yelled at him. 'Leave them.'

Ned knew that they came from families filled with paramilitary headcases. It would be a mistake to antagonise them. Ned jumped over the bonnet and wrapped his arms around his incensed fighter while the joyriders disappeared. Barry leant against the bag he had been hitting while he watched Ned calm Francie. Two policemen carrying automatic rifles appeared at the ruined door and looked in quizzically.

'It's all right, lads,' Eddie Shaw said with a cheery wave. 'Just another day in the madhouse.'

The policemen shrugged and turned away. Barry McGuigan, just weeks from his professional debut, returned to work. He sank jabs, hooks and uppercuts into the swaying bag as if the solitude of boxing might offer him peace from the lunacy.

*

On Sunday 1 March 1981, a BBC newsreader confirmed the news to the world beyond Belfast: 'A Republican prisoner at the Maze prison refused food this morning, and said he would fast to death to achieve his aims of achieving political status. Bobby Sands, who is 26, and serving a 14-year jail sentence for firearms offences, suggested that other prisoners will join the hunger strike in the coming week.'

Sands made a more personal statement in his cell in H3 block of the Maze. Starting a hunger strike diary, which the IRA encouraged him to write, Sands printed out his opening line on a sliver of toilet paper that would be smuggled out of his cell. 'I am standing on the threshold of another trembling world. May God have mercy on my soul.'

The early days unfolded peacefully. The prison warders brought extra helpings of food into Sands' cell at every mealtime and in the first week they ensured he could often smell his favourite prison dish, an Irish stew. Sands found it easy to resist and he enjoyed reading the newspapers, books and collections of poetry. He was also heartened on the ninth day of his hunger strike, on Monday 9 March, the evening of his 27th birthday, when word was shouted from one cell to the next in the H-blocks. Sands was doing well, everyone heard, and his weight was still a relatively healthy 132 pounds.

'One more thing,' a voice shouted out from D wing. There was a pause before the starving man heard all the prisoners shout out in Irish: 'Happy birthday, Bobby!'

Gerry Adams and Bernadette McAliskey (née Devlin) were in the midst of hatching a piece of propaganda that would give the hunger strikers an immense boost of publicity. On 5 March, Frank Maguire, the Irish Republican and Independent MP for Fermanagh and South Tyrone, had died of a heart attack. It was thought initially that McAliskey would stand in the by-election but, prompted by Adams, she agreed quickly that it would be far more effective to the Republican cause if Bobby Sands was put forward as a candidate.

Before then, two more IRA prisoners joined the hunger strike. Francis Hughes refused food for the first time, on 15 March, exactly two weeks after Sands started his fast. The following Sunday, 22 March, Raymond McCreesh also stopped eating. Another seven men were ready to take their place alongside the first trio of strikers.

News from the Maze dominated television and radio bulletins and newspaper headlines around the world – especially when, on 26 March, Sinn Féin announced that Bobby Sands would be standing for British parliamentary office in Fermanagh and South Tyrone. When the only other Nationalist candidate, Noel Maguire, decided to step aside it meant that Sands would be in an electoral battle with the Ulster Unionist Party representative, Harry West, who had led the workers' general strike in May 1974 against a power-sharing deal between Unionists and Nationalists.

In his light-headed reverie, as the world drifted away just as his name echoed around the globe, Sands slipped back into memory to sustain his resolve. He could still remember growing up in the mainly Protestant Rathcoole estate in north Belfast. His dad, John, worked for the post office while his mum, Rosaleen, looked after them in the same shy manner that characterised her husband. They were good people and steered clear of politics. But trouble found them. When Bobby was 17, they had been among a thousand other Catholic families who had to leave Rathcoole after a campaign of Loyalist intimidation.

In west Belfast, where the family moved, they were still tested. The UDA marched down their street at night, as Protestants outnumbered the six Catholic families on their road, and the Sands family huddled inside in the dark. Bobby and his sister Marcella sat on the top of the stairs and waited. He held a carving knife in case anyone stormed inside.

His arm was cut by two Loyalist men who casually stopped him for a light before they slashed him. Bobby was a fine cross-country runner and he relied on his speed and endurance to escape local gangs. They still came back to the house in large numbers and chanted 'Taigs out!' When a dustbin was thrown through their front-room window they knew it was time to move again.

They found refuge in a Catholic estate, Twinbrook, and soon afterwards Bobby became an active member of the IRA. He was only 19, and working as an apprentice coachbuilder, when he was first jailed in 1973. Bobby was put into the same cage in the Maze as Gerry Adams, who was then 24 and an emerging Republican leader.

The trauma of his youth had turned Sands into a hard-edged rebel. He read Che Guevara, Frantz Fanon, Camilo Torres and Amilcar Cabral to fuel his politicisation. But there was a softer side to Sands, who loved writing and reading poetry, and playing the guitar, banjo and bodhran drum. Waking from his disjointed dreams, and starving in the Maze, he often spoke of how he had been running in his sleep, or singing and writing, as if he wanted to escape the weight of his place in history.

He kept writing smuggled messages to his comrades. Bobby signed the letters in the name of his sister Marcella. In a note to Adams, who was called 'Brownie', he wrote on 2 April, 'Seen ya on TV, ya big ugly hunk, you haven't changed a bit. I'm not building hopes on anything. I'm afraid I'm just resigned to the worst but I'm ensuring I'm giving my family some hope. I've been reading poetry and the papers and listening to whatever traditional music there is on the radio and generally carrying on – so for a change I'm taking it easy (such an excuse, are ya jealous?). Watch your big self and *Beannacht Dé ort* [God bless you], comrade. Marcella xxxxxxx'

Sands weakened steadily. He lost 25 pounds in his first month without food. He consumed at least six pints of water a day, containing salt tablets, but even drinking had become repulsive and he no longer yearned to taste soft wholemeal bread covered in butter, or sample a hunk of cheese or even a spoonful of honey. He was moved from his cell to the prison hospital, where he spent most of his days lying in bed while, in Fermanagh and South Tyrone, Republican supporters from the North and the South poured in to campaign on behalf of their dying candidate.

Loyalist voters in the constituency were determined to block Sands, and 'a vote for IRA violence', and they tore down posters within an hour of them being pasted to walls and fences. Campaigning was bitter and fierce and, on polling day, 9 April, the vote was tight. West won 29,046 votes. The returning officer at the Fermanagh College of Further Education in Enniskillen then confirmed, after a dramatic pause, the votes gathered by his rival: 'Sands, Bobby, Anti-H-Block-Armagh, Political Prisoner . . . 30,492.'

Bobby Sands had been elected as a British Member of Parliament by 1,446 votes.

The positive impact on the hunger strike was profound. It was no longer being led by just another IRA man; the hunger strike was being led by Bobby Sands, a Member of Parliament. The electorate had essentially decriminalised Sands – and enshrined his status as a political prisoner.

Thatcher and her government were furious and became even more determined not to yield to public pressure. Bernard Ingham, the Prime Minister's press secretary, was pugnacious and scathing. 'If Mr Sands doesn't want to eat, then Mr Sands will not be an MP for very long,' Ingham sneered, 'assuming he has the courage to go through with it.'

On his hospital bed, the new MP's gaunt face sank into itself, skin tightening around a bony skull, while his body wasted away both inside and out. He was soon joined in hospital by the next hunger striker, Francis Hughes. On 15 April, Patsy O'Hara, who felt terrible pain whenever he touched his sunken stomach, and Raymond McCreesh were carried out of the Maze. The Republican prisoners chanted their names and banged the doors of their cages in appreciation of the courage they saw in the hollowed-out faces of the two men. Death would soon come and the next hunger strikers, led by Joe McDonnell, prepared for their own demise.

Bobby Sands was more popular than he had ever been. Significant figures, from the Pope to Charles Haughey, the Irish Prime Minister, called on the British government to find a compromise that could end the hunger strike before Sands died. On 25 April, members of the European Commission on Human Rights, including its Danish president, Carl Aage Norgaard, travelled to Belfast to meet with Sands so that they could make a formal complaint to Britain over his treatment. Sands insisted through his lawyer that he would only see them if they were accompanied by Gerry Adams and Danny Morrison of Sinn Féin.

A fellow Maze prisoner, 'Bik' McFarlane, who ran the hunger strike, went in to see Sands. His friend was barely well enough to talk, but he made it plain that he wanted Adams and Morrison with him. The British government refused and after eight futile hours the European delegation gave up. They slipped out of a side exit and avoided the demonstration led by Ian Paisley and 200 Loyalist supporters.

In late April, the Pope's secretary, Father Magee, travelled from the Vatican to Belfast and he saw Sands three times. He also met Humphrey Atkins, the British government's Secretary of State for Northern Ireland. Sands refused to end his hunger strike and Atkins was intransigent. There would be no concessions from Westminster.

It became difficult for Sands to drink. He gagged as his stricken body recoiled at the prospect of swallowing even a mouthful of water. His skin had become so thin and papery he had to be lifted onto a water bed to ease the pain. It looked as if his bones could break through and pierce the mattress at any moment.

The Pope called on the world to 'Pray for our Catholic and non-Catholic brethren in Northern Ireland in this time of grave tension'.

Father Magee tried again to see if the prisoners might compromise on any of their five demands, so Charles Haughey could take something to Margaret Thatcher. His request was refused.

The end, meanwhile, came for Bobby Sands. On the 63rd day

of his fast, Sands was visited in hospital by Jim Gibney, a senior Sinn Féin official. Sands wore the crucifix that Father Magee had given to him on behalf of the Pope.

'How are you?' Gibney asked.

'Jim?' Sands said in a cracked, whispery voice. 'Is that you?'

'Yes, Bobby, it's me,' Gibney said as he took hold of Sands' skeletal hand.

'I'm blind,' Bobby Sands whispered again. 'Tell the lads to keep their chins up.'

Sands was visited by Gibney one last time, later that day. He managed to ask if there had been any change in the attitude of the Brits. When he heard the single word of 'No', he sighed and murmured: 'Well, that's it. Keep my ma in mind.'

The next day, on Sunday 3 May 1981, he slipped into a coma. Forty hours later, at 1.17am on Tuesday 5 May, surrounded by his parents, his brother Sean and his sister Marcella, Bobby Sands died. The British government's Northern Ireland Office released a brief statement an hour later. 'The prisoner took his own life by refusing food and medical intervention for 66 days.'

Newspapers, radio and television stations around the world, from America and India to France and the Soviet Union, quoted their leaders expressing sympathy for the loss of another life in Northern Ireland. Sands was number 2,308 on the list of dead during the Troubles.

West Belfast was already burning with torched barricades lit by Molotov cocktails that had been hurled through the air at British soldiers. The call to arms, to full-scale rioting, had begun just before 2am. Hundreds of women had left their homes and taken to the streets. Armed with metal dustbin lids in their hands, they had begun to strike the pavements in sadness and fury. The terrible din of the metal lids used to be a warning sound during internment. Ten years on it spelt out a different and even more ominous message. From one street to the next, from house to house, the echoing clatter rose into the night. Republicans across

Belfast understood the meaning of crashing dustbin lids at the dead of night.

Bobby Sands is dead. Take up your arms. Bobby Sands is dead.

Thirty-six hours later, after his emaciated body had been brought home to the Twinbrook estate in west Belfast, Bobby Sands was carried from St Luke's Chapel just after 2pm on Wednesday 6 May. The funeral cortège, flanked by IRA men wearing combat gear and balaclavas, moved slowly along the four miles to the cemetery, with over 100,000 mourners lining the streets. People cried openly while a piper played 'The H-Block Song':

> *I'll wear no convict's uniform,*
> *Nor meekly serve my time,*
> *That Britain might call Ireland's fight*
> *Eight hundred years of crime*

Inside the cemetery, Sands' coffin was removed from the hearse. A trio of IRA gunmen fired three volleys of shots over the coffin. Gerry Adams took charge of the ceremony, while the funeral oration was delivered by Owen Carron, Sands' election agent and the man who would replace him as the Member of Parliament for Fermanagh and South Tyrone.

'They tried to compromise Bobby Sands,' Carron said as his voice boomed through a megaphone. 'They tried to compromise his supporters. But they failed. Around the world, Bobby Sands has humiliated the British government. In Bobby Sands' death they have sown the seeds of their own destruction.

'Bobby Sands has gone to join the ranks of Ireland's patriotic dead. He will be remembered by freedom-loving people throughout the world as a freedom fighter and a political prisoner hungering for justice. I have no doubt that the name of Bobby Sands will mark a watershed in Irish history and will be a turning point in this struggle for Irish freedom.'

A young man had still died. There was no thought of historic milestones or political watersheds among the grieving Sands family at the graveside. Bobby's seven-year-old son, Gerard, was among those who helped cover his coffin with sand.

CHAPTER 11

A Funeral and a Wedding

Dalymount Park, Dublin, Sunday 10 May 1981

Charlie Nash turned 30 on his day of reckoning. It was cold and rainy in Dublin and, beneath the gravity of the hunger strike, there was no birthday cheer for the European lightweight champion. The funeral of Bobby Sands had been the largest and most sombre display of Republican mourning since the Bloody Sunday burials in Derry. Memories of Willie and that awful day had been dredged up again.

There was little escape in Dublin. The Irish capital was also consumed by the Maze crisis. On 8 May, a fifth IRA man, Joe McDonnell, joined the hunger strike as if to prove that the resolve of the prisoners remained undented. Even before Sands had died, there had been rioting in Dublin by young people sympathetic to the Republican cause and angry with the Thatcher government. A boxing promotion, even featuring a European defence by Nash and a professional debut for the highly touted Barry McGuigan, had little chance of breaking through the oppressive pall.

Charlie was already full of unsettling concerns. He did not feel completely fit or prepared for Giuseppe Gibilisco, who had won 19 of his 27 fights. His training had gone badly after he had twisted his ankle while out running one evening. Charlie had stuck to the footpath because, amid all the strife surrounding Bobby Sands, few street lights were on in Derry. His foot caught in a hole where there had once been a lamp post and he fell to the ground.

His badly sprained ankle had to be strapped heavily in the last few weeks before the fight and Charlie could only do limited training. But he was loath to cancel the fight as, with even just one good leg, he believed he could handle Gibilisco. The Italian had started boxing in Australia, where they called him Joey rather than Giuseppe, and returned to Europe in 1978. Charlie knew he was a crude slugger who had never previously fought at championship level. He had been promised another world title shot, against Sean O'Grady, if he retained his European title.

'You'll be fine,' his promoter Mickey Duff reassured Charlie.

Barry McGuigan was convinced about his own fight. He was sure he would shine against Selvin Bell, a journeyman featherweight from Manchester. Bell's fight record was distinctly modest – 16 victories, 42 defeats and two draws – so Barry felt excitement rather than trepidation in the week of the fight, and not even the bleakness of the hunger strike could dim his enthusiasm.

He began to experience some misgivings in his dressing room. It had been a filthy day and the rain had eased only as night-time descended on Dalymount Park, a football stadium in north Dublin. Barry had expected to box in the first bout of the evening and so, 15 minutes before the start, he tied plastic bags around his boxing boots. He wanted his feet to stay dry as he walked through the muddy outfield to the ring. After his hands had been wrapped, and he pulled on his gloves and gown, he made a surreal sight in the dressing room as he shadow-boxed and danced around in his shopping bag-covered boots. Barry didn't care what anyone thought until his momentum was halted by a young woman from the television crew. She opened his dressing-room door to tell him that his fight would now be held after the main Nash–Gibilisco contest to suit the television schedules.

Barry was deflated and the first sign of nerves began to eat away at him. Still wearing the plastic bags on his feet, he sat on a hard wooden bench in the dressing room and listened to the fight commentary echoing through a tinny little Tannoy. He suddenly realised how different the professional fight game was compared to amateur boxing as Charlie Nash and Giuseppe Gibilisco were introduced. Barry might have sparred Charlie twice in Derry, but it felt momentous to be on the same bill as the most famous fighter in Ireland.

Harry Carpenter was the BBC's commentator and, as Nash and Gibilisco met in the centre of the ring, he suggested that, 'These two boxers have stripped off at the last possible moment because it really is a very cold night. It's going to be very difficult for them to keep warm.'

The white canvas had turned a grimy brown with muddy foot-prints as no one else had latched onto the McGuigan plastic bag trick. In his corner, Nash, as usual, sank down onto his knee to say a small prayer. He wore green boots and green shorts trimmed with gold, while Gibilisco was dressed in all white with his black hair styled in a bubble perm. At five foot four, Gibilisco was three and a half inches shorter than the champion. But he looked fear-less as he barrelled forward and caught Nash with a couple of left hands in the first minute. Nash settled himself and, with his right jab snaking out from his southpaw stance, he won the first round, picking off the Italian with ease.

It was different in round two. A series of long left hands rocked Nash and sent him reeling towards the ropes. Two more swinging left hooks hit him on the top of his head and left him dazed. It would emerge later that one of these punches in the second round caused Nash to be concussed because, after the fight, he could not remember anything from that moment. He swallowed a right uppercut and, towards the end of the round, struggled to withstand a barrage of blows when the referee jumped between the fighters to give him a standing count.

In the corner, at the end of the round, Tommy Donnelly tried to remove Nash's gumshield. Some of his front teeth had broken off and the mouthpiece came out with a gush of blood. Nash spat a red stream into the steel bucket at his feet and then gazed groggily at Donnelly, who urged him to box Gibilisco at distance.

Nash looked forlorn in the third as, swallowing blood, he was punished by Gibilisco's roundhouse swinging. It was as if Nash was moving in slow motion, unable to avoid even the most telegraphed punch. When he was cut over his right eye the referee called in the doctor. The cut was examined and, after 20 seconds of deliberation, Nash was sent back into the fight.

'If Nash pulls this off it will be a miracle,' Carpenter suggested.

Nash was caught again early in round four, and made to take another standing count, before he somehow found the will to rally. He outboxed Gibilisco over the next minute and throughout the fifth round. Carpenter suggested that, 'Nash is looking like a champion again.'

His comeback did not last. In the sixth, blood sprayed from his mouth as he was hit by a right uppercut and a left cross. Nash tried to back away, but Gibilisco sensed the conclusive moment. He came steaming in, swinging crudely, and Nash could not hold him off. A big left hand staggered him and, as he sank against the ropes, another left dropped Nash heavily. He clutched at the middle rope and pulled himself up slowly to his feet.

The fight should have been stopped then but the referee waved them on. Gibilisco fired in punches furiously, catching Nash with four blows. The last, a crunching right hand, left Nash stretched out flat on the muddied canvas. He managed to lift his head, as blood streamed down his face, but the champion would not be able to get up.

As the referee counted Nash out, Carpenter delivered an equally decisive verdict: 'On this cold night in Ireland, the Irishman

Charlie Nash has lost his European title. And it might be worse than that. Nash looked to me, on his back, as though that might be the end of his championship career. This is a very sad night for Irish boxing.'

Nash looked in such a bad state that Gibilisco, the new champion, started crying. His tears were not of pride but of concern that he might have done lasting damage to the old champion. Eventually, Nash was helped to his feet and preparations were made to take him to hospital so he could be stitched up. It was the beginning of the end for a brave fighter.

In the dressing room, Barry's feet rustled inside the plastic shopping bags. He looked pale as he absorbed the fact that Charlie Nash, a boxing hero, had been knocked out badly in the very ring where he would now make his professional debut. Yet McGuigan was a born fighter and as he walked to the ring just before ten o'clock that night, with half of the crowd already heading to the exit, certainty coursed through him. He knew he would win. Eddie Shaw reminded him to start carefully, as Bell was an awkward veteran, and so McGuigan took the measure of his opponent in the first round.

At the start of the second, having ascertained that Bell was no match for him, the 20-year-old McGuigan cut loose. He drove Bell into a neutral corner, hurting him with spiteful combinations, before he dropped him with a left hook to the body. Bell had already had enough and he made no protest as the referee spread his arms to confirm the end.

Barry, Eddie Shaw, Barney Eastwood, his father Pat, his brother Dermot and a large entourage from Clones swarmed around the ring in jubilation. Sandra Mealiff and Sharon McGuigan were jumping up and down and shouting and screaming so much that Harry Mullan, the venerable editor of *Boxing News*, observed dryly from ringside: 'You would think that young Barry McGuigan had just won the world title – instead of being the 43rd man to beat Selvin Bell.'

The elation melted away in the dressing room. Barry watched, feeling suddenly sombre, as Charlie Nash's entourage disappeared. The loneliness of defeat was etched across the former champion's face. Only Tommy Donnelly, his trainer, remained. Tommy would take Charlie to hospital, where he would spend the night. Boxing, Barry McGuigan realised with new clarity, was like nothing else. It offered up joy and misery in equal measure.

Two days later, on 12 May 1981, another hunger striker died. Francis Hughes stopped breathing 59 days after his last mouthful of food. Heavy rioting broke out on the streets of Belfast and Derry. Young men, carrying petrol and nail bombs and with their faces covered by balaclavas or handkerchiefs, ran blindly at the RUC and the army. Their rage and desperation, as well as their masked faces, made them look fearless against a smouldering backdrop of burning cars, tear gas, plastic bullets, flaring incendiary devices and incessant gunfire. Ordinary young people were caught up in the madness or simply struck down.

On 13 May Emmanuel McLarnon, 21, was shot in the Divis Flats, near where Barry McGuigan trained, while a 14-year-old Catholic schoolgirl was killed when she was shot in the head by a plastic bullet fired by soldiers in west Belfast.

Protestant families also suffered. On 7 May, a Republican mob on the New Lodge Road, not far from the Holy Family, had stoned a Protestant milkman and his son after the death of Bobby Sands. Eric and 14-year-old Desmond Guiney died after their milkcart crashed into a lamp post. The Guiney family lived in Rathcoole, the Protestant estate where Sands had spent his early years.

The routine presence of death, in a relentless loop of retaliation and revenge, numbed Northern Ireland while the hunger strikes ground on in the Maze. Raymond McCreesh and Patsy O'Hara were both seriously ill and, on 21 May, they died on the same day. Both men had clung on for 61 days. Within another week, three more prisoners had joined Joe McDonnell on hunger strike as they replaced the four dead men. Kieran Doherty, Kevin Lynch and Martin Hurson each refused any more food.

Gerry Storey felt bereft when he learnt of the death of one of his favourite old fighters. Joe Lynch had been victorious on the night in 1969 when the Holy Family whitewashed the British paratroopers boxing team. Twelve years later, aged 33, Joe was killed by an RUC Land Rover that mowed him down in the Republican district of Oldpark in north Belfast. The police claimed to be fleeing a rioting mob, inflamed by the hunger strikes, but local witnesses offered a different account. They stressed the streets were quiet when Joe and his companion were targeted by the Land Rover. The driver aimed his speeding vehicle straight at them. Joe pushed his friend out of the way but he could not save himself.

He died on 23 May 1981 – victim number 2,327 of the Troubles. But, to Gerry Storey, he would always be Joe Lynch, an all-action Holy Family fighter and a kind, amusing man.

The death rate was rising, and the political stakes were climbing. Publicity for the IRA and Sinn Féin had reached unprecedented levels as the hunger strikes dominated news headlines around the world. In the United States there was particular affinity for Republican objectives in the Irish-American community where a romanticised vision of Ireland did not square with the violent realities of the Troubles. Donations poured in from across the Atlantic to boost the IRA. The fact that much of this money would be used to cause further death and despair, often for innocent people, was lost amid the surging waves of support for the Maze prisoners.

The British government was under increased pressure to resolve the crisis, but Republican leaders were also subjected to heightened tensions. All four of the hunger strikers who had died were in their twenties. There was disquiet within the Maze. There was no end in sight and more young men were likely to die of starvation.

Margaret Thatcher made no sign of buckling. 'The prisoners have taken their own lives deliberately,' she said. 'I do not know of any religious leader or politician who is urging me to give political status. Every single one knows that to do so will be tantamount to giving some people a licence to murder innocent men, women and children.'

In the face of her unyielding conviction, other prisoners and even senior members of the IRA began to ask difficult questions in private. How many men were they willing to sacrifice? Were they ready to lose another eight or ten men? When would enough be enough?

The deterioration of Joe McDonnell, the fifth hunger striker, could not be ignored. On 24 June 1981, he was taken from his cell to the prison hospital. McDonnell had reached his 48th day without food. He could only be expected to survive for another two or, at the most, three weeks. Garret FitzGerald and his Fine Gael party had won the Irish general election on 11 June. As he prepared to replace Charles Haughey, Ireland's new leader resolved to help end the hunger strike. FitzGerald lent his full support to a new initiative launched by the Irish Commission for Justice and Peace that aimed to break the deadlock.

The commission made progress and in early July they seemed to have secured a breakthrough. They met Mike Alison, the minister for Northern Ireland, and obtained the basis for an agreement. The commission then spoke to Bik McFarlane, the IRA's commanding officer in the Maze. They suggested the five key demands made by the prisoners would be fulfilled. McFarlane and the other prison leaders remembered how they had been duped by the British after the first hunger strike and so they demanded unequivocal proof. On 4 July 1981, the prisoners released a conciliatory statement saying they were open to a concrete new offer.

The Irish Commission had no idea that the British government and the IRA were conducting clandestine talks through their intermediary – the mysterious Mountain Climber. Both parties were ruthless in trying to outfox each other and the brinkmanship was dangerous as McDonnell neared death. But a step forward was made when Danny Morrison, one of the most articulate members of the IRA, was allowed into the Maze to outline the secret offer that had been pledged. Morrison met with 80 prisoners, including McDonnell, who was blind and in a wheelchair, and discussed the proposals. McDonnell was defiant. His hunger strike would continue until written guarantees were in place.

The government agreed that an official from the Northern Ireland Office would arrive at the Maze prison on Wednesday 8 July at 8.30am to provide the guarantee.

It was too late. At 5.11am McDonnell took his last breath. His death marked the end of any hopes of an immediate deal. The loss of a fifth hunger striker had a terrible impact in and outside the Maze.

There was another catastrophic blow for the hunger strikers when Martin Hurson died unexpectedly on 13 July, on his 46th day without food. The crisis deepened and there were angry exchanges between Denis Faul, the Maze chaplain, and Bik McFarlane. Faul accused McFarlane of choosing unfit men to join the hunger strike and of, effectively, killing Hurson. McFarlane responded angrily that Maggie Thatcher was responsible for the death of six hunger strikers. Faul's rebuttal was stinging as he accused the IRA of wanting more funerals to fuel their publicity train. Yet the IRA could not back down after coming so far, and Thatcher's government – while prepared to make concessions in secret negotiations – was not willing to blink first in public. A conveyor belt of death would grind on.

It needed the families of the hunger strikers to intervene. On 28 July, they met with Faul in a small hotel 30 miles north of Belfast to stress their concern at the lack of any settlement. Faul arranged for them to meet Gerry Adams later that day and he agreed to ask the IRA leadership to order the prisoners to end the strike. When Adams then obtained permission to visit the six surviving hunger strikers in the Maze, they all refused to abandon their mission and stressed that it would betray Bobby Sands and the five other men who had died before them.

Paddy Quinn had joined the hunger strike on 15 June and after 46 days he looked close to death. Faul had established that, when the prisoners fell into a coma, their families had the legal right to make decisions on their behalf. So Quinn's mother stepped in to save him. In later years, he described the pain of starvation and the depth of his resolve to endure.

'Maybe it crossed your mind to go off the hunger strike, but I wouldn't give up,' Quinn told Melanie McFadyean of *The Guardian* in 2006. 'Maggie Thatcher wasn't going to criminalise me. I came round in intensive care. My lips were swollen, chapped and cut. They said I'd been biting them. I could hear the scraping of the blood on the back of my brain. I could feel this terrible pain ... You watched the deterioration of your own body, thinking, "I have to do this; I'm going to keep going." It was just pain, day after day. I was in a wheelchair. My eyes had gone, all I could see were shadows. I had reached a point that I was looking forward to death. I felt contentment. I had accepted I was going to die. I was happy with my decision.'

Quinn had told his mother not to take him off the hunger strike when he lapsed into a coma: 'You either back me or you back Maggie Thatcher.'

On 31 July, when Quinn lost consciousness, his mother insisted on medical intervention. Her decision seemed timely as Kevin Lynch died the next day, followed by Kieran Doherty on 2 August. Thomas McElwee died on 8 August, and 12 days later Michael Devine became the tenth and last fatality.

That same day, 20 August 1981, Pat McGeown's family took him off the strike after 42 days. Five other men – Laurence McKeown, Matt Devlin, Liam McCloskey, Patrick Sheehan and Jackie McMullan – still refused to eat. Another five men prepared to join them.

Belfast's boxers found hope and harmony in each other's company. Davy Larmour came from near the Shankill Road, and Paddy

Maguire from near the Falls Road. Yet the Protestant boxer and the Catholic boxer had become best friends. Boxing allowed them to establish this unusual rapport. Ordinary Protestants and Catholics could become friendly in a work setting, but there were limits on their interaction. They could not easily mingle in the same neighbourhoods or pubs. Sectarian divisions ruled their lives. But boxing obliterated these borders for its fighters.

Paddy had retired in 1977, having fought for the British, Commonwealth and European titles. He had been unlucky that his career coincided with the near-impossibility of staging professional boxing in Belfast. But he could not shake his addiction to the old game and had begun to train Davy, who was still struggling to get fights. Davy's record was a modest 8–4 but, with Paddy in his corner, he wanted to give boxing one last crack.

The two friends criss-crossed Belfast together and, when they were stopped at security checkpoints at night, their different backgrounds confused the British soldiers. Davy's identity document showed that he lived in Protestant Glengormley while Paddy's ID proved he lived just off the Catholic Falls Road. One night a soldier shining a light into the car recognised Davy as the boxer but he was confused to see a Catholic next to him.

'Who's this?' he asked Davy.

'Paddy Maguire,' Davy said. 'He's my friend.'

'Where are you off to?' the soldier asked suspiciously.

'I'm taking Paddy home.'

The soldier gave him a hard look before waving them on. As he wound up the window, Davy heard him say to another squaddie cradling his rifle: 'I wonder what those two are up to . . .'

On 7 August 1981, in the depths of the hunger strikes, Paddy's father had died. Davy knew he needed to be with Paddy at the funeral. The dangers in crossing the peace line and moving from Loyalist Belfast into the Republican heartland were irrelevant. The night before the funeral, he told three of his friends at the Albert Foundry Boxing Club that he was going to pay his respects to Paddy's father and support his friend. All three Protestant boxers, who knew Paddy well, immediately said that they would join him. Davy was heartened, but unsurprised. Perhaps being punched hard in the face and the gut gave boxers a purity of purpose that lifted them above petty discrimination.

The four boxers met an hour before the funeral and together they walked from a fiercely Loyalist to a staunchly Republican neighbourhood. At the erroneously named peace wall – a bare concrete wall with barbed wire on top that provided a physical and symbolic barrier between two warring communities – they passed through the heavy steel door and headed along Cupar Street. When they turned left onto Springfield Road, they were in the heart of Republican territory. Mothers bringing their children home from school hurried inside at the sight of four unknown men walking down the street. It usually meant only one thing: trouble.

On Kashmir Road, where Paddy's large family lived, most of the Catholic houses had been the first to be burnt out at the start of the Troubles in 1969. Yet a deep-seated community spirit prevailed and hundreds of people had arrived for the Maguire funeral. They watched the four men turn off Springfield Road and walk towards them down the Kashmir Road. Apprehension rippled through the mourners as the men approached them. And then Paddy's voice rang out amid the surrounding grief and trepidation.

'It's Davy Larmour,' he shouted.

Everyone relaxed and even smiled as Paddy broke through the huddle to walk towards them. 'Davy!' he called out. His friend lifted his hand in greeting.

The two men walked towards each other, the Protestant boxer and his Catholic trainer, as if all the surrounding tension and strife meant nothing.

'You came,' Paddy said simply as he stretched out his hand.

'Of course,' Davy replied, gripping his friend's hand tightly. 'Your father was a good man.'

'Aye,' Paddy nodded sadly. His face brightened again as he saw his fellow boxers from the Albert Foundry club. 'You're very welcome, lads,' he said softly. 'Thank you for coming.'

The five fighters moved back towards the house where the funeral cortège was preparing to leave. People gazed at them with respect and admiration.

Barry McGuigan had hit the most troubling period of his young boxing life. On Monday 3 August, at the Corn Exchange in Brighton, he suffered a terrible shock. He lost his third professional contest on points against Peter Eubank – the older brother of Chris Eubank who would rise to the peak of British boxing in the 1990s. McGuigan moved up to super-featherweight to fight Eubank, a journeyman pro, and he dominated the eight two-minute rounds. He hurt Eubank repeatedly and dropped him. But Eubank, like his younger brother, had an incredible chin and he was a tough 29-year-old. He was also the home fighter and the referee Roland Dakin gave him the decision by the narrowest of margins: 78½ points to 78.

It was a shameful decision and the Brighton crowd booed the verdict in favour of their fighter. McGuigan cried bitter tears as he walked along the seafront to his hotel with Barney Eastwood. 'Don't worry about it,' the promoter said. 'You won the fight. It was just a bad decision.'

But it also made Eastwood wonder if Gerry Storey had given him a bad steer in persuading him to sign McGuigan. He resolved to give Storey's protégé an acid test in his next fight against the unbeaten Belgian Jean-Marc Renard exactly a month later. In peak condition, aged 25, Renard had won all his six fights in imperious fashion. He had excellent technique and punched hard – as his two most recent TKO victories proved. It was as if Eastwood decided that if McGuigan was going to sink then it was better it happened before they wasted any more money on him. McGuigan's career was on the line in only his fourth contest.

McGuigan took one look at Renard and he knew. 'Renard was a

very serious dude,' he said later. The Belgian went on to become European champion and fight for the world featherweight title.

The beautiful old Ulster Hall was half-full for McGuigan's first home fight as a pro on 3 September 1981. As if he wanted to avoid the magnitude of the contest for as long as possible, McGuigan turned his back on Renard and danced quietly in his corner. He only turned to face his opponent when they were summoned to the ring for their final instructions by the referee Harry Gibbs. A tough London docker, Gibbs was scrupulously fair and McGuigan would receive no favours from him.

Cries of 'C'mon, Barry!' cut through the low rumble of anticipation as the bell for the first round rang. McGuigan, at five foot six, was two inches taller than Renard, an orthodox stylist with noticeably bandy legs. They were evenly matched. McGuigan's jab was relentless and he ripped the Belgian on the inside with his left hook. Renard had a smart left hook of his own and, whenever McGuigan threw a right hand, Renard seemed to connect with his best punch. McGuigan was canny, though, and he began to feint with the right and then glide away as Renard threw a left hook. He would then fire back a counter-punch and clip the Belgian. McGuigan also kept up a high tempo, never allowing Renard to settle into a rhythm.

It was the most absorbing fight the Ulster Hall had seen in years and the crowd, sensing the rise of a new hero in the bleakest of times, became deeply involved. The acoustics of the hall, which made it such an evocative venue for music, accentuated the drama. It seemed to both McGuigan and Renard that the spectators were so loud that they were inside the ring with them. Every shouted word and cry resonated in their heads, driving them to fresh heights.

They fought with controlled ferocity in a see-sawing battle. In the seventh, it seemed as if McGuigan had begun to shade another round, with the crowd chanting 'Baaaa-rry, Baaaa-rry, Baaaa-rry!', when his double jab was followed by an overhand right from

Renard. It caught McGuigan flush and he went down. Renard peeled away to a neutral corner but it was just a flash knockdown. By the time the Belgian had spread his arms on top of the ropes, as if to admire the impact of his punch, McGuigan had bounced back to his feet. Referee Gibbs was fooled by the alacrity with which he got up because he assumed the Irishman had tripped and fallen. He did not bother with a count.

McGuigan's head was clear. When Renard threw a sharp combination in an attempt to reassert his fleeting supremacy, McGuigan weaved out of the way. McGuigan took back control of the centre of the ring and he forced Renard to retreat with some crisp hitting. He had survived a small crisis with heart and skill. Sustained applause rang around the Ulster Hall as the knowledgeable crowd revelled in the engrossing drama.

In the break between rounds, a young woman in a short white dress and high heels walked around the ring, holding a card with the number eight. Wags in the hall catcalled and wolf-whistled her. But before the start of the eighth and final round, the two corners had no eyes for the ring-card girl. One of Renard's seconds swung a white towel in fast circles in an attempt to cool down his fighter while Eddie Shaw and Ned McCormick worked on McGuigan.

'Did you trip?' Shaw asked his fighter.

McCormick answered before McGuigan could respond. 'You must be joking,' he said. 'He was knocked down by a great right hand.'

Dunking his arm deep in a bucket of iced water, McCormick brought out a soaking sponge and shoved it in McGuigan's face. He then squeezed the rest of the cold water over his fighter's head to make sure he was alert. McGuigan listened intently as Shaw reminded him to close the show. He was just ahead but he needed a big last round.

It had been a hard and bruising contest that was replicated again in the final three minutes. McGuigan was slightly the busier and more effective boxer and, in the last seconds of the fight, he reeled off a blistering combination that rocked back Renard's head and forced him to clinch. There was time only for Gibbs to separate them when the bell rang.

After a warm embrace between the fighters, Gibbs wasted no time in moving towards McGuigan. As the only judge in the fight, he knew the decision and so he raised McGuigan's right hand. He had won the fight by five rounds to three. Shaw and Eastwood soon engulfed him and McGuigan had to fight his way out of their delighted arms to meet Renard again. The Belgian had crossed the ring to offer his congratulations.

Ten- and 50-pence pieces showered the ring in a traditional Belfast tribute. Whenever a crowd had seen a 'nobbins fight', a Belfast classic, they would throw coins as a thank you to the boxers. The canvas was covered in money and it sounded as if the roof of the Ulster Hall might lift when McGuigan began blowing kisses to the rafters. This was just the first of many 'nobbins fights' and tumultuous Belfast nights.

The hunger strikes withered away. Following the decision of Paddy Quinn's mother to call for medical intervention once her son slipped into unconsciousness, three more families followed her lead. Between 20 August and 6 September 1981, Pat McGeown, Matt Devlin and Laurence McKeown were all saved. Their health would never be the same as they had endured a terrible ordeal. McKeown was on his 70th day without food when his family took him off the strike. Liam McCloskey also gave up after 55 days, on 26 September, when he realised his family would intervene as soon as he became too ill to respond.

On 3 October 1981, the hunger strike was finally abandoned and the six remaining prisoners accepted nourishment again. One of the most distressing periods in Irish history was over – but its impact would resonate for decades.

In Britain the end was presented as a victory for Margaret Thatcher – the Iron Lady. The truth was more tangled. Within two years, the British government met most of the prisoners' original demands. The hunger strikes had also served as the IRA's most powerful weapon since Bloody Sunday in terms of winning new recruits and legitimising the aims of the Republican movement. The electoral success of Bobby Sands persuaded the IRA and Sinn Féin to adopt a new Armalite and ballot-box strategy, combining terrorism with political manoeuvring. Gerry Adams stressed that victory for Bobby Sands in an emotive by-election 'exposed the lie that the hunger strikers – and by extension the IRA and the whole Republican movement – had no popular support'.

Yet there was lasting regret that ten men had died horrendously. For many Republicans it had been a cost too high. Bernadette McAliskey said years later, as she cautioned against rewriting a miserable time as glorious history, 'Those of us who lived through it would counsel against ever doing it again.'

There had been carnage outside the Maze and, during the seven months of the hunger strikes, a further 68 lives were lost. The wounds of Northern Ireland were deeper than ever.

Hugh Russell had begun to see the wounds through a lens. Brendan Murphy had helped him become a trainee photographer at the *Irish News* while also taking him out on assignments so that Hugh could shadow him. A life lived in New Lodge had made Hugh accustomed to the violent realities of the Troubles. Bombs and gunfire, rioting and army checkpoints had all become so routine that, as a teenager, Hugh almost skimmed over the daily problems. He was also fortunate that, in Gerry Storey and the Holy Family, he had found a refuge. Boxing protected and nurtured him. But working with a camera, and seeing Belfast with new clarity through the gaze of a master photographer in Murphy, changed Hugh.

He spent his days working on the photographic beat and it was clear that, if he stuck to the grisly task, a full-time job could be his in another year. Murphy also helped him feel the pain and pathos of his home city in deeper ways than he had ever experienced. Murphy taught him to be both dispassionate and compassionate with a camera. It was important that he approached each new story without prejudice and with calm scrutiny. At the same time, his photographs should capture the humanity beneath the brutality of Belfast.

It was difficult because the hurt seeped through the camera and down into the photographer. Murphy had blunted his own pain with drink, but a life lived on the edge of alcoholism was no life at all. He learnt to use the hurt he felt to deepen the texture and meaning of his photographs. Hugh was still young, at 21, and it would take years for him to develop the sensitivity and craft of Murphy. But he had found his vocation. The former tugman at Belfast docks was certain he would be a news photographer for most of his adult life.

He was still a boxer and, with an Olympic medal in his fight résumé, Hugh was Barney Eastwood's second big signing after Barry McGuigan. He was given the nickname of Little Red and he made his debut on the same bill as the heavily anticipated rematch between McGuigan and Eubank at the Ulster Hall. McGuigan was in the mood to avenge his loss against Eubank. With the debut appearance of 'Little Red' Russell adding to the allure of another Eastwood promotion, the Ulster Hall soon sold out.

In the last weeks before his fight, Hugh worked as a photographer in the day, and at night sparred in the Castle Street gym that Eastwood's fighters had begun to use. McGuigan and Davy Larmour engaged in fierce sparring sessions when Hugh was still at work for the *Irish News*. It was hard for Eastwood to find suitable opponents for Hugh at his natural weight and so he moved up two divisions for his debut, where he would face the super-bantamweight Jim Harvey who had won only two of his nine fights. He looked set for an easier night than McGuigan.

Peter Eubank was full of confidence on his arrival in Belfast. Having beaten McGuigan four months previously, he glossed over the controversy and insisted he would be better than he had been in Brighton. Eubank even took to beating up his manager, Terry

Brazil, in sparring. Eastwood had arranged local sparring partners, but Eubank also liked to go in the ring with his manager – who was in his early fifties. Eubank set about Brazil and the poor manager looked as if he had been in a bad car smash. His nose was broken and he had cuts and bruises under both eyes. It was a novel way of trying to send a message to Barry McGuigan.

Hugh Russell, meanwhile, immersed himself in training. He ran in the early mornings before work, and he was surprised one day when he jogged straight over the top of British soldiers who had dug a trench-style hideaway for themselves amid a row of hedges in New Lodge. Hugh ran still faster, his mind whirring like a camera as he imagined the kind of photograph he might have taken had he been shooting a future champion boxer running over the top of a startled pair of soldiers. Boxing and photography had become the cornerstones of his new life.

Ulster Hall, Belfast, Tuesday 8 December 1981

Exactly one week before he turned 22, Hugh felt young and vulnerable. Professional boxing was much more serious than the amateur game and, without his Holy Family vest, he felt exposed as he made the long walk to the ring. He also had tiny six-ounce gloves on his fists, which meant there was little padding. Punches would be thudding into skin and bone with raw force. It was a timely reminder that boxing was a dangerous business.

Russell, however, had been fighting for years and the familiar rush of adrenaline coursed through him. He was reassured within a minute of the first round and knew Harvey would be no match for him. Russell had faced far superior fighters in the upper echelons of amateur boxing and so he could relax and take his time to chop down Harvey. He won on a fifth-round TKO as the Ulster Hall stomped its approval for Little Red. Only his mother, who covered her eyes for most of the fight, could not bear to watch his easy victory.

Sandra Mealiff, just days from becoming Mrs Sandra McGuigan, was different. She was so convinced Barry would win she kept her eyes riveted on the ring. It was a sign of how little the boxers and their families were pampered by Barney Eastwood that Sandra did not receive a free ticket. Her expensive seat in the second row was paid for by Pat McGuigan, who would soon become her father-in-law.

Pat loved the fact that Sandra kept telling her mother not to distract her with wedding arrangements. 'Mum, I'm really busy,' Sandra would say. 'I have to go and train Barry.' Her mum would point out that this was her wedding day. 'Yeah,' Sandra smiled, 'but Barry needs me to record his punch rate.'

Her wedding dress had already been made, for just £25, by a lady in Clones. Sandra's only stipulation was that it should include Clones lace. She looked beautiful when she tried it on and she was happy that Barry's aunt made all the bridesmaids' dresses. The rest of her attention fixed on her fiancé's preparations for Eubank.

Such concentration paid off because McGuigan ground Eubank down round after round, tattooing him with punishing combinations and jolting uppercuts. McGuigan was intent on knocking Eubank out, but his rival's jaw seemed unbreakable. In the sixth round, McGuigan had him in desperate trouble. Eubank sagged beneath the assault, and the referee, Bob McMillan, jumped in to separate them. McGuigan thought he had won, but the ref assumed that he had heard the bell somewhere in the Ulster Hall cacophony. By the time he had realised his mistake, Eubank had been given over ten seconds to recover.

In the eighth and last round there was no saving Eubank. McGuigan attacked him ferociously, pummelling him around the ring, and with 20 seconds left the referee reacted mercifully. He put his arms around the stricken Eubank. The contest was over. McGuigan had won his third straight fight in ten weeks and obliterated the pain of his shock defeat in Brighton. He really was as good as Gerry Storey had predicted.

*

Six days later, back in Clones, Barry McGuigan had six stitches removed on his wedding morning. Eubank's head had cut him above the eye and marked him up. But he was a fighter and so neither he nor Sandra minded. His new in-laws had been less impressed by him fighting so close to the wedding, but Sandra reassured them that Barry would win and they wanted to marry as soon as possible. His career was about to take off and she was hard at work in a hair salon. They wanted to start a family and there seemed little time to waste.

Money was so tight that Barry and Sandra had to marry on a Monday – a day when the hairdressing salon was closed. She and her friends from the salon had to work on the Saturday because it was the busiest day of the week. It gave Barry two more days for the wounds on his face to fade.

Snow fell that Monday and, even though the treacherous conditions made it difficult for Sandra to walk up the stairs to the church, their winter wedding looked beautiful. They were married in Sandra's church, which was part of the Protestant Church of Ireland, and then received a blessing in Barry's Catholic church. His brother, Dermot, was best man and the reception was held at the Lennard Arms – his father-in-law's hotel.

After the grief and pain of 1981, which saw 118 people die by the end of the year, Barry and Sandra McGuigan lit up Clones. The distressing impact of the hunger strikes still lingered but the Troubles were forgotten – at least for one day. Yet boxing had to remain at the forefront of their minds. Rather than tearing up the night at an Irish shindig of a wedding reception, Barry had to travel back to Belfast for an evening press conference that Barney Eastwood had arranged to announce his fighting plans for 1982. The boxer and his bride were already used to the demands of the ring. They headed out into the freezing night, eager for a new year and their new life together.

CHAPTER 12

Into the Maze

The walls, fences, gates and locks kept shutting Gerry Storey in tighter and tighter the deeper he moved into the Maze for the first time late in 1981. The prison bus had driven him across the flat bog that opened up into 270 acres of confinement designed to control its 2,800 highly politicised and dangerous prisoners. Unlike any other prison in Europe, the Maze was populated entirely by men convicted of offences relating to terrorist activities. They were united in their determination to be treated as political prisoners, to resist jailhouse discipline and to retain their paramilitary structures within the Maze.

Ten miles south of Belfast, on the outskirts of Lisburn, Her Majesty's Prison Maze had come into existence in 1971, at the start of internment, when it was known initially as Long Kesh. The original detention centre was turned into a sophisticated and forbidding jail in 1976 to cope with the spreading influx of prisoners from both sides of the sectarian divide. This new structure was named after a nearby village called Maze, but it resembled a utilitarian fortress with high walls and watchtowers surrounding eight identical cell blocks that each resembled an H.

The design of the Maze meant there were no stairs anywhere in a vast prison. Each H-block, with its four single-storey wings, was self-contained. Every wing within the block then made up its own separate entity with 24 cells each measuring eight feet by seven, ablution facilities, a dining area, an exercise yard, a governor's office, a control room, staff toilets and a storage room. Each cell and each H-block looked identical both inside and out.

New prisoners, many political dissidents and violent inmates were consigned to the H-blocks, while the lifers tended to be imprisoned in the 'cages', as the compounds of the Maze were known. Each cage contained four Nissen huts measuring 120 feet by 24 and housing 40 prisoners who slept in two-tier bunks packed tightly together.

Gerry was taken to the cages and, on the long drive into the confined heart of the Maze, he was made to feel like every prisoner did on his first morning of incarceration. It began with him being searched at the first massive gate and then led to the bus. Once they were cleared to pass, the gate closed behind them. As they drove through the bleak and alien landscape, Gerry noticed the watchtowers and the security cameras attached to each 17-foot-high gate that blocked their path at regimented intervals. He would be checked at every gate before it opened and then closed behind him.

The further he went, the more Gerry understood that the two-and-a-half-mile expanse of the Maze was designed to isolate its occupants. As functional and rigid as it appeared architecturally, the Maze echoed its name by being bewildering and repetitive. The stark labyrinth became even more confusing because the monotonous H-blocks and cages were separated by blank spaces called 'Inertia' and 'Sterile'.

Gerry had cleared three gates when he finally reached the cages. The uncertainty of his task rose up as he was told to step down from the bus in order to be searched again. He still could not quite believe that prisoners in the Maze, on both the rival Loyalist and Republican sides, had asked to see him.

Conditions in the cages were harsh and, after the hunger strikes, morale was lower than ever. The paramilitary leaders were concerned because their men, whether they were Loyalists or Republicans, had lost their willingness to exercise. Discipline was lax and motivation had virtually disappeared. It was then, in desperation, that an appeal was made to Gerry Storey.

Realising the need for some compromises after the distress of the hunger strikes, the Maze governor agreed to contact the Ulster Sports Council on behalf of the prisoners. They had made the unusual request that Gerry should be allowed to visit them regularly in the cages in order to give them boxing training. Gerry assumed the Republican prisoners had asked for him and so he was taken aback when it was stressed that the request had been lodged jointly with the Loyalists. He was being asked to train both sides of the prison – with one afternoon a week set aside for the Loyalist cages and another for the Republican cages.

'I'll need to speak to the men first,' Gerry said.

And so, on an oppressive December afternoon, with snow falling from a leaden sky, he was allowed into the cages. His nephew, Big Bobby, having recently started his latest 18-year sentence at the Maze, was in the H-blocks with Bik McFarlane and other Republican prisoners who were still recovering from the death of the ten hunger strikers. Gerry would be meeting instead with prisoners who had been given life sentences.

He knew his arrival was considered significant because, once inside the first cage, he was led into an office where the deputy-governor waited for him. It was explained that they would meet first with Gusty Spence, the UVF's leader in the Maze. Fifteen years earlier, Spence had been sentenced to life imprisonment for the murder of an 18-year-old Catholic boy, Peter Ward, in a pub on Malvern Street. That early sectarian murder made Spence one of the most infamous figures in Northern Ireland – even though he had always denied killing the boy.

Spence's notoriety had increased when, after he had been given two days of leave from prison in July 1972 to attend his daughter's wedding, he went on the run with the help of the Red Hand Commando Unit. He was a fugitive for four months and, during that time, he gave an interview to ITV's *World in Action* and called on the UVF to increase their military onslaught against the IRA. Nicknamed the Orange Pimpernel as he evaded the security forces, Spence was finally caught in November 1972.

Taken to Long Kesh to resume his life sentence, Spence established himself as the UVF's commanding officer on the inside. He was moved to the compounds of the Maze in 1976, where he ran his cage with military discipline, and the deputy governor suggested that Spence had pushed hardest to meet Gerry. He would he accompanied by Bobby Rodgers – another Loyalist hard man convicted of murdering a 19-year-old Catholic girl, Eileen Doherty, in 1973.

Spence and Rodgers were an intimidating duo and most people would have quaked at the prospect of meeting them. Gerry welcomed the opportunity. He had never met either man but he felt neither apprehension nor animosity. He had faced many tough-nut paramilitaries in the past and, by treating them politely and fairly, he could speak to such men on an equal footing. They usually respected the iron resolve of his commitment to peace.

When the two UVF men walked in, Gerry immediately liked Gusty Spence's manner. He was courteous and respectful – and clear in his objectives. Spence explained that the cages were divided along paramilitary lines. He and Rodgers ran an UVF cage and Gerry would soon meet with commanding officers in charge of cages for the UDA, UFF, Provisional IRA, Official IRA and the INLA. Spence revealed, almost nonchalantly, that he had spoken to the Republican leaders in the adjoining cages. Despite their murderous differences with the Loyalist groups, they backed his hope that Gerry would train all interested prisoners.

'We know you don't think along sectarian lines,' Spence said to Gerry with a wry smile.

He pointed out that prison, like boxing, made men understand that they were not so different after all. They faced the same doubts and fears. Spence opened up about his boys in the UVF cage. They were struggling and they felt forsaken. Most of them were in for life and the Maze had messed with their heads. Spence wanted to help them regain self-worth and unity and to stop their petty squabbling. It was easy to see that, before he joined the UVF, Spence had been a British army military policeman. He craved order and structure.

He did not shy away from the terrible deeds done by many of his men. Spence had already spoken in public about the fact that it was UVF policy to kill Catholics. 'The UVF took a conscious decision to give the British government a message that if Republican violence could get them to the conference table, the use of indiscriminate violence with a terrible rationale, a "terrible beauty", the UVF could commit more violence than the IRA. Our violence was not totally indiscriminate. It was directed at male Catholics.'

Just like their Republican counterparts, the UVF bombed and shot and killed people. But Spence argued that they needed to remember the political principles and values that had shaped them. Without them, they were merely violent gangsters rather than well-drilled soldiers. Spence spoke of the UVF as being an army, with a political purpose, but they would become a shapeless rabble without the core attributes in which he so believed. He also said the cages had become consumed with self-loathing. Spence wanted to help his men learn to like themselves again. If you hated what you had become, it would be impossible to like anyone else or be liked yourself. He was convinced that boxing, and Gerry, could regenerate them.

They had been following Gerry's work for years. The way he helped Protestant fighters like Davy Larmour was legendary – as were all the nights when his boxing shows lit up the Shankill Road and briefly blinded all forms of prejudice. They knew all about the

Shankill Road summit, nine years earlier, and how the Loyalist Army Council had endorsed Gerry's work so powerfully. He had never let them down and, despite the appalling strife, Gerry still used boxing to inspire people. He humbled them.

'I want my boys to get the best,' Spence said simply at the end, 'and you're the best, Gerry.'

The logistics were far more complicated than the praise. As they began to discuss the ways in which he might bring boxing into the cages, Gerry noticed a surreal shift in the conversation. The deputy governor had been silent until that point but, as he began to talk about rules and regulations, Spence and Rodgers ignored him. When they were asked specific questions by him, they offered their answers to Gerry – as if he was their new prison translator. If they wanted to make points to the deputy governor, they would say them directly to Gerry. They soon reached agreement that Gerry would start his boxing tuition of the Loyalist prisoners the following Tuesday afternoon. One cage would be set aside for his use and all UVF, UDA and UFF inmates interested in boxing would spend the afternoon with him. He would offer to work on a similar basis in a cage with the Republican prisoners drawn from their various groups every Thursday.

'That's grand, Gerry,' Spence said. 'You'll be very welcome.'

They wished him an effusive goodbye – but they did not ask him to translate a fond farewell to the deputy governor.

It was exactly the same when Gerry met the IRA and INLA commanding officers. They refused to acknowledge the presence of the deputy governor and spoke only to Gerry. He had to again play the mock part of translator when the prison official demanded answers to his queries. The Republicans had eyes only for Gerry.

They welcomed him as one of their own, for the Storey name carried significant weight in Republican circles. But there was respect for his insistence on non-sectarian attitudes. There was acceptance, too, that every Tuesday would be given over to the Loyalists. Gerry smiled when he was told the mood of the

Republican prisoners would be lifted by news of his plans for the following Thursday. The power of boxing surged through him again.

It had been a draining afternoon in the Maze. Gerry felt weary as he waited in the watchman's hut for the bus to take him back to the prison exit. In the silence, his gaze moved across the hundreds of ID photos that covered the walls. The names and sentences of each prisoner in the compound were listed below their mugshots. One word echoed: *Life ... Life ... Life.*

Almost every man he would train in a makeshift boxing ring in the Maze cages was serving a life sentence. Their faces blurred on the wall, but the youth of most of them was a unifying factor. One young man after another, Republican after Republican, Loyalist upon Loyalist. They all seemed likely to spend most of their lives in this miserable setting. The barren stretches of cages and H-blocks made their life sentences look the very opposite of life. Gerry resolved, in that austere setting, to try to make Tuesdays and Thursdays seem like afternoons of freedom in the ring.

He was alone on the prison bus when he made the same journey from earlier in reverse. One high gate after another opened and closed behind him as one search party after another searched him and his bag. The clank of the gate shutting after him, the clatter of the bolt sliding into place and the clink of the lock turning stayed in his head when he left the bus and climbed into his car. He could hear the sounds of the prison even as he drove back to the Holy Family. It would take a long time to get used to the Maze.

Gerry's first session with the Loyalists proved the extent of Gusty Spence's resourcefulness. Spence had made a boxing ring using the sheets from their beds and around 50 prisoners were crammed into the Nissen hut that served as a recreation centre in this part of the compound. Gerry had also shown his ingenuity and had brought in a giant sling that was usually used to hook onto the boats in the docks. It was flat and over 20 feet in length and Gerry connected it from one end of the hut to the other. The sling worked perfectly for the exercise routines he conducted as the prisoners weaved and bobbed under it.

At the end of the session, with the men glowing from their exertions, Gerry asked Spence if he could leave the sling with them as it was heavy and it took up a lot of space in his bag. He knew the prison wardens wouldn't like it but, as long as Spence promised not to use it for any dramatic escapes, he was happy to hand over the sling to the UVF cage.

'Of course, Gerry,' Spence said.

'I'll need it on Thursday,' Gerry said cautiously, not sure how Spence would feel about sharing the sling with the Republican cage.

Spence nodded. 'No bother. I'll have a word with them boys and we'll toss it over the wall of the cage when no one's around.'

Gerry knew that 'them boys' meant the IRA. Spence said it so casually that Gerry knew it would be done.

Two days later he discovered that the Republican prisoners had safely received the secret sling from the UVF cage. Gerry was encouraged – as he was by another successful session of training with the IRA and INLA boys. Afterwards they crowded around him, looking re-energised and happy, as they fired boxing questions at him or asked about fighters they admired or people they remembered from the docks. He knew many of the prisoners, like Big Rob Maguire, whose younger brother, Martin, he trained at the Holy Family.

'Gerry, keep looking after our kid, will you?' Maguire said earnestly.

'I will, Rob,' Gerry assured him. 'Young Martin's doing well. He'll box for Ireland.'

Maguire peppered him for more details about his brother's prospects at welterweight. News from the outside lifted everyone in the Maze.

Gerry soon thought of new ways to raise spirits in between hard training sessions for both cages. He brought in old fight movies. Black-and-white footage was fine for classic fights, but he knew how much the boys would love to watch the *Rocky* movies in colour. He convinced the wardens to loan him one of their colour TVs so that he could screen *Rocky* and *Rocky II* to the happy prisoners. Gerry was not done yet with his television plans. While he told the wardens of the additional basic equipment he would need for his boxing classes, he also said two colour TVs and a video recorder were essential for his boxing instruction videos.

'Colour TVs?' a warden snorted.

'They can't see the instruction videos clearly on a black-and-white set,' Gerry said.

A week later, two colour TVs and a video recorder were waiting for him. The prisoners in the cages were ecstatic. Gerry's credentials as a hero of the Maze had been established.

They were soon enshrined when, in front of many of the prisoners and wardens, Gerry stood up to the governor. It began, after he had been away at the European championships, when the prison bus driver said to him: 'There's been some fun and action, Gerry, since you were away. The Sweeney found this massive sling. They can't find out where it came from.'

'That's my sling,' Gerry said.

'Oh good Jesus, Gerry, don't be saying that.'

'You won't get into trouble,' Gerry reassured him. 'I'm happy to tell them it's my sling.'

The governor was less impressed. He stormed into the cages and, in a long rant, told Gerry that he had committed a treasonable offence in the most secure prison in Europe.

'Have you finished?' Gerry said coolly.

He knew the governor was an ardent Unionist and so he chose his words carefully. 'I think you'll be talking to Mr [Ian] Paisley and telling him what has gone on in your high-security prison. I was asked to come in here, for the prisoners, and you didn't direct me about anything. So you tell Mr Paisley that as well and then maybe he will be speaking to my barrister because you have embarrassed me in front of these people.'

Gerry could see that many of the wardens were in stitches behind the governor's back. He kept talking quietly. 'Maybe I should be on my way now that I am up for treason.'

The governor huffed and puffed before storming out. Gerry had delighted the wardens and the prisoners, who were impressed by his refusal to be cowed by the governor. He was more pleased by the collaboration between the UVF and the IRA. They had been passing the sling back and forth between cages 18 and 19 as a way of helping each other's boxing training.

That collaborative spirit deepened and Spence and Billy Hutchinson, one of his young UVF protégés, came over regularly to ask Gerry: 'How are the boys doing?' Gerry knew they meant the IRA. He responded honestly: 'They're doing okay but they don't have as much equipment as you fellas.'

'What do they need?' Spence asked. Once Gerry had listed the items, Hutchinson said: 'Let them have our stuff.'

'Are you sure?' Gerry asked, thinking of the retaliatory murders unleashed for years by such embittered paramilitary rivals.

'Of course,' Spence agreed. 'As long as we get it all back by next Tuesday.'

The Troubles were still raging outside but, inside the cages of the Maze, the UVF and the IRA would share the same boxing gloves, pads and headgear.

'I know the boys will appreciate it,' Gerry said.

'We're happy to do it,' Spence replied.

Gerry had come into the Maze with a high reputation – not only for his boxing work but also for the way in which he kept so many young men out of paramilitary violence. Spence and Hutchinson were committed to the UVF but they also hoped that, one day, peace would return. They knew Gerry's narrative was steeped in non-violence and cross-sectarian unity and they admired him. The purity of his even-handed approach in the Maze resonated.

He poured everything of himself into his training sessions in the Loyalist cage – and he did the same with the Republican prisoners who he knew so much better than them. His fairness and refusal to judge anyone because of their background made the Loyalists respect him even more.

Hutchinson, working towards a postgraduate degree in geography, was more interested in long-distance running than boxing but he and Gusty Spence were fascinated by how Gerry uncovered the best characteristics in everyone he trained. Before he had met him, and knowing of his work on the Shankill Road, Hutchinson had thought Gerry must be either very stupid or very brave. He now knew, having seen the man from New Lodge working so warmly with 45 life prisoners from the UVF, the UDA and the UFF, that Gerry was very smart. He was also uncluttered in his thinking. Gerry believed that working with both sides was the right thing to do. There was no confusion, no agonising, no debate. He did not ask people about their sectarian aims or beliefs. He just spoke to them as ordinary human beings whom he wanted to help.

Gusty Spence was depicted as an imposing hard man outside the Maze – but Gerry found him to be thoughtful and even vulnerable. 'We talk about you often, Gerry,' Spence said one Tuesday afternoon when the boxing trainer was packing up his gear. 'We always say we don't want any of the politicians in here. They can't do what you're doing. We don't believe them. A lot of our politicians told us the Troubles would be over in three months. And here we are – most of us boys in for life.'

There was no bitterness in Spence's voice. He told Gerry about how reporters always wanted to interview him. 'But all they want to hear about is Gusty the gunman,' Spence said with a sad shrug. 'I just tell them about crying when them gates closed on me on my first night in the cages. When I heard that sound I cried like a child. They stop writing then. They don't want to hear how it feels to be inside. They just want to hear about the guns.'

Gerry understood. They all felt good when they were training but, afterwards, as he prepared to leave the cages, Gerry felt their incarceration deeply. It was even more acute when he waited in the empty hut for the bus to drive him out of the prison and he looked up at the lifers on the wall around him. Something clicked inside him and made it feel as if his heart had turned over when the gates opened and shut behind him and the bolts and locks slid back into place. Gerry could not shake from his head the story of Gusty Spence crying on his first night in the cages of the Maze.

Barry and Sandra McGuigan finally had their own home, a little bungalow close to Clones and right on the border of the Republic and Northern Ireland. As if in keeping with his desire to ignore all borders, they paid for the electricity from a company in the South while their water bills were sent by a utility in the North.

Seven roads make Clones a crossroads. Five of those roads lead to the North, including the country road that wound past their bungalow. The remaining two roads stretch back towards the Republic. If they took a short walk to send a letter in the South, the postboxes were painted green. Just across the border, half a mile away, the postboxes were red. The different coloured postboxes were a constant reminder that they straddled two countries and two warring communities. Armed police, soldiers and paramilitary bandits echoed the fact that they were surrounded by danger on both sides of the divide.

Yet Barry and Sandra, a Catholic and a Protestant, were married and in love. They ignored the boundaries and borders, the sectarianism and strife, as they looked ahead to the future. A much more personal and deadly battle loomed.

World Sporting Club, Grosvenor House Hotel, Mayfair, London, Monday 14 June 1982

Barry McGuigan had been paid a flat £500 for each of his first ten fights. He earned £600 for knocking out Gary Lucas in Enniskillen in his 11th contest in April 1982 – on a bill that saw Hugh Russell's record improve to 6-0. The young Irish Olympians would headline Mickey Duff's promotion at the plush Grosvenor House Hotel on Park Lane in London. Both were fighting in eight-round contests at featherweight and Barry would make £700, his highest purse to date. Barry's was the third bout – against the West African bantamweight champion, Asymin Mustapha, the Nigerian who boxed under the name of Young Ali. Hugh would follow in the final contest of the evening, against Stuart Shaw.

The atmosphere in the Great Room of the Grosvenor House, where the World Sporting Club held their black-tie boxing and dinner nights, could hardly have been more different to the raucous Ulster Hall where McGuigan and Russell usually fought. As businessmen in tuxedos ate dinner at tables covered in pristine white tablecloths, their silver-service cutlery chinking above the murmured conversations about stocks and shares and golf games, McGuigan and Young Ali ducked through the ropes. There was a smattering of applause and a few shouts of encouragement from family and fans up in the balcony. Some of the businessmen looked up and made shushing gestures.

Inside the ring it felt serious. Despite Ali's slender build, he looked strong and hard. McGuigan sensed it could be a testing night. In his corner, Paddy Byrne, the cutman, had come from Brighton to help Eddie Shaw and Barney Eastwood look after McGuigan and Russell. Byrne's voice rang out above the thud of punches landing against skin and bone. The fighters made small noises, grunting in exertion or pain when a big punch was absorbed.

Ali was slick and lively in the opening round as McGuigan boxed patiently, trying to work out the calibre of a fighter he had never even seen on tape. In the second, as McGuigan cranked up the intensity, Ali was forced on the back foot. But he was tough and durable, walking through some hard punches as if they merely bounced off his head. McGuigan knew that African fighters rarely folded early. He dug in for the long haul.

The first three rounds were relatively even. Ali had a tight defence when McGuigan went to the body but he was easier to hit around the head. He was still quick and awkwardly effective when throwing plenty of leather at McGuigan. But the young Irishman was edging the fourth when he cracked Ali on the temple. The Nigerian tottered but he recovered and was punching again at the bell. He was similar to Peter Eubank in his ability to absorb a hard punch and come back in the same determined manner.

Shaw and Byrne assured McGuigan he had won every round and reminded him to be patient. McGuigan coasted through round five, conserving his energies for a big push in the last nine minutes of the fight.

Ali returned to his corner and complained that he could not feel his jaw. It was numb and felt like it was floating away from his face. His trainer encouraged him, suggesting that McGuigan was tiring and that Ali just needed to take the fight to him to regain control.

Ali came out fast for the sixth round but McGuigan was waiting. He lured the Nigerian in and then he let rip with a right hand that crashed into Ali's nose. The force of the punch made Ali sigh and wilt and McGuigan, like a cat leaping on its hurt prey, followed up with three scything punches – another right, a left jab and a straight right hand. He had never seen an opponent crumple like Ali did. When the last punch landed Ali's eyes rolled back into his head, which almost swivelled round on his shuddering neck. He bounced off the ropes and fell face down on the canvas.

McGuigan's uncle and cousin were the only ones to shout in delight as the black-tie diners chewed and chatted while staring casually at the stricken figure of the young African. Eastwood, Shaw, Byrne and Barry's brother Dermot ducked through the ropes to congratulate him. Barry wanted to see Ali, to console him, but Eastwood held him back. The beaten fighter was still stretched out on the canvas and surrounded by his cornermen.

Barry had knocked out many fighters before and they always got up. He allowed Shaw to remove his gloves and slipped on his gown while Eastwood went over to talk to Ali's trainer. Barry was just about to join his promoter when Eastwood held up his hand to indicate that he should wait. After another minute, Eastwood returned to Barry's corner.

'This kid is hurt,' he said quietly. 'The doctor's on his way.'

There were no paramedics on site and a solitary doctor took a few minutes to reach the ring and climb through the ropes. The huddle around Young Ali was much larger now and Barry was forced to stand and watch from the other side of the ring. He could only see Ali's legs and began to worry as they did not move for five and then ten minutes. Finally, they lifted him onto his stool but he looked as lifeless as a ragdoll when his trainer propped him up.

Barry saw the worry on the face of a man he knew only as Al. A second-generation black Londoner, of Nigerian descent, Al was an agent and a fixer who looked after all the African fighters who came to London. Al and two other men had reached the ring. They held a table that they had brought in from the back of the room. They had folded away the legs so that it resembled a stretcher.

'Come on, Barry,' Eastwood said, 'let's get out of their way.'

Barry climbed out of the ring and walked towards the dressing room. He turned back to see what was happening. Young Ali was stretched out on the table. He was utterly still.

'They'll look after him in hospital,' Eastwood reassured him. 'Don't worry.'

Barry felt better in the dressing room. Hugh Russell was shadow-boxing and looking totally unconcerned. 'Well done, Barry,' he said.

'Thanks, mate,' Barry said. 'Good luck.'

Barry stepped into the showers as Hugh walked to the ring. The cascading water eased his tension and he told himself that Eastwood was right. Young Ali would soon be well again.

Fate took a different tack. While Russell outpointed Shaw over eight rounds, Ali was taken to the wrong hospital. He needed immediate neurological attention and so the ambulance had to turn round and, with its siren blaring, race to the correct hospital. Over an hour had passed since Ali had been knocked out. His chances of avoiding brain damage had reduced drastically.

Barry watched the last two rounds of Hugh's routine victory and then hung around afterwards until everyone was ready to return to the Piccadilly Hotel. He slept fitfully that night, wondering if Ali was recovering and hoping that they would hear good news in the morning.

There was nothing more than a brief message from the British Boxing Board of Control to say that Ali was still in hospital when Eastwood called just after breakfast.

'He'll be okay,' Eastwood said. 'They're just monitoring him.'

They had a plane to catch back to Belfast and so there was no option but to head for Heathrow. Barry just wanted to get back to Sandra, who was pregnant with their first child. He would be himself again as soon as he was with Sandy.

The days passed slowly and there was little news. It was only late the following week when Eastwood received the shattering blow. Young Ali remained in hospital after the surgeons in London had operated on him. They had discovered a bleed on his brain and to ease the pressure they had cut open his skull and removed the sub-dural haematoma. Barry had never heard the medical phrase before, though it would haunt him for decades. In a new century, he would learn a great deal about brain injuries caused by blows to the head but, in the summer of 1982, he had to ask Eastwood what he meant.

'They say it's like a kind of blood clot on the brain.'

'I caused that?'

'You can't be thinking like that,' Eastwood said reasonably.

Barry shook his head. He could feel the tears rising. 'Is he going to be all right?'

'I don't know,' Eastwood said simply. 'It seems as if the operation did not go too well.'

Barry walked away. He needed to see Dermot. His brother

listened intently while Barry told him the bare outline of what he knew.

'It sounds like he might die,' Barry said. He shook his head as the tears streamed down his face. 'I did it to him.'

Barry cried silently, his mouth crumpling into a tight little ball as if he wanted to stop himself from howling out loud.

'You can't blame yourself,' Dermot said.

'I do,' Barry said through a broken sob. 'I don't want to box again.'

Three months passed, and as the seasons turned, Barry refused to return to the ring. He could not bear the thought of hurting another fighter. Young Ali had been flown back to Nigeria but the hospital prognosis was bleak. He remained in a deep coma. Barry's resolve had been hardened by the revelation that Ali's wife was pregnant. He felt tormented by the irony that he and his stricken opponent were both due to become fathers. It seemed unlikely the Nigerian baby would ever hear a father's voice.

Sandra had handed in her notice as a hairdresser after their wedding and she and Barry's sister, Sharon, had started their own salon. But it took time to grow the business and she was heavily pregnant. 'We'll be all right,' Sandra reassured him. She wanted to take away his worry about money when his heart was set against boxing. Barry's anguish did not ease. The larger Sandra's belly grew, the more he also realised that, without boxing, he had no obvious way of supporting her and the baby.

'Boxing is what you're best at,' Dermot reminded him.

Barry looked down at his hands. He hated their deadly impact. But he trusted Dermot, and Sandra, and so his mind turned over the options amid the sadness. If he did not box again, how could he make the kind of money he would earn if he continued working and fighting so hard? Barry rested his hands on Sandra's swollen belly and then leant down to kiss her tummy and their unborn child. Sandra pulled Barry towards her and held him for a long time.

On 25 August 1982, Barry and Sandra McGuigan's first son,

Blain, was born. A week later, amid the joy, a decision was made. 'I've spoken to Barney,' Barry told Sandra, kissing her head while she held their baby. 'I'm going down to Castle Street tomorrow.'

He could not say the words 'boxing' or 'gym' quite yet. But, at the age of 21, it was time to face his greatest test.

In late September 1982, a week before Barry McGuigan would make his comeback on a bill headlined by a compelling and dramatic fight between Davy Larmour and Hugh Russell, their old trainer waited in his usual old hut just outside the cages of the Maze. Gerry Storey kept thinking of all his fighters – about poor grief-stricken Barry, and the bout between wee Hugh and wee Davy. A headline fight between a Catholic boxer and a Protestant fighter had already begun to transfix Belfast. Gerry knew he would not go to the Ulster Hall that coming Tuesday, 5 October. It was best for both Davy and Hugh that he kept his distance from a contest that he thought would be bloody and savage.

A mizzling rain fell outside in the gathering gloom of that late Thursday afternoon. Gerry looked at the faces all around him. As he scanned the mugshots, putting a human being to each face he knew, the same word echoed in his head: *Life . . . Life . . . Life.*

Some of the lifers he trained were as young as 19. They were so youthful and yet it felt as if their lives were already over. There were older faces on the wall, men he had come to almost admire, like Gusty Spence, but most of the boys he worked with were just kids. Gerry could have cried as he stared at the waste of life.

He felt no better when the bus arrived. Instead of chatting away as usual to the driver, he gazed at the steady drizzle falling across the cages and H-blocks. The driver sensed Gerry's changed mood and drove them silently towards the exit. Each massive gate opened and closed with a scrape of metal and the heavy thudding clank of a key turning in a lock. The slamming of one gate after another locked Gerry even more tightly inside himself. As he drove slowly home towards New Lodge, he could not shake the despair he felt for all the lifers, on both sides, and all the people they had hurt so terribly on the outside.

At home he got ready to go back out to the Holy Family that evening, to train his innocent young boxers, while Belle prepared dinner for all six of them. His sons Gerry Jr and Sam, both fine fighters, would accompany him to the Holy Family. Sam, in particular, was a star boxer. He was on the path to a place in Ireland's 1984 Olympic squad, and a future professional career as a world championship contender. Gerry would be there to guide him. But that night, as he sat quietly over his dinner, hardly eating, Belle spoke sharply: 'Gerry, where are you?'

Her husband looked up in surprise. Belle recognised the faraway look that had replaced his typical crinkly grin. She knew the answer before Gerry even replied.

'You're still in there, aren't you?' she said softly.

Gerry nodded. Belle was right. He had begun to dread going into the Maze every Tuesday and Thursday. He liked the men, and the work filled him with immense pride. But the cages made him feel like a prisoner.

'You're a good man, Gerry,' Belle said, 'but you can't stay in the Maze for ever. We need you out here.'

CHAPTER 13

A Bloody Battle

Davy Larmour's car idled outside the Lansdowne Hotel on the Antrim Road. There was just a week left before the biggest fight of his life, but one last night of taxi driving would help pay the month-end bills. He could then give everything to his final week of preparation before stepping into the ring against Hugh Russell on 5 October 1982. This was the fight Davy had been waiting for his whole career.

It was nearly midnight and he felt a bone-deep weariness. He had worked all day as a stager for Harland and Wolff, erecting scaffolding needed to build new naval boats or to carry out repairs on ships that had been at sea for months. Davy had been hoisted high in the air, fitting heavy scaffolding while a cold wind whipped off the water. He knew it was dangerous but, tethered with ropes and harnesses, he felt safer on the towering scaffolds than he did in his car at night. In the taxi game an edgy uncertainty lurked just beneath the surface. He could pick up a paramilitary or simply run into trouble while taking someone home.

Davy wanted one more fare from the Lansdowne and then he could finish and head home. While he waited for a customer to stagger out of the hotel in search of a taxi, his mind drifted to

Russell and his big night. He had headlined a boxing bill at the Ulster Hall before – most recently in May 1980, when he beat Isaac Vega while Charlie Nash featured as the main support. But that had been a low-key bill without the hype of his clash with Russell.

Barney Eastwood knew it was the biggest fight in Belfast since John Caldwell and Freddie Gilroy had staged a bloody and epic bantamweight battle at the King's Hall in October 1962. Caldwell, from the Falls Road, and Gilroy, with a fanatical following in Ardoyne, were Catholic fighters, former Olympic teammates, and rivals. In the words of Jack Magowan of the *Belfast Telegraph*, 'they went at each other like alley cats' and reduced the crowd to 'gibbering, uncontrolled hysteria'.

Exactly 20 years later, Eastwood knew Belfast was ready for a momentous showdown in the ring between a Catholic and a Protestant. He was certain a sold-out crowd would rise above sectarian strife and lose itself in a ferocious contest. There was still a real risk because 66 people had been killed by paramilitary groups or the army in the first nine months of 1982. Eastwood's instinct was to trust the boxing fervour of Belfast and the respect both communities had for each fighter. Larmour was well known in New Lodge and other Republican areas; Russell had fought on the Shankill Road and was seen often in Loyalist Belfast while working as a trainee photographer for the *Irish News*.

Davy was neither a jealous nor a bitter man. But he was overdue the opportunities that McGuigan and Russell had been feasting on for more than two years. Russell had his Olympic medal and an unbeaten professional record of 8–0. McGuigan was still reeling from the Young Ali fight, but Davy – who sparred often with him at the Castle Street gym – knew the young featherweight was destined for world title fights. McGuigan's brilliance was obvious.

Eastwood's patronage also meant McGuigan and Russell were plastered all over the Belfast papers every week. They were the special guests at beauty pageants like Miss Lovely Legs or at civic functions. Their avoidance of sectarian bias meant they were in demand across Belfast. Sponsors and fans clamoured to be near them and, more importantly, they fought often. Russell had boxed eight times in ten months; McGuigan 12 times in 17 months.

Davy's two measly fights in the last two years had both been in London. He had lost controversially to Dave Smith in Southwark in March 1981 and, with Paddy Maguire spurring him on in the corner, got back on track against Ivor Jones at the Albert Hall in April 1982. After the first round, with Jones bullying him with his elbows and head, Davy took an even bigger crack when he sat down on his little stool. Paddy slapped him hard in the face.

'What's that for?' Davy asked in angry surprise.

'To fucking wake you up,' Paddy shouted. 'Start fighting.'

Davy outboxed Jones for the rest of the fight, winning an easy decision on points. 'See?' Paddy said with a grin afterwards. 'The hardest punch you took all night came from me!'

Davy's record was patchy: nine victories and five defeats. He knew Eastwood regarded him as a washed-up 30-year-old who only deserved a headline fight because his Protestant background drew such a stark contrast with the 22-year-old unbeaten Catholic, Little Red. Davy believed there would be no room for market-ability when he started smacking Russell in the face. It would just be the two of them between the ropes. Davy would pour all his frustration into the fight. He was determined to finally feel some sunshine in the ring.

A young woman came tottering out of the Lansdowne on high heels. She wore an expensive coat and lots of make-up, but he could tell she was just an ordinary Belfast girl. He wound down his window and confirmed he was for hire.

'Would you take us to New Lodge, mister?' the woman asked. She had no idea of Davy's background, but most Protestant drivers would refuse to enter Republican territory.

'No problem,' Davy said without telling her he was from the Shankill. There was no point making her twitchy. She said she would be back in two minutes with her friends.

At the end of a night of drinking Davy knew two minutes could stretch to 20. He waited patiently. As long as they didn't vomit in the back of his car, or pull a gun on him, he would be happy. He got lucky. They rolled out and were inside his car in five minutes. The man who slipped into the passenger seat next to him gave him the street name.

'Near the Star Boxing Club?' Davy asked.

'You know it?'

'I've been there many times.'

The men in the car chattered away to each other and the woman. Davy became an invisible taxi driver again, his face lost in the shadows and only occasionally lit up when they passed a yellow street light. He wondered what they might say if they knew he was fighting the pride of New Lodge, Hugh Russell, the following Tuesday. But Davy was content in his silence.

'Listen, pal,' the man next to him said as they neared the end of their seven-mile journey from the Antrim Road, 'could you do us a favour after you drop me and the boys off?'

'What might that be?' Davy asked.

'We'll pay our fare but could you take the young lady up to the Shankill Road?'

Davy sighed in relief. He thought they might have been about to ask him to let them off the fare or, more ominously, to deliver a package to an unknown address. He would have refused but he was glad to avoid any aggravation. 'That's no problem,' he said.

They paid him as soon as he pulled up outside the Star Boxing Club. Davy then asked the young woman to get in the passenger seat next to him. He didn't want to be given a hard time by the army. It was best they looked as routine as possible.

After she had said goodbye to her friends the woman joined Davy up front. They fell into an easy conversation and Davy asked her why she was heading to the Shankill.

'I live there,' she said. She could tell that Davy knew she was a Catholic and so she added an explanation. 'My husband's from there.'

Davy nodded. As long as you were happy with each other, he thought, what difference did your religious background make? Nothing.

'Are you okay going up to the Shankill at night?' the woman asked.

'Aye,' Davy said with a smile, realising that she had not guessed he was a Protestant. 'How long have you been married?'

'A couple of years,' the woman said before pausing, unsure if she should continue. 'I'm married to a fella called James Craig.'

'Jimmy Craig?'

The woman laughed wryly. She knew her husband, a Loyalist paramilitary and a gangster, struck fear across many quarters of Belfast. 'Most people have heard of him.'

'I know Jimmy very well,' Davy said.

'Really?' the woman said in surprise.

'I used to spar on the Crumlin Road with Paddy Maguire. Jimmy was often there. He liked watching the boxing.'

'Jimmy loves boxing,' she said. She was interested in Davy now. 'What's your name?'

'Davy Larmour.'

'The boxer?'

He grunted, and then smiled. 'The boxer – and your taxi driver.'

'Aren't you fighting soon?'

'On the fifth … against Hugh Russell.'

The woman had seen posters all across Belfast. She and Jimmy would be rooting for him.

Davy had just spotted a roadblock. 'They're going to stop us,' he said, pointing to the soldiers moving into view. 'Don't tell them this is a taxi. I'm just giving you a lift.'

He slowed as they reached the security checkpoint. A soldier shone a torch into the car and asked for Davy's ID and their destination.

'Just off the Shankill Road,' Davy said. 'I'm giving my friend a ride home. And then I'm onto my place in Glengormley.'

'Davy Larmour? The boxer?' the soldier said.

'Yes.'

The soldier handed back his papers and waved them through.

'I should have known I was getting a lift with a famous boxer,' the woman said when they pulled up outside her house.

'I'm not as famous as Jimmy.'

'Infamous might be the word.'

Davy laughed. 'Send Jimmy my best.'

'I will, Davy. Good luck next week. Are you going to win?'

'I'm planning on it,' he replied.

Barry McGuigan was back but all the fight talk centred on Russell and Larmour. The Irish, and especially people in Belfast, loved a good fight. But a good fight with a sectarian edge made it even more meaningful. It fitted the old Belfast adage: put a good Catholic and a good Protestant in the same ring and you've got yourself a sold-out venue.

Hugh Russell didn't care about his religious differences with Larmour. He wouldn't carry a crucifix into the ring and Davy wouldn't bring in an orange banner. They were just fighters, and Hugh knew Davy was tough and determined. He would have liked to ask Gerry Storey for his advice on how best to plan for the fight. Yet he would never put his old trainer on the spot – and, anyway, Gerry would insist on being scrupulously fair and not favour him over Davy. Hugh was now trained, like McGuigan, by Eddie Shaw.

Hugh knew Larmour thought everything had come much more easily to him. But nothing was easy if you came from the New Lodge. Hugh was also blighted by the fact he could have dominated at strawweight. The 112-pound mark would be a beast to reach, but he could do it and he would have been the strongest little man in the fight game. Even at flyweight, 115 pounds, Hugh was too powerful at domestic level. But he could not get many fights and so he had to fight mostly at bantamweight, where Larmour was comfortable at 118 pounds.

Hugh still looked cherubic with his round, freckly face, full lips and curly ginger perm. But he was a real fighter and ready to go to war with Larmour. He knew they would give Belfast the fight it had been craving for decades. After all the years of the city being like a ghost town, scarred by violence and death, he and Larmour would give them something to cheer about. Only a few Irish singers and pop groups, such as Chris de Burgh and Thin Lizzy, dared visit Belfast in the early 1980s. It was time Belfast saw stars of a different kind – little sparks of explosive hitting that Russell planned on landing on Larmour. He would have to hit Larmour many times, and hard, to dent his drive. He also knew he would be hit and hurt himself, but he was going to prove himself tougher than anyone thought.

At the weigh-in on the morning of the fight, Larmour was the bigger man. He stepped on the scales and was bang on the bantamweight limit of 118 pounds. Wee Hugh Russell ate more than he normally would in the week of a fight and scaled 116 and a half pounds. They shook hands, posed for the photographers and then broke apart. They were tense, but ready.

Barry McGuigan sustained himself by visiting the Poor Clare nuns of the Cliftonville Road in Belfast. He asked them to pray for Young Ali, stretched out in deep unconsciousness in a hospital bed in Lagos, Nigeria. He prayed with them, too, for Jimmy Duncan, his next opponent.

Afterwards, as they sat together in the nunnery and drank tea, Barry admitted his guilt towards Young Ali and expressed concern that a similar tragedy might occur again. The nuns were kind and helped the 21-year-old fighter feel a little better. They knew he had not meant to cause any harm and they advised him to let God guide him. They encouraged him to keep fighting. Just as they had a calling to serve God, so did he, as a boxer. Barry promised them that if he ever won a world title he would dedicate it to Young Ali.

He asked Father Brian D'Arcy to be with him in the dressing

room at the Ulster Hall. The Catholic priest sat with the hard-hitting young boxer and tried to reassure him that God would protect him and his opponent. He also suggested they pray together. It was a prayer that Barry had learnt as a child in Clones and he found it strangely comforting as they murmured the words together in the stark dressing room, just minutes before he walked to the ring:

Angel of God, my Guardian dear, to whom God's love commits me here; Ever this day, be at my side, to light and guard, to rule and guide.

Barry thanked Father D'Arcy and stood up to lead Eddie Shaw, Paddy Byrne, Barney Eastwood and his brother Dermot to the ring. As he walked into battle he repeated the prayer quietly to himself, over and over.

Ulster Hall, Belfast, Tuesday 5 October 1982

The tough little featherweight in the blue trunks bounced up and down on the turquoise canvas, lost in a dance of his own, before lifting his arms happily when he was introduced by the MC to the Ulster Hall: 'Ladies and gentlemen . . . weighing 126 pounds, from Liverpool, Jimmy Duncan!' The Belfast crowd offered respectful applause to the visitor. They knew it had taken courage for an Englishman to fight in Belfast.

There was no need for any grand flourish in his introduction of the home favourite and so the MC made a simple shout: 'And on my left, also weighing 126 pounds, is Barry McGuigan!'

There was no need to say he was from Clones any more. McGuigan belonged to all of them. He lifted his arms briefly in recognition of the roar that greeted him.

They were brought together to the centre of the ring by referee Bob McMillan. McGuigan kept his gaze fixed on Duncan, willing himself to make eye contact even if he wanted to just look away and be elsewhere. He was dressed in sober black, his skin ghostly beneath his dark hair. Duncan kept staring at him, rolling his neck, making it plain he believed in himself. He was a contender, having won six out of his seven fights, and the winner would be in prime position to push for a shot at the British featherweight title.

At the first bell, Duncan came at McGuigan with intent. He was an awkward, compact opponent who often ducked down so that he was almost fighting out of a crouch, making him difficult to hit. At the same time, he swarmed towards McGuigan, throwing flurries of blows. McGuigan was much smoother, gliding away from most punches, but he lacked his typical fire in an even opening round.

The ring-card girl ducked through the ropes while the fighters were sponged down by their jabbering corners. She was dressed in white shorts, a white long-sleeved top advertising Smirnoff vodka on the back, and red high heels. Looking embarrassed as she held up the card for round two, she made no effort to milk the applause or smile at the whistles. She wanted to be out of the ring as much as McGuigan did.

Duncan was the aggressor in the second and backed McGuigan into a corner after he had been clipped by a long left. It had been a good punch from McGuigan but he lacked the mean attitude to follow it up. Duncan had taken the initiative, but McGuigan deflected most of the punches. McGuigan landed a few decent digs to the body but his work was sporadic, as if he was questioning himself constantly. It was only at the end of the round that he finally let loose some fast combinations. Duncan took the punches well but the referee intervened. The Liverpudlian was cut over the eye and the ref brought him back to the corner. They wiped down his face, cleared the cut and were about to send him back to work when the bell rang.

As if to prove his eye was not troublesome, Duncan came after McGuigan fiercely at the start of the third. McGuigan preferred to concentrate on his body-punching. It felt important to avoid

Duncan's head as images from the Young Ali fight still drifted into his mind. His work downstairs began to make an impression and Duncan wilted. McGuigan nailed him with a left hook and there was a clear tremor in Duncan's legs.

Seeing vulnerability in Duncan, McGuigan paused. He was afraid of causing lasting damage to his opponent. Two seconds passed and then Duncan, showing the vicious instinct McGuigan lacked, threw a left hook. This was the punch that always caused McGuigan problems and he felt the force of the blow down to the soles of his boots. He realised Duncan could knock him out if he didn't fight back. McGuigan fired a left hook of his own. But Duncan, heartened by that momentary hesitation in McGuigan, landed a big right hand.

'What was that about?' Eddie Shaw said in disbelief when McGuigan sat down on his stool.

'Nothing,' McGuigan shrugged.

'Don't fucking do it again!' Shaw shouted. 'Start fighting.'

McGuigan almost ran out of his corner for round four. He kept punching to the body, hurting Duncan and grinding him down. A left hook to the gut dropped Duncan.

McGuigan watched from a neutral corner, willing the fight to be over, but Duncan hauled himself up. The fight continued. McGuigan attacked with force but Duncan fought back valiantly. His bravery was rewarded by applause from an appreciative crowd. Just before the bell, McGuigan caught Duncan with a right to the jaw. The Belfast fans stood up and applauded the best round of the fight.

Shaw used a sponge to flick water into McGuigan's face. 'Much, much better,' Shaw shouted, 'but go out there and finish the job. He's almost gone.'

McGuigan nodded and drank some water before he looked up to a roar. Across the ring, in the opposite corner, Duncan's trainer shook his head and waved his hands again. It was over.

Shaw, Byrne and Eastwood all congratulated him, but McGuigan shook them off. He needed to see Jimmy Duncan. There was a surge of relief when, unlike Young Ali stretched out on the canvas, Duncan walked towards him. The fighters embraced. McGuigan stepped back and praised Duncan's courage and skill while also checking he was fit and well.

'I'm fine, mate,' Duncan said in his Scouse accent. 'You're just too good.'

McGuigan could have kissed him but, instead, he lifted Duncan's hand high in the air. The Ulster Hall cheered both fighters while McGuigan led the applause for Duncan. He finally could smile. God had answered his prayer. They had both survived the fight. Jimmy Duncan would go home, fight again and live for years to come.

The Ulster Hall was so full it felt as if it might burst. Heavy clouds of smoke hung in the air as most of the 1,250 crowd puffed away excitedly while they waited for Russell and Larmour. The acrid smell of cigarettes was so thick it filled the separate dressing rooms where the boxers had their hands wrapped and went through their last warm-up routines.

Davy Larmour had fought at the Ulster Hall dozens of times before. He had won four Senior Ulster titles in this venue and picked up two Boxer of the Year awards here. Even as an ordinary fan, he loved the Ulster Hall. You could feel the crackle of anticipation before a night of boxing from three blocks away. Spectators would chatter loudly about the upcoming bouts. Humour and intensity were trademark features of a night at the Ulster Hall.

There was no room for any wisecracks as Paddy Maguire repeated his instructions. The sight of a beaten Jimmy Duncan drifting down the corridor was another reminder of the seriousness that awaited.

Russell felt on edge. Larmour presented a different challenge to every one of his previous opponents. Eastwood had tried to assure him that Larmour was on the far side of the downward slope – but

Russell knew he was in for a difficult night. He was up against a proud man whom he had admired for years. Russell also knew that the winner was guaranteed a shot at John Feeney's British bantamweight title within the next three months.

The Ulster Hall was crammed. An additional 550 tickets had been sold, illegally, such was the demand to see Russell and Larmour, and the crowd spilled out into the aisles. The fighters had to push their way through the smoky throng, a tunnel of light picking out a path for them as they were cheered all the way to the ring.

Catholics and Protestants were jammed against each other. The ongoing tension and violence between the two communities should have turned the beautiful old Ulster Hall into a tinderbox. Instead, it became a roaring sea of unity; people were bound together by boxing. There was no trouble outside the ring that night, no discord or sectarian chanting, no blood was spilt and no lives were threatened. It was a shimmering miracle in the depths of the Troubles.

It was different, of course, between the ropes. So much blood fell in a savage battle that the referee, Mike Jacobs from London, looked like a butcher working in an abattoir. As Larmour tried to walk down Russell, throwing heavy combinations that were answered by spiteful punches from the slicker and younger man, the blows thudded into skin and bone. Cuts opened and blood spurted, mostly from Russell's eye but also from Larmour. Jacobs wiped the blood off his face after every round while his shirt turned crimson. It looked as if he had been shot in the heart and stabbed above his right breast.

Each corner worked hard to stem the flow of blood, with Eddie Shaw pouring in a cement-like mix of coagulant to close the wide gash above Russell's eye. Larmour would open it again and Russell threw his spearing jab in reply. By the time they reached the end of the ninth, with just three rounds left, Russell and Larmour were level on the scorecards.

He might have been more badly cut, but Russell found new

reserves of energy, and produced a stunning tenth round, only to be met with Larmour's equally determined resolve. The Ulster Hall was enraptured, each telling blow eliciting another roar as the two fighters gave everything of themselves for 12 rounds. At the final bell they hugged, their faces matching each other again through grinning masks of blood. Jacobs wiped his hands one last time on his butcher's apron of a shirt and turned to the red-headed fighter. He lifted Hugh Russell's hand, confirming that he had won the narrowest of victories by 117½ to 116½ points.

Davy Larmour scrunched his face up in disappointment but he congratulated Hugh. He turned back to see Paddy Maguire shaking his head furiously and talking to Barney Eastwood. The trainer told the promoter that his boy had been lucky. Davy deserved a rematch.

'We can do it again,' Eastwood said with a grin as he looked around the Ulster Hall. Everyone was on their feet, applauding, cheering or shouting about it being a battle for the ages.

Davy just wanted to get back to the dressing room and sit down in a quiet corner. He looked over at Hugh one last time and saw his bloodied opponent move towards his mother. Eileen Russell clutched her glasses in her left hand. She had hardly worn them all night as she could not bear to watch her son. Hugh, still in the ring, walked towards her with his arms outstretched as if to tell her he needed his mum. Eileen looked up at him, the belt of his trunks resting against a thick and gnarled rope as he stretched over to reach her.

Brendan Murphy, the great photographer who was Hugh's mentor, sensed the moment. He prepared for a shot that would illuminate the front page of the *Irish News* the following morning. He framed his photograph perfectly so that he caught his battered and bloodied protégé leaning through the ropes to kiss his mother. Love and relief, mingled with tears and horror, were unmistakeable on Eileen's face. Murphy pressed the shutter just before they kissed. He captured the fighter and his mother, bound together by love, in a black-and-white photograph that distilled the gory drama and bruising intimacy of boxing.

Eileen Russell cried as she kissed her son. Hugh looked so tired and vulnerable she wished she could tell him never to fight again. She wanted him to throw away the boxing gloves and pick up his camera for good. But she knew that the urge to fight still pumped in his blood, which kept dripping down onto the turquoise canvas.

'I won,' he said simply as he gazed down at her from the ring.

'Yes, son,' Eileen smiled up at him through her veil of tears. 'You won.'

The loser sat in the corner of his dressing room. Davy sank into the familiar pain as his adrenaline faded. He hurt all over – and in his heart most of all. Paddy was still raging, convinced that Davy had won, but promising him they would get the rematch. They would make sure there were no mistakes next time.

Davy just wanted to get showered and stitched up in hospital. The doctor had already been to see him and said Davy would probably need a dozen stitches.

Davy allowed Paddy to unwrap his hands and untie his boots, removing his sodden socks, in that unique bond a fighter and a trainer share after a vicious encounter. In the shower he watched the blood run from his face, his chest and his legs before it disappeared down the plughole as the water turned red beneath his feet. He lifted his tender face up to the shower and winced. He had come so close to winning. It echoed the story of his career. Davy knew he would have to keep driving his taxi at night while he waited for the rematch.

He felt a little better as he towelled himself dry. Davy had told Paddy he wanted to drive up alone to the Mater Hospital on the Crumlin Road. Quiet time in the car would do him good. Paddy looked dubious but Davy reassured him. The dressing room was silent as Davy pulled on his shoes and socks. His hands were bruised and sore. He had hit Hugh very hard and very often. He was just about to pull on his jacket when there was a sharp knock. A boxing official popped his head around the door.

'Davy, how are you getting up to the hospital?' the man asked.

'I'm driving over to the Mater.'

'You wouldn't take Hugh up?' the official asked. 'He has no way of getting to the hospital.'

'Aye, no problem,' Davy said. 'Tell him to come over when he's ready.'

'Good man,' the official murmured.

Hugh didn't make Davy wait long. They shook hands and Hugh thanked him for the lift.

The streets around the Ulster Hall had emptied and few would have seen two fierce rivals, a Protestant and a Catholic, leave the scene of their epic fight together. When they got to Davy's car, Hugh spoke softly. 'Would you mind if I stretched out in the back? I'm a bit sore.'

'No bother,' Davy said with a small smile. 'I know the feeling.'

Davy knew the route, from all his taxi-driving nights, and it was just under a mile and a half from the Ulster Hall to the Mater. He reversed slowly out of his parking spot and headed north on Bedford Street. He turned left onto Franklin and took the first right at College Square.

It felt strange to be driving again, as if he was back on his taxi beat, and so he looked into the rear-view mirror. He saw Hugh's face, cut and swollen beneath the gauzy street lights.

'How you doing, mate?' he asked.

'I'm okay, Davy,' Hugh said. 'You?'

'I'm sore too. It'll be good to get these stitches out of the way.'

He reckoned Hugh would be needing more than him and so he changed the subject. He said they should avoid any army checkpoints.

'We'll confuse them if they do stop us,' Hugh said with a wry laugh. They imagined the scene if British soldiers stopped a battered Protestant driving a bloodied Catholic to hospital.

Davy drove up Carrick Hill. It helped that he and Hugh had known each other for years. They were not close, as their difference in age separated them, but they were friends.

'I reckon Gerry would have enjoyed tonight,' Davy said as he turned left on Clifton Street and aimed for the Crumlin Road.

'Yeah,' Hugh replied. 'But he wouldn't have wanted us taking so many punches. He'd be having words with both of us.'

They gave their names at the front desk of the Mater Infirmorum and waited. The hospital was not far from the Crumlin Road Gaol and, for once, it was quiet in A&E. A night nurse led them down an echoing corridor. Would they mind seeing the same doctor? Both fighters smiled. They had shared a much more dangerous space in the ring. They were each shown to a bed in the same room. The nurse pulled a screen between them to offer some privacy.

Davy was closest to the door and he had stretched out on the bed and closed his eyes. The pain and the fatigue made him ache now. He knew Hugh felt just as bad.

Eventually, a doctor walked in and came over to the bed. He took a long look at Davy's face. 'Oh my,' he said. 'You've been quite badly hurt. Who did this to you?'

Davy leant across and pushed the screen away. 'He did,' he said with a laugh as he pointed at Hugh who was also spread out, on the adjoining bed.

The doctor's eyes opened wide as he stared at a freckly face that would need many more stitches. 'You might not believe it, doc,' Davy cackled, 'but Hugh won the fight.'

'It looks as if you've both had quite a night,' the doctor murmured.

Davy was examined and needed a dozen stitches to seal his cuts. Hugh's face was even more of a mess. Thirty stitches were threaded through his skin. They had both been through the bloodiest fight of their lives.

A couple of days later, in London, Mike Jacobs went to pick up the shirt he had worn in the ring. It was soaked in so much blood he had taken it to the dry-cleaners. The laundry man had been so shocked when he opened the bag and discovered a shirt stained crimson by blood that he had called the police. He was convinced Jacobs must have murdered someone.

Jacobs was confused when, instead of his shirt, he was handed a letter instructing him to report to the police. The dry-cleaning manager looked away and wouldn't answer his questions and so Jacobs walked to the police station. He was even more bewildered when he was taken into a small room and two CID detectives began to grill him.

When he told them he had been in Belfast they became even more suspicious. His claim that he had refereed a British title fight eliminator seemed highly unlikely. At Jacobs' urging, they agreed to phone the British Boxing board of Control. Eventually, after they had been reassured by the board that Jacobs had indeed been in the middle of a bloody battle between two Belfast bantamweights, an amused policeman released Jacobs. They also returned his bloodied shirt.

'I'd frame it on the wall if I were you,' a detective said. 'That could become a very famous shirt.'

A different kind of phone call floored Barry McGuigan two months later. In December 1982, Barney Eastwood spoke gently but there was no easy way to break the news. The hospital in Lagos had switched off Young Ali's life support machine.

Eastwood knew this was the moment his fighter had dreaded ever since that terrible night in London almost six months before. Barry could hardly speak through the tears. Remorse welled up inside him. His punches, his very fists, had killed Young Ali.

Dermot was soon at his side. 'Don't say that, Barry,' his brother urged. 'You never meant it.'

'I'm sorry,' Barry said, crying helplessly. 'I'm sorry.'

CHAPTER 14

The Body and the Briefcase

Ulster Hall, Belfast, Tuesday 25 January 1983

A fighter is the first to recognise the end and, usually, the last to admit it. Davy Larmour knew before anyone else that his fighting days were fading. He sensed the gathering darkness in the Ulster Hall. There was little he could do as he felt slower and heavier than Dave George, a slick little Welshman who was in the midst of dishing out a hiding to him. Larmour was beaten to the punch again and again as George won four of the first five rounds.

In the corner Paddy Maguire urged Larmour to dredge up the grit he needed. His rematch against Hugh Russell would be ruined if he did not derail the onrushing train of punches.

'Are you going to let Russell off the hook?' Maguire asked angrily, using all the fight psychology he could muster.

Larmour felt the water from Maguire's sponge run down his face and he shook his head – both to answer the question and to clear his mind. He knew he could not fight on much longer. But, after so many unfulfilled years, he needed one great night under the hot lights, against Russell, to feel vindicated. He drew in gulps of air.

The Ulster Hall was as smoky as ever, but Larmour didn't care. He just needed to fill his lungs and heart with fire.

'Show this kid you're so much better than him,' Maguire said, jabbing his thumb accusingly at the 23-year-old George.

Larmour, according to the official British boxing records, would turn 29 in less than three months. But he would actually be 31 that April. On the advice of his first promoter, Gerry Hassett, he had shaved two years off his age when he became a pro. Hassett had believed, wrongly, that Davy would get more fights by claiming to be younger. The truth remained that all his years of work in the docks and driving his taxi late at night had left their mark.

Maguire applied thick swathes of Vaseline above Larmour's swollen eyebrows. Davy swallowed one last slug of water. He turned to Maguire and opened his mouth. The trainer shoved in his gumshield.

Larmour bit down on his mouthpiece and lifted himself from the stool. He banged his gloves together. George, flowing with confidence and expecting the pattern of the fight to remain unchanged, took charge of the centre of the ring. Larmour met him and opened round six with a barrage of punches. The hurtful blows surprised George. He stepped back, but Larmour kept after him. His powerful arms moved like pistons, fists thudding into George's body before he switched to the head. The ferocity was new.

The tide of the fight had not only turned – it now surged in waves against George. He struggled not to be overwhelmed, holding onto Larmour to stay on his feet. But Larmour pushed him back and resumed his attack, clubbing George repeatedly until the Welshman slid to the canvas. The fight was over. Davy Larmour could dream of his rematch again.

'Did ya see that?' Maguire yelled to Barney Eastwood at ringside.

Maguire jerked his thumb at the crowd. 'And did ya see what they thought of Davy Larmour?' People stood and cheered Larmour as he consoled his bewildered opponent.

Eastwood grinned and nodded. Maguire shouted again: 'Don't forget that promise you made, Barney. We want that rematch.'

Hugh Russell faced a more difficult examination. There would be no immediate rematch with Larmour if he was beaten badly in his first British title fight against the bantamweight champion John Feeney in the headline bout. Feeney was a skilled stylist who regarded Russell as little more than a flyweight. He thought two weight divisions would be too much for Russell to cross.

Davy knew a different truth. He had fought Russell at bantamweight and had learnt the hard way that the wee man they called Little Red had a massive fighting heart. Yet Feeney had won 25 of his 30 fights as a pro and he was still only 24, just a year older than Russell. He was fit and tough and the best fighter Russell had faced. But Davy, fuelled by feelings of hope and redemption, believed in the Holy Family man. He thought Russell might shock Feeney in the last 15-round British title bout before all future title fights were reduced to 12 rounds.

Davy showered quickly so he could cheer on his rival from ringside. He pulled on his clothes and, with his hair still damp, ploughed through the throng of Belfast fans who wanted to shake his hand and slap his back. His own fight had been a small ordeal, but he now needed Russell to produce the best performance of his career to seal their rematch.

At ringside, Larmour offered vociferous support. It became plain that his unstinting backing for Hugh was not just motivated by personal ambition. His desire for a Russell victory was rooted in their shared bond as Belfast fighters. All their differences melted away and he just saw a fellow Ulster boxer, raised in the same Holy Family gym where Davy had prospered under Gerry Storey, and he shouted even louder: 'C'mon, Hugh!'

Russell fought cannily and Feeney found it difficult to tag him. The challenger was far quicker and kept picking off rounds while Feeney was warned for using his head. Russell was not a concussive puncher but, fighting as a southpaw, he was effective.

Feeney landed the odd heavy blow but Russell did not buckle. It was still a close and absorbing contest when, in the 13th round, a frustrated Feeney headbutted Little Red yet again. He had been warned repeatedly and the referee, Sid Nathan, disqualified him. Feeney's protests were muted – in contrast to the wild celebrations that engulfed the Ulster Hall.

Hugh Russell was the new British bantamweight champion in just his 12th bout. The belt, once held by Paddy Maguire, was back in Belfast. In a crammed dressing room, Maguire pushed his way through the crowd to find Barney Eastwood. The two men liked each other, but Maguire would not go easy on the promoter.

'You're keeping your word, Barney,' Maguire said.

'I'll keep my word,' a beaming Eastwood said.

'So Davy will get his rematch – and a shot at the title?'

Eastwood nodded. 'We'll take it to the King's Hall.'

'Now you're talking,' Maguire growled. The King's Hall, which had not been used for boxing since the famous Caldwell–Gilroy fight in 1962, would be packed with 9,000 fans.

Eastwood offered his hand to seal the agreement. Maguire clasped the promoter's hand and said one urgent word: 'When?'

'Soon,' Eastwood grunted.

'We want it now, Barney,' Maguire said. 'Belfast wants it now.'

Davy woke just after seven o'clock on the morning of 2 March 1983. As soon as he opened his eyes his empty gut and parched mouth were stark reminders that yet another weigh-in loomed, followed by yet another fight. A mere 36 days had passed since he and Hugh Russell had won their contrasting fights in the ring. It was hard to believe Paddy Maguire had got his wish so soon. They would meet again at the King's Hall that night.

Starting with his punishing battle against Davy in October 1982, it would be Hugh's fifth fight in less than five months. He had stepped into the ring twice more than Davy in that time, beating George Bailey and Juan Rodriguez before he faced Feeney. Hugh had a glittering reason for wanting to win another title fight, for he and Davy agreed that the Lonsdale Belt was the prettiest prize in boxing.

A 22-carat gold belt, containing an enamel medallion featuring a small painting of a boxing match in its centre and inscribed with the names of its winners, the Lonsdale Belt had first been awarded to a British champion in 1909. It had since assumed a gravitas in British boxing that, for men like Davy and Hugh, almost matched a world title. Any champion involved in three successful British title bouts becomes the owner of his own Lonsdale Belt. Hugh knew that if he could beat Davy again he would need only one more winning defence of his title to be awarded a Lonsdale Belt for permanent keeping. His desire to reach that goal was so strong that he signed for the immediate rematch with Larmour.

Hugh thought it would be easier to beat Davy the second time round. He was fitter, younger and on a roll of victories. He had not forgotten his 30 stitches from their first fight, but Hugh was convinced Davy could not summon that same intensity. Davy carried a bleaker conviction. He was ready to die before losing again to Russell.

Davy kept out of the kitchen while his wife, Ellie, made breakfast for her and the kids. There was no point being in smelling distance of food when he would not be able to eat or drink until after the 1pm weigh-in. He looked at himself in the mirror. He was gaunt and almost skeletal. The battle to make weight seemed harder with each new fight.

He followed his usual pre-fight ritual and, after everyone else had finished their breakfast, Davy and his eldest son, ten-year-old David, left for the gym. It would be easier passing the slow hours before he could eat again in the company of his closest allies. Father and son were quiet as they left Glengormley in Davy's night-time taxi. Davy drove them deep into Belfast, passing the usual checkpoints and burnt-out cars, the rumbling Saracens and the barricades.

The Troubles ground on year after year but Davy thought only of how many of these roads he had run along in training while wearing his American marine boots and plastic sweat gear under his hooded tracksuit. He knew the roads so well, having shed so much sweat and pain on them, that he could remember some of the cracks still visible in the tarmac. For eight years, since 1975, he had run the same route, criss-crossing Loyalist and Republican terrain, slogging down the Crumlin Road, passing Ardoyne, turning right onto Twaddell Avenue and jogging to the West Circular junction where he turned left and headed for Paisley Park.

Davy was back at this point, in his car, with his son, on the day of the biggest fight of his life. He drove slowly down the track that led to the Albert Foundry Boxing Club. Davy had been skipping and sparring, hitting the speed ball and the heavy bag in this gym for over 20 years, since he was a boy of ten – now the age of his son. It was as if everything he had worked towards for so long would culminate in one last big night in the ring.

Paddy Maguire, Harry Robinson from the Albert Foundry, and Davy's brother John were waiting for him. 'Here he is,' Harry shouted out. 'Did you get some sleep, Davy?'

'Aye,' Davy said. 'I slept fine.'

Paddy was all business. 'I hope you weren't on the Cokes last night?' he said with a grim little smile before he gave his first order of the day. 'Get stripped and get on them scales.'

'Good morning to you as well,' Davy replied dryly.

Davy took off his shoes, his socks, all his clothes and even his underpants. There was no room for modesty in his struggle with the scales. He shivered a little as he stood on the icy metal plate, its coldness rising up through his bare feet and making his legs tremble. He felt light and spacey while Harry fiddled with the balance arm on the measuring mark. Paddy fretted anxiously, thinking Davy was over the bantamweight limit.

'No, Paddy, you're wrong,' Harry reassured him.

Davy was bang on the limit. 'Eight stone six,' Paddy exclaimed. 'Brilliant!'

After Davy had dressed and they hung around chatting for an hour, Paddy said they should walk the two miles to the Europa Hotel. 'It'll do you good,' he told Davy. 'And it will keep your mind off grub.'

Davy was starving. His cheeks were sunken hollows and his stomach an empty cave. Even his head felt airy as if it had been punched full of holes. Only a fighter would understand how he felt in these low hours before the weigh-in. At least he was lifted by people shouting out good luck or by cars beeping him in recognition as they made the long walk to Great Victoria Street.

Davy knew that many reporters from around the world used the Europa as a base while they reported on the Troubles. Most of the newspapermen he could see now were familiar faces from the Belfast boxing beat. There were also many radio and TV journalists and production staff and hundreds of ordinary fans who had taken an early lunch to watch two hungry fighters try to make weight.

They found a corner of the lobby and Paddy led Davy to a seat. 'You're going to win tonight,' Paddy said quietly.

'I know,' Davy replied. He also knew he would feel better once he had been fed and watered.

He was soon whisked away to do a round of TV and radio interviews where the same questions were put to him again and again. How did he feel? Would he change tactics for the rematch? Would Russell's youth be a decisive factor? What did he think of fighting in the historic King's Hall? Would he win? Could Belfast expect another classic fight?

Davy was positive in all his answers and, to the last query, he always answered with the same words: 'It's going to be a cracking fight.'

Russell and his entourage had also arrived and they were being interviewed on the opposite side of the ballroom where the weigh-in was being staged. If Russell was quiet, the champion's promoter, Barney Eastwood, and cutman, Paddy Byrne, were boisterous. It seemed to Davy as if they were trying to introduce some American-style razzmatazz to the promotion even though the King's Hall had sold all 9,000 seats weeks earlier.

Davy felt a tap on his shoulder. 'Right, this is it,' Paddy murmured. 'Let's go.'

At the side of the stage Davy stripped down to his trunks. After all his talking his mouth felt dry. The MC for the weigh-in boomed into his microphone: 'First to the scales for this British bantamweight title fight, the challenger … *Davy Larmour!*'

Raucous cries of 'C'mon, Davy son!' and chants of 'Lar-mour! Lar-mour!' broke out.

On the scales the balance arm quivered once Davy stood on the metal base. Byrne, playing the part of Russell's chief cheerleader, shouted out: 'You're overweight!'

Byrne had moved to the very front as he pointed to the marker that skittered over the eight-stone-seven mark.

'The scales are wrong,' Davy said coolly, knowing that he would have lost weight rather than put on an extra pound after his two-mile walk from the gym.

A member of the British Boxing Board of Control asked Davy to move aside so that he could check the scales. After he had tweaked the balancing arm, he asked Davy to step back up.

Davy looked down in relief as the MC confirmed his weight: 'Davy Larmour weighs in at eight stone five and three-quarter pounds.'

He was a quarter of a pound under the bantamweight limit. It showed how close Davy was to being completely drained because his long walk and continuing lack of food and water should have knocked off at least a pound. But the nightmare was over. He accepted a bottle of water and drank it greedily while Russell stepped onto the scales.

'The champion, Hugh Russell, weighs in at eight stone three and a half pounds,' the MC announced.

Davy and Paddy exchanged glances. Russell was two and a half pounds under the limit.

'He's way too light,' Paddy said. 'He'll not have the strength to keep you off.'

Davy was more interested in eating. Paddy led the way as Davy and his brother and son, John and David, headed for a café on Queen Street. Davy ordered egg and chips and a large glass of cold milk. He noticed how David looked tired and queasy. It was far harder being the son of a boxer than the fighter himself.

By the time they got back to the Albert Foundry and he picked up his car, Davy was ready for bed. He just had time to have a cup of tea with Ellie while David and his younger son Steven sat with them in the living room.

'Are you all right, Davy?' Ellie said anxiously.

'Aye, I'm grand,' Davy nodded. 'I just need some sleep. Could you wake me at six?'

Two hours later, after he had slept deeply, Ellie woke him. 'It's six o'clock, Davy,' she whispered. 'Time to get up.'

Davy opened his eyes. He watched Ellie moving about the dim room, switching on a small bedside lamp and making sure all his clothes and kit were laid out ready for him to pack. It was not a perfect marriage, but Davy appreciated the way in which Ellie never tried to persuade him to walk away from the ring. He knew his wife did not like him fighting. She had only ever watched one of his bouts as a pro and, from the ring, Davy had seen how she covered her face for most of the fight.

Boxing was his business and Ellie trusted him not to take any unnecessary chances, despite the dangers. Her business was looking after the family and she never complained once to him that she was tired of her work or wanted a break. She patted him lightly on the arm as he lay in bed for a minute more. They both knew it would soon be time for his own serious work to begin. After a shower he dressed and went downstairs for some of Ellie's scrambled eggs and toast. It was all he could stomach this close to a fight.

Paddy and John arrived in a blur of movement and noise to pick up Davy. The little trainer, was buzzing with nervous energy and, when Davy and Ellie took a while to pack his fight bag, Paddy barged up the stairs.

'What are youse two doing?' he shouted, worried Davy and his wife had slipped into bed.

Davy walked to the top of the stairs. 'Packing my gear. What did you think?'

He wasn't sure if Ellie or Paddy blushed a deeper shade of red. It was good to share a laugh with his brother at Paddy's expense.

Davy was more sober when saying goodbye to Ellie.

'Good luck, Davy,' she said, remembering how her husband had ended up in the Mater the last time he fought Russell.

'It's going to be fine,' he said. 'Don't worry.'

Davy walked down the stairs, hugged his sons and turned to Paddy. 'Let's go,' he said.

King's Hall, Belfast, Wednesday 2 March 1983

A mile from the famous old venue they began to see small crowds of people walking together along the dusky pavements. It looked as if they were heading for a football match rather than a fight. The strangeness of a Protestant and a Catholic fighting, in front of a crowd that mixed supporters from both sides of the divide, rose up inside Davy all over again. Gerry Storey had been right all those years ago. Boxing, for all its brutality and danger, was a force for good.

The crowds thickened the closer they came to the King's Hall, with fight fans pouring in from the Shankill and the Falls Road. People seemed good-humoured and excited.

As they drove past the main entrance on the Lisburn Road they saw how the King's Hall was lit up both inside and out. The grand old building looked beautiful. They turned off at the next exit and found the Balmoral Golf Club. Security guards blocked their entrance, but as soon as they shone their torches into the car someone shouted: 'Oh, Davy Larmour! In you come ...'

Paddy led them to a set of double doors at the back. He hammered against them and shouted 'It's Davy Larmour!' until they opened up.

Davy's team was ushered to a long room at the rear of the venue. This was to be the makeshift dressing room for both Larmour and Russell.

'We'll take this end,' Paddy said, gesturing to the right-hand side of the room. 'Russell can take the other side.'

The cutman, Joe Glelland, laid out all his equipment while John and Harry set up camp. Davy found a stool and his mind settled on the fight. He thought again that Hugh Russell would have to kill him to win tonight. And he would not allow that to happen.

Paddy knelt down in front of Davy. He spoke in an unusually soft and sympathetic voice: 'How do you feel?'

'I'm okay,' Davy replied.

Paddy, who remembered those same feelings from his own career, winked at him.

Russell and his team arrived and, in their wake, the reporters followed. They all passed the Larmour camp, occasionally saying a muted hello, and gravitated towards Russell and, especially, Barney Eastwood. Davy didn't care. They would all want to talk to him after he won – and he realised again how much he loved the nerve-jangling rush of adrenaline coursing through him. He felt more alive when waiting for a fight than at any stage of his life.

He was so immersed in his own thoughts that the rituals of preparing, of changing and wrapping his hands and limbering up, reeled past. Occasionally he looked over at Russell. He was also lost in his own world. As the noise of the crowd during the preliminary bouts seeped into their room, it was as if they were ancient gladiators getting ready to fight in a baying arena.

'Right,' Paddy said abruptly. 'It's time to go to work.'

The champion, Russell, wore royal blue trunks trimmed with yellow; the challenger, Larmour, had chosen an eye-catching dark red pair. Larmour's trunks were made out of velvet and he slipped out of his matching gown once he was inside the ring. Russell and Larmour were summoned to the centre of the ring by the referee, Harry Gibbs, who spoke to the two fighters with characteristic Cockney bluntness.

'I want a clean fight,' he said. 'No holding and no rabbit-punching. When I say "Break" I want you to break clean and take a step back. Shake hands and may the best man win.'

Briefly, and barely looking at each other, the fighters tapped gloves. Twelve rounds of hell awaited them.

'Well, this is the one that everyone has been waiting for,' Jim Neilly told his BBC audience as the first bell sounded. 'For the second time it's Hugh Russell against Davy Larmour. Great friends outside the ring but, as everybody knows, there is no friendship in there whatsoever. But there's tremendous support in the hall for both boxers.'

Russell started well, throwing punches in fluid combinations, while Larmour was content to work behind his jab. After a minute, Larmour felt the crack of bone on bone just above his left eye. He wasn't hurt but he knew at once that he had been cut by Russell's head. The old sensation of his flesh being opened up made him swear to himself. As blood slipped down his face, Larmour fought hard but Russell was slick and evasive while using his right jab.

In the second, with Russell targeting his eye, Larmour was the aggressor. He stalked Russell and caught him with a slicing right hook that forced the champion back on the ropes. Larmour swarmed over him but Russell calmly slid away. They were soon battering each other with fierce body punches.

A solid right hand from Larmour caught Russell flush in the third. He took the punch well, but it had shaken him down to the soles of his dancing feet. Both fighters began to clinch and hold, their heads clashing, and the hulking figure of Gibbs, who was so much larger than the little bantamweights, waved to the timekeeper to signal a pause. He brought Russell and Larmour together. 'There's too much holding and clinching,' he warned them. 'People have paid good money to see a great fight.' He ruffled the hair of each man, as if to confirm that they were doing well, apart from the holding and head-banging.

On his stool at the end of the round, Larmour remembered a piece of advice given to him years earlier by Jimmy Hamilton, his first trainer at the Springmount Boxing Club: 'The best way to beat a southpaw is to throw plenty of right hands.' He could hear Jimmy's voice so clearly in his head that a shiver ran through him. Old Jimmy had been dead for years.

Advice from the grave did not help much in the fourth round as Larmour was again caught by Russell's flashing red head. A much deeper gash opened up above his right eye and, within another minute, Larmour's cheek was covered in blood that soon spread to Russell's shoulder as they brawled and clinched. They were warned again by Gibbs, but Larmour was worried. It felt as if the new cut was a bad one.

'Don't worry about the cuts,' Maguire told his fighter in the corner. 'That's my job.'

The trainer smeared Vaseline over the cuts and Larmour spat into a yellow plastic bucket just as the bell for round five sounded.

Larmour threw much heavier punches, with mean intent, grunting loudly each time he landed. He knew he had to regain some control and, as single shots began to penetrate Russell's guard, he felt encouraged. It seemed to him as if Russell sighed each time he was hit, as if he was tiring a little. Larmour was turning it into a war of attrition with lots of in-fighting, which suited him much more than a will-o'-the-wisp like Russell.

'Get out of there,' Eddie Shaw yelled to Russell, reminding him to get on his bike and back-pedal away from another bloody brawl.

Russell couldn't get out of the pocket, and a big hand caught him on the jaw and knocked him down. Larmour was sent to a neutral corner before Gibbs began to count. Russell rested on his bended left knee. He waited for Gibbs to say 'Eight' before he stood up and lifted both hands to indicate he was not badly hurt.

Larmour trapped Russell in a corner and poured on the pressure. The wilting champion clung on with less than 20 seconds left in the round – but his upper left cheek had now opened up in a deep gash of its own. Larmour let rip with punch after punch, but Russell caught him with an answering blow just before the bell. Both fighters were bleeding. They touched gloves in mutual respect as the King's Hall thundered its approval of another fierce but strangely uplifting round.

A crescent-shaped cut had sliced open the skin of the cheekbone beneath Russell's right eye. It would scar him for life. He sat on his stool while Paddy Byrne stemmed the blood flow.

'Don't go mad,' Maguire urged Larmour. 'Box smart and this fight will soon be over.'

Larmour came steaming out in the sixth, throwing punch after punch, but Russell was still alert and he landed a couple of beautiful counters. As they fought up close, Larmour's left eye began to bleed again, but he responded by rocking Russell with a jolting right uppercut. The challenger seemed to be landing the more punishing blows but Neilly confirmed that, 'Larmour's face is now a mask of blood. It's quite a mess.'

In his corner after another brutal round, Larmour felt his legs stiffening with fatigue. He was worried that all the newspapermen had been right in predicting he was too old to beat the undefeated younger champion. Maguire wiped the blood from his face and tried to seal the two cuts. The fight was on a knife-edge.

'Be busy, Davy,' Maguire yelled at him as Larmour climbed off his stool. 'Be busy.'

The next three rounds were gruelling. If Russell provided the most impressive moments, catching Larmour with a series of sweet combinations, the challenger always came firing straight back at him. Russell landed more punches, but Larmour's individual blows looked punishing. Chanting filled the hall, the rival supporters jammed together so closely that 'Russ-ell, Russ-ell!' and 'Lar-mour, Lar-mour!' echoed each other.

On his stool between rounds, there was discord in Larmour's head. He felt the sponges and swabs at work on his face, as Maguire tended to his bloody skin, but he could not concentrate on his trainer's instructions. It was as if his skull had split his brain in two. On one side he heard an insistent voice telling him that he could not go on, he needed to rest, and he would feel better if he just sat on his stool and closed his eyes. A second voice reminded him that when the bell rang he had to get up and start all over again.

Larmour's reverie was broken when the referee joined them in the corner. 'You'll have to stop that bleeding, Paddy,' Gibbs said.

'It's okay, Harry,' Paddy said urgently. 'I've got it under control.'

The voice in Larmour's head urging him to rest was silent now. Dread that the fight might be stopped surged through him. 'It's not too bad, Mr Gibbs,' he said. 'There's no problem.'

Larmour knew he could not afford to be cut again. The warning gave him fresh impetus.

Russell's right jabs were not quite as stinging and Larmour could tell the champion was weakening in round ten. But then, as if to snap him out of such complacency, Russell caught Larmour with a sneaky left hand. Larmour responded with a left and a right to prove that he was back in the groove. Another big right hand shook Russell just before the bell.

'He's nearly done,' Maguire said in the corner.

Larmour hoped he was right. Only two rounds were left. Six more minutes. Larmour remembered how Russell's late rally in the final rounds of their previous fight had swung the decision his way. He could not allow a repeat and so Davy prepared himself for yet more exhaustion and pain.

The right hand from Larmour again rocked Russell with the first meaningful punch of the 11th round. Russell responded with another flurry of punches and the King's Hall echoed with the sound of both fighters' names. 'Two proper battleships,' Neilly yelled above the bedlam. Larmour wobbled Russell with another right and the champion clung on. At the bell, Larmour landed one more right to seal a big round in his favour.

'You've got him, Davy,' Maguire shouted. 'Three more minutes and you're the champ.'

Larmour knew he still had to convince the referee. Harry Gibbs' decision would be the only one that counted. Larmour rose with renewed vigour before the start of the 12th round.

Russell met him in the centre of the ring and raised his gloves in tribute. Larmour tapped them in acknowledgement of a fine champion. Their faces were both cut, bruised and swollen, with the gash above each of Larmour's eyes being matched by the crescent embedded into Russell's cheek. It had been another terrific contest to watch, and an ordeal for the boxers.

Larmour's favourite right hand landed first in the final round. Another two rights were followed by a left. The champion clinched in a bid to stem the flow of punches. Gibbs warned him to break and not to use his head in the close exchanges. The next right hand from Larmour lifted his supporters even more and their chanting of his name reverberated around the hall. In the last 30 seconds, Larmour kept pressing, forcing Russell on the retreat yet again. They swapped weary punches at the bell and, then, it was all over.

It took Gibbs only a couple of seconds to lift Larmour's hand as the winner. The new champion leapt into the air and, by the time he landed on the blue canvas, his trainer had climbed into the ring and was running towards him.

Paddy Maguire from the Falls Road embraced Davy Larmour from the Shankill Road. They had done it. Larmour was the new British bantamweight champion.

'Paddy, you seem just as pleased as Davy,' Neilly said a few minutes later in the ring.

'Well,' Paddy said, clutching the Lonsdale Belt, 'he's the first fighter I ever trained and he's just won the bantamweight title. I told his son today: "Your dad's getting one of them Lonsdale Belts tonight," and he laughed at me. But I've now got it in my hand. It's Davy Larmour's. I'm really proud – more than when I won the title myself.'

'He's not a bad talker is he, Davy?' Neilly said, turning the mic to Larmour.

'No, he keeps on going,' Davy said wryly. 'He's been in my head the past week: "Do this, do that!" He's been treating me like I'm a pregnant woman. I'm not allowed to do this or that.'

'It's all paid off, hasn't it?'

'Yeah,' Davy said. 'I just feel some pity for Hugh, losing his title in his first fight as champion. But he knew the risk he was taking by giving me a chance. He must have been mad.'

Davy knew that they would both be back in hospital for yet more stitches within the hour.

'But you're still great pals?' Neilly asked of him and Hugh.

'We're great pals. I told him we can fight again. Who knows? A third encounter?'

There would be no more ring encounters for Charlie Nash. Two nights later, on 4 March 1983, his boxing career ended in Cologne. He suffered his second straight defeat when, having been stopped by Tony Willis in Birmingham three months earlier, he lost on a fifth-round TKO against Rudy Waller. The German's record rose to an impressive 18–0. He was a good fighter and he had also been Charlie's last opponent as an amateur. But Charlie was a shadow of himself in Cologne.

Unable to get any fights in Derry, Charlie had gone on the road and faced unbeaten fighters who were being promoted heavily. He had become a famous old fighting name who would look great on a rising star's résumé. He was offered £3,000 to fly to Cologne at short notice. The fact that he had had flu the previous week and done little training had to be set aside. His family was growing and the money was too good to turn down.

Waller's style didn't suit him. Charlie fought out of a stand-up southpaw stance and Waller came at him with a rolling gait, his head flashing as he rose up. They clashed heads repeatedly and Charlie, always a bleeder, was cut again. Waller kept nailing him with combinations and, as there was only going to be one winner, the referee rescued Charlie.

It was a lonely end to a brave career and, on the flight home the next morning, Charlie told Tommy Donnelly his decision: 'I can't go on. It's over.'

Tommy nodded sympathetically. All the old fire and determination in Charlie had burnt out. The pride of Derry could not become just another hapless journeyman after seven and a half years as a professional fighter and being a former British and European champion.

The trainer, who had been with him since even before the night that Mousey Harkin lost his life, understood the gravity of Charlie's life. He had suffered since Bloody Sunday. Two months before he turned 32, it was time for Charlie to find peace in retirement.

'Thank you, Tommy,' Charlie said quietly. He looked out of the plane window at the heavy banks of cloud. He was crying, but he was happy he would not have to fight again.

Barry McGuigan took a risk. The following month, on 12 April 1983, he became the first fighter from the Republic of Ireland to fight for the British title. He had taken out British citizenship, while retaining his Irish passport, in order to be eligible for a crack at the title. Boxing realities, rather than any political statement, drove his decision. He knew that to move up to the European and world stage he needed a National title first, and no Irish belt carried any status internationally. The British title would open the way to big-money fights.

No one in the Republican movement said a word to him. But Barry knew that they were whispering about him in Belfast, in Clones and in Dublin. The slogan 'Barry the Brit' was painted on brick walls in mockery rather than tribute. He had alienated the hardcore element, the IRA and INLA supporters, but he had no desire to accept the embrace of the Loyalist UDA and UVF. As a statement of neutrality, he wore a dove of peace on his boxing trunks.

A death threat was made against McGuigan. Barney Eastwood expressed his disbelief in a television interview. 'For the life of me I don't understand why anyone would want to hurt Barry McGuigan. He brings joy and happiness to us all.'

Vernon Penprase, a baby-faced 24-year-old Englishman, had cause to dispute that line after he had faced McGuigan for the British title in the Ulster Hall. There were meant to be question marks over the young Irishman. His nationality and appetite for savagery in his first fight since the death of Young Ali were concerns. McGuigan had also just recovered from a debilitating virus. But he blew away each question, and Penprase, in two brutal rounds.

In the first he battered Penprase to the body before breaking his nose. Round two was even more violent: McGuigan backed Penprase into a corner and then uncorked a brute of a left hook. It was so perfectly timed, from such a close trajectory, that Penprase was knocked clean off his feet. He managed to get up but he was as wobbly as a fawn on spindly legs as McGuigan tore at him. Harry Gibbs had to pull McGuigan away and lambast him for fighting on even before he had completed the standing count.

Penprase rallied bravely and for the next two minutes – stalked by McGuigan while the Belfast crowd chanted 'Easy, easy, easy!' – he somehow stayed on his feet. But a chopping right hand dropped him heavily near the end of the second. Penprase dragged himself up but his face was smeared with blood. The referee took one look at his dazed and gory expression and showed Penprase the compassion he needed.

Barry McGuigan, an Irishman from Clones, was the new British champion. He had crossed another border with venomous precision. Yet there had been silent anger, too, because McGuigan had been furious to hear of the grumbling dissent. He did not believe in terrorism, in the way in which both Republican and Loyalist paramilitaries bullied and intimidated their own communities. He was sick of the bombs and the balaclavas, of the kneecappings and the punishment shootings. He had had enough of people being told what they could or could not do by hooded men who sometimes seemed to him to be no better than gangsters.

McGuigan could say none of this in dangerous times. He knew that they could kill him in an instant. Far worse, they could kill his family and other innocent people around him. So he listened in silence to the whispers around him. But, in his head, he was thinking of the hardcore militants and saying 'Fuck you' to every one of them. This was his boxing career and he would do what was best for him and his family. He bore no ill will to poor Vernon Penprase, whom he actually liked, but when he stepped into the ring that night Barry was fuelled by suppressed fury. He had lived, along with everyone else, for too long in the pressure cooker of the Troubles. He was not willing to be cowed into submission by anyone.

Gerry Storey applied the same principles of training when working with his sons as he did while acting as a coach for thousands of other amateur boxers. Two of his boys, Gerry Jr and Sam, had made the finals of the Irish Nationals in March 1983. Sam had only had his first bout outside the Juniors just over a year earlier, when he fought in the 1982 Ulster Seniors. He made it all the way to the final and pushed the heavily favoured Tommy Corr from Tyrone hard in front of a packed Ulster Hall. A few months later, with Gerry Storey in his corner, Corr returned from the world championships in Munich with a bronze medal, having reached the semi-finals to prove himself one of the four best amateur light-middleweights in the world.

Corr and Sam Storey met again the following year in the 1983 Ulster Senior finals. Their rivalry had grown and Sam sat in the dressing room and heard his name and Corr's name being chanted by the crowd outside. He felt a shiver run through him but his dad took over. Gerry sat down and quietly listed the reasons why Sam could beat Corr. Sam listened to his dad. His voice was soft and gentle but it drowned out the chanting crowd.

'Okay, Pop,' Sam said when Gerry finished his talk with the certainty that he would win.

It was a fierce and testing fight, but Sam proved his father right. He beat Corr clearly to win his first Ulster Senior title at light-middleweight. Gerry Jr was the Ulster lightheavyweight champion. The hall rocked as Gerry Storey's Holy Family boys, assisted by Bobby McAllister in the corner, tore through the tournament to win six Ulster Senior titles. It equalled the record for a single championship and the Holy Family might have made history if their American wildcard, Rory O'Neill, had not been such a spectacular flop. Rory's father had flown him out from America in a bid to win an Ulster Senior title that would have looked magnificent in his bar back home. Gerry agreed to take on young Rory as he was meant to be a great talent.

It soon emerged that Rory ate, rather than fought, like a world champion as he settled into the Storey home. He still promised Gerry he would win the Ulster title for the Holy Family and his dad. Gerry had his doubts but, with a clean sweep of titles until then, he sent out Rory for the seventh and last fight of the night. Rory came out of the corner like Rocky Marciano but he ran straight into Danny Ogle, who dropped him. It was a disaster and Ogle blitzed the American. The dream was over for Rory's Irish-American dad and for the Holy Family's record bid. They remained locked on six Ulster Senior titles with the St George's club from the markets area of Belfast.

After making sure that Rory was okay, Gerry could smile after an unforgettable evening. He knew the Ulster Seniors had confirmed that his two eldest sons, Gerry Jr and Sam, both had a real chance of fighting for Ireland in the 1984 Olympics in Los Angeles. His aim was to be in the corner for his boys at the Games.

Yet boxing was rarely easy and neither of them became Irish Senior champion shortly afterwards. On 25 March 1983, in Dublin, in the middleweight category, Gerry Jr was stopped by Tony de Loughrey in the second round. In the light-middleweight division, Sam was meant to meet Corr in the concluding bout of a gripping trilogy. But he was so stricken with a sore throat that he actually fainted when the Irish team doctor, Sean Donnelly, gave him an injection a day before the bout. Sam woke up with Donnelly berating him as a big so-and-so because, despite being a small man, the doctor had lifted him off the floor and onto a bed.

Corr became Irish champion on a walkover but he then decided to take a short break, which meant Sam was drafted into the Irish Senior team to face Scotland in an international. Mickey Hawkins from the Holy Trinity club in Belfast took charge of the squad that travelled to Glasgow to fight the Scots. Gerry, despite being National coach, stayed at the Holy Family to work with his young boxers. He knew that Hawkins was a fine trainer and so he felt content.

In Glasgow, the night before he pulled on an Irish Senior vest for the first time, Sam had a light workout on the pads with Hawkins. 'Do you know who you're fighting tomorrow night?' Hawkins asked.

'No,' Sam replied.

'You really don't know?' Hawkins said in a tone of voice that told Sam he would not be ducking through the ropes to face Mickey Mouse. 'You're fighting Davy Milligan.'

'Who's he?'

'He fights in the ABA final in two weeks,' Hawkins said, confirming that Milligan was one of the two best amateur middleweights in the UK.

'Jesus,' Sam said.

When he got back to the hotel, Sam rang his dad: 'Pop, do you know who I'm fighting tomorrow night?'

'No,' Gerry said, echoing his son's earlier ignorance. 'Who?'

'Davy Milligan – who is an ABA finalist in a couple of weeks.'

Gerry paused before saying just one word: 'And . . .?'

Sam wanted to remind his dad that this would be his first fight in the green vest of Ireland but that 'and', followed by another loaded pause, resonated.

'There's no need to worry,' Gerry told Sam. 'You'll have too much for him.'

All at once, Gerry's belief and confidence surged inside Sam. No one knew amateur boxing as well as his dad. If Gerry was convinced he would win, then Sam could have no doubts.

Twenty-four hours later Gerry Storey's insight, and the wisdom of his simple 'and . . .?', was vindicated. Sam won his first bout in an Irish vest – and the power of his father, both as a trainer and an inspiration, was evident all over again.

Belfast, Wednesday 7 December 1983

Hugh Russell heard the news soon after 11 o'clock that morning. There had been a shooting outside the library at Queen's University just a few minutes earlier. The rumours were unconfirmed, but it sounded like one of the big news stories of the year. Edgar Graham, one of the most brilliant young minds in Unionist politics, was said to have been shot by the IRA. Graham was a lecturer at Queen's, a barrister and an Ulster Unionist member of the Northern Ireland assembly. He was only 29 but regarded as the most intellectually driven and fair-minded politician on the Unionist side. Graham was spoken of often as an alternative future leader of the Unionist cause ahead of the far more draconian Reverend Ian Paisley.

Brendan Murphy was out of the *Irish News* office, working on a different job, and so the picture editor barked out his order: 'Hugh, I want you down there now! Get as much as you can. We're leading on this for the main edition.'

'Who am I going with?' Hugh asked.

'You're doing this solo, wee man,' replied the editor. 'Everyone else is out. Get cracking.'

Hugh packed his camera bag hurriedly. Ripples of anxiety ran through him at the prospect of missing the shot every other snapper out there might get before him. He had only done a few jobs on his own and they had been minor skirmishes, kids rioting or tense soldiers cocking their rifles in readiness for yet more trouble.

The picture editor had grunted on previous occasions when he saw the stock images Hugh had offered him. They must have been adequate because they had been in the following day's edition and he had felt a little thrill when he saw the caption: 'Photograph: Hugh Russell'. His photos had been tucked away on the inside pages, but at least they had been used. Until now, though, he had never been sent on an assignment attached to a major news story.

All the big boys would be there from the photography pack. The hardcore Irish photographers who had covered the Troubles for years and the foreign star snappers who had come over for the hunger strikes and simply stayed on. They were grizzled men used to working in war zones from Beirut to Belfast.

Hugh remained a professional fighter, but he felt like an amateur photographer. He had fought twice more, winning both, since his first loss in the ring against Davy Larmour. His next fight, against the tough Welshman Kelvin Smart for the British flyweight title, was scheduled to take place at the King's Hall in another seven weeks, on 25 January 1984. He was deep in training. Every morning, around 5.30am, he ran through New Lodge and into the heart of Belfast. It was freezing and he wore a black balaclava and gloves. He knew he looked like a Republican militant on the run, but the army seemed to know him because he was hardly ever stopped. Even when he was pulled to one side, he was released quickly after he removed the balaclava and the soldiers saw his curly red hair. Everyone seemed to know he was a boxer.

He would skip and pummel the heavy bags in the Castle Street gym before clocking into the *Irish News* around mid-morning.

Hugh worked as a trainee snapper with the established photographers all day and then returned to the gym in the early evening for sparring. He knew his boxing career had a year, or two at the most, to run. A reminder of the finite nature of this violent business had been evident the previous month when Davy Larmour had been sent into retirement. On 16 November, on the same bill as Barry McGuigan becoming European featherweight champion, Davy's first defence of his British bantamweight title had ended in a third-round stoppage and defeat against John Feeney. Davy knew it was the end of the road.

Hugh, being younger, had a few more fights left in him. By the time he quit the fight game he hoped to be working full-time for the *Irish News* – unless he totally messed up his first big job that morning at Queen's University. He left the office on Donegall Street and grabbed a lift with a news reporter. It was less than two miles to the university and Hugh had little time to compose himself. He simply tried to remember how he calmed his nerves in the ring.

The streets around the university library had been sealed off and they left the car as soon as they could. They ran through the freezing streets, and the reporter found it hard to keep up with the little boxer – even though Hugh carried his heavy camera bag.

At the army cordon they showed their press passes. Hugh felt amazed that he was a genuine photographer. Most people in Belfast had no choice but to turn away from the security barricade. Even in the city there was little freedom to move. Hugh's wife was pregnant and when she went shopping the British soldiers would sometimes check she really was expecting a baby – rather than carrying a bomb. But here, at the scene of a murder, he was let inside the roped-off area.

The reporter, being so much more experienced than him, had established the facts. Edgar Graham had been gunned down by suspected IRA gunmen who had been carrying clipboards and mingling with students to obscure their identity. As soon as

Graham and his fellow lecturer and friend Dermot Nesbitt had appeared on the street outside the library, between four and six shots had been fired. Graham was dead after being hit in the head at point-blank range. Nesbitt was unharmed.

Hugh walked slowly down University Square – approaching the carnage from the University Road end. He could see the black body bag with the body of Edgar Graham inside it. RUC officers and soldiers swarmed around the area. Hugh kept walking. He needed to see his first body in a different way. Edgar Graham was in his head. It didn't matter that Hugh was a Catholic boxer and Edgar had been a Unionist politician. He had also been a man with a close and loving family. This innocent man was now dead on an ordinary Wednesday morning just two and a half weeks before Christmas.

By the time Hugh had circled the square and approached the body from a new direction, most of the soldiers and policemen had drifted away. The street behind the body was eerily littered. But, in front of the body, the pavement stretched out in clean blocks of concrete. Hugh's eye snared on an image.

A black briefcase stood in front of Edgar Graham's body, like a small sentry. It was black with a gold buckle that snapped it shut. Hundreds of academics, barristers and politicians probably carried the exact same briefcase wherever they travelled. The briefcase looked very ordinary next to the strange sight of the body bag. It was made of leather but it looked human.

Edgar Graham had not been carrying a rifle or a petrol bomb when he had spotted his friend. He had been carrying that simple briefcase. When he and Dermot stopped to chat, Edgar must have placed his briefcase on the pavement next to him. It remained in the same place, neat and upright. The briefcase accentuated the loneliness of this sectarian death.

Hugh knelt down. His boxer's hands were steady as he held the camera and aimed it at Edgar Graham. The briefcase was in the middle of the frame, the body just behind it. Hugh squeezed the shutter and it whirred in the silence. He shot another frame, and another. His mind emptied and the image became everything.

The following morning, with his photograph of Edgar Graham on the front page of the *Irish News*, Hugh was called in to see the picture editor.

'This was your first body?' his editor asked.

'Yes,' Hugh replied.

'Edgar Graham,' the editor said, as if confirming the significance of the photograph. 'The briefcase makes this photograph very powerful, and very touching.'

'Thank you.'

'You've done well, Hugh,' the editor said as he looked up from the photograph to the famous Belfast boxer. 'Your future is here.'

CHAPTER 15

Collect Work

Nineteen eighty-four was meant to be a landmark year for the Holy Family boxing club and the Storey family. Gerry had coached Ireland in three successive Olympic Games, from 1972 to 1980, in Munich, Montreal and Moscow. There seemed little doubt that he would retain the position in Ireland's corner at the 1984 Los Angeles Olympics – especially as he had doubled up as both head trainer and manager in Moscow. His boxing knowledge was unparalleled and no one in Ireland came close to matching his experience and insight.

Sam Storey looked a certainty for the team at light-middleweight and Gerry Jr was pushing hard for the middleweight slot. At the 1984 Ulster Senior finals, the Storey dominance continued. Tommy Corr, the excellent world championship medallist, was beginning to feel sick of the Storeys. He had lost his Ulster Senior title to Sam in 1983 and when he moved up to middleweight he faced another Storey in the 1984 final. Gerry Jr beat Corr to become middle-weight champion, while Sam retained his light-middleweight title that same night.

Gerry, both as a father and a club coach, made sure he kept his boys grounded and that he paid equal attention to all his Holy

Family fighters. He never favoured one boxer over another and he was even more scrupulous in not putting his sons ahead of the other fighters. Gerry Jr and Sam liked and respected his fairness to all. But they were furious when there was little equity inside the murky machinations of Irish boxing politics.

It might have been jealousy of the Storey name and the success of Belfast boxing, or simply a desire to promote a coach close to Dublin, but plans were made to oust Gerry as head coach. He was the biggest certainty to take Ireland to a fourth successive Olympics since Arkle won three Gold Cups in a row in the 1960s. But he would be denied his rightful place at the heart of the team when boxing administrators in the South chose to promote his number two, Paddy Muldowney from the Transport Club in Dublin, to Olympic coach. There was outrage, and boxing officials in Ulster protested vehemently. When their anger proved ineffective they began a campaign to elevate Gerry to the role of manager. They were denied again.

Only Gerry was unmoved. The change had happened when he was out of the country, taking an Ulster team to fight in New Zealand. The Dublin administrators had waited for him to be on the other side of the world before they cut him loose. Gerry smiled and said nothing. The boys were bereft. Gerry Jr, who was more hot-headed than both his dad and Sam, raged against the decision. Sam pointed out that Paddy Muldowney was a good timekeeper in the gym, and a decent man, but not a patch on Pop when it came to tactics and preparation.

There was further misfortune in early 1984 when Gerry Jr broke his hand in an international against Scotland. He was out of the Irish Seniors and his chances of being picked ahead of Tommy Corr as the team's Olympic middleweight were ruined. Sam won the Ulster Seniors and in the final of the Irish Nationals he easily beat Paddy Ruth on points. There had been so much pressure on Sam, as Gerry's son, that winning his first Irish Senior title in such style meant relief flooded through him.

Sam was selected to box for Ireland in the 1984 Olympics alongside Gerry Hawkins, Phil Sutcliffe, Kieran Joyce, Paul Fitzgerald and Tommy Corr. Without his dad in the corner, Sam's mood darkened. The team was run badly and there were arguments every day. Sam had injured his hand while boxing for Ulster in New Zealand and, to protect it when sparring, he wore a special glove with the thumb sewn down. Sparring against Joyce, who was a tough nut at welterweight, Sam felt comfortable until the team manager Art O'Brien instructed him to switch to ordinary gloves.

'But I've got a sore hand,' Sam protested. 'I'm nursing it.'

O'Brien waved away his concerns and made Sam change gloves. In the next round Sam hit Joyce with a right hook – and cried out in pain. He had suffered a hairline fracture of his thumb and he was out for the next five weeks. Unable to throw a punch, he had to restrict his training to jogging and shadow-boxing. He felt out of sorts when the team reached Los Angeles, with the injury having been kept secret even from his dad back in Belfast.

Sam put on the gloves again, for the first time since the fracture, when he fought his opening Olympic bout against the Italian world champion Romolo Casamonica. He boxed well, and aggressively, for two rounds and he was ahead going into the third and last. But his exhaustion caught up with him and Casamonica stopped him with 30 seconds left of the fight. The Storey Olympic dream was over.

When he got home to Belfast, Sam could have been consumed by bitterness – but he looked at his dad. Sam learnt a profound lesson in humility and acceptance when he saw how his father was devoid of anger or resentment.

'Don't worry about it, Sam,' Gerry told his son. 'Let's stick to fighting in the ring ... not outside of it.'

The ragged cry echoed again and again when the sadness seemed unbearable: 'Leave the fighting to McGuigan!' Beyond the Falls Road and the Shankill Road, amid the wounding and the killing, people also whispered this phrase to themselves. They were sick of the sectarian hatred and the incessant violence and so they said it in Belfast and Derry, in every forsaken corner of Northern Ireland: 'Leave the fighting to McGuigan!'

The paramilitary headcases and zealots on both sides of the divide were so rooted in bitterness and intransigence that they resolved to fight each other until the end of time. They were wedded to their bombs and guns, their vengeful shootings and retaliatory explosions, but everyone else was fed up with misery and death. They had had enough. The only fighting they wanted to see, and exalt, was in a boxing ring. Unless you were Barry McGuigan or one of his fellow boxers, it was time to lay down your arms and accept the truth.

There had been too many years of fighting and too many deaths, with fatalities in the Troubles stretching to 2,670 people by January 1985, and nothing had changed. Division and discord were woven into the fabric of everyday life. More fighting outside the ring would bring down more woe on the world. It was time to let go and leave it all to McGuigan.

When McGuigan fought there was so much joy in the crammed King's Hall, and in delirious pubs and living rooms across the land. The dove of peace on McGuigan's boxing trunks could have been cloying but instead, in a time of brutality and war, it gleamed with hope. It meant that you could support the Belfast-based feather-weight from Clones whether you lived in the North or the South, whether you were a Catholic or a Protestant, a nun or a gangster, a man or a woman, young or old, lost or sad.

Three months earlier, on 12 October 1984, the IRA had taken the Troubles to the Conservative Party Conference at the Grand Hotel in Brighton. At 2.54am a bomb under the bath in room 629, one floor above Margaret Thatcher's suite, exploded. It had been planted in mid-September, when the IRA's bomber Patrick Magee had hidden 20 pounds of gelignite attached to a long-delay timer while staying at the hotel under the alias of Roy

Walsh. The bomb was meant to kill Maggie Thatcher and most of her cabinet.

Thatcher was still awake, working on her conference speech, when the explosion occurred. Her bathroom was badly damaged but she and her husband Denis escaped injury. Others were far less fortunate. Five Conservative Party members were killed, including the MP Anthony Berry, and 34 were injured and taken to hospital. Walter Clegg, another Tory MP, and Margaret Tebbit, whose husband Norman was the Secretary of State for Trade and Industry and one of Thatcher's most loyal cabinet ministers, were both disabled permanently.

The IRA had come close to achieving their objective, but Thatcher had left the bathroom just before the bomb detonated. She personified a steely calm in the immediate aftermath, and her determination to face down the IRA intensified, but at the end of that dramatic week she knew how close she had come to death.

The IRA had already responded with chilling simplicity on the morning of the bomb: 'Mrs Thatcher will now realise that Britain cannot occupy our country and torture our prisoners and shoot our people in their own streets and get away with it. Today we were unlucky, but remember we only have to be lucky once. You will have to be lucky always. Give Ireland peace and there will be no more war.'

Yet the idea that only more terror could bring peace, on both sides of the divide, had become frayed with the weariness of conflict. Thirteen years had passed since the McGurk's Bar atrocity in New Lodge, and the Balmoral Furniture Company bombing on the Shankill Road, and Bloody Sunday in Derry. How many more years would need to pass, and how much more death would it take, to bring peace to Northern Ireland? The unknowable answers were shrouded in exhaustion and grief, in the muck and murkiness of sectarian warfare. And so most ordinary people, who carried neither a gun nor an incendiary device, took in a deep breath and repeated the consoling call for peace: 'Leave the fighting to McGuigan!'

America had also begun to fall for McGuigan. On 13 October, the night after the Brighton bombing, the US network CBS had screened McGuigan's second-round knockout of the tough Colombian Felipe Orozoco, whose only previous defeat had been in a world title fight against Jaime Garza. It followed an earlier CBS broadcast of another sensational McGuigan stoppage – of the American Paul DeVorce, whose record had been 22-1 before he was blitzed in Belfast on 30 June 1984. The American television executives were entranced by McGuigan's ferocious fighting style and his polite charm outside the ring. They had never experienced a fight atmosphere as fevered and riveting as they discovered in the King's Hall.

Time magazine readers were equally absorbed after a glowing feature described some of McGuigan's significance in Northern Ireland and the peaceful path he was trying to cut through the Troubles. This was a story that transcended boxing and sport. McGuigan was a source of fascination in America – and not just in Britain and Ireland.

The CBS moneymen were convinced they could claim even higher ratings for McGuigan if he was able to overcome a serious challenge – against the New York-based Puerto Rican, Juan LaPorte – and win the right to fight Eusebio Pedroza for the WBA world featherweight title. It was McGuigan's dream to fight Pedroza. The imperious Panamanian had not lost for nine years and had sailed through 19 successful title defences. McGuigan knew he would have to beat LaPorte to earn a shot at Pedroza.

McGuigan exuded confidence on the outside but, deep down on the inside, he could be besieged by doubt. He knew he had never faced a man as hard as LaPorte, or as experienced and skilled, and so in his quieter moments he grew pessimistic. LaPorte had knockout power, which he used to stop Rocky Lockridge in two rounds. He had lost his first two WBA world featherweight title challenges, but they had been narrow points defeats to the brilliant Salvador Sanchez and Pedroza. LaPorte had become the WBC world champion in September 1982 and he had only relinquished the title in March 1984 against another legendary fighter in Wilfredo Gomez. He had broken his hand in the fourth, but fought on for eight more rounds before losing on points to Gomez.

'He's one tough hombre,' McGuigan said when asked to distil LaPorte's best feature.

Hidden uncertainties rose up inside him in the last two weeks before the bout. LaPorte had arrived early in Belfast to acclimatise and he used the same Castle Street gym as McGuigan and Hugh Russell. They were kept apart by Barney Eastwood's rigorous scheduling, but it was difficult for McGuigan to avoid the rumours of how hard LaPorte was working and how good he looked in sparring. His invisible presence began to grow in McGuigan's head.

There was no relief when, finally, they crossed paths. McGuigan was climbing the stairs to the gym a few days before the fight. He looked up and saw LaPorte walking down towards him.

'Barry, at last,' LaPorte said as he stretched out his hand. 'It's really good to meet you, man.'

'Juan,' McGuigan said in surprise. 'It's good to meet you too.'

'I've been waiting to catch you every day but we train at different times,' LaPorte said. 'You're watching your weight and I'm not telling you the truth about mine.'

LaPorte cackled and McGuigan was taken aback by the warmth of his opponent. His usual rivals were aggressive, dismissive or non-communicative. He also wondered if LaPorte could tell he was struggling with the weight even though the Puerto Rican had stipulated that they would fight at two pounds over the feather-weight limit.

'I hope everyone's treating you well in Belfast?' McGuigan said as a way of changing the subject.

'Your people are fabulous, man,' LaPorte enthused. 'We're going to give them a hell of a fight. You're a real good fighter.'

'You too, Juan,' McGuigan said, almost sheepishly.

The two featherweights exchanged another handshake and a brief embrace. LaPorte was then gone and McGuigan resumed his climb up to the gym. LaPorte was a classy guy but that mild observation churned up yet more anxiety in McGuigan. The best fighters didn't have to resort to cheap tricks of intimidation. They were content to allow their fists to do all the work. The nicer they are, McGuigan thought, the harder they hit. LaPorte looked supremely assured. He did not look like a fighter who had come all the way from Brooklyn to Belfast to lose.

McGuigan wondered if he would be able to find the resolve and panache to overcome a world-class fighter. Would LaPorte expose him as a fraud rather than a saviour? The closer they came to the fight, the more doubt grew in the young Irishman.

King's Hall, Belfast, Saturday 23 February 1985

Juan LaPorte was kept waiting in the ring for five long minutes by Barry McGuigan. The Puerto Rican didn't seem to mind as, in his long red gown, he shadow-boxed intently in his corner, ignoring the chants of 'Ba-rry! Ba-rry! Ba-rry!' from 9,000 supporters. He only looked a little quizzical when the familiar opening to the *Rocky* soundtrack was accompanied by a roar that gathered in volume as McGuigan and his entourage made their long walk to the ring. McGuigan kept his head down, his arms resting against the shoulders of Eddie Shaw, and by the time the vocal refrain of 'Gonna fly now, flying high now' had reached its crescendo the King's Hall was seething with noise. As McGuigan finally climbed through the ropes, Harry Carpenter sounded stunned on his BBC television microphone.

'It is the most incredible sound,' Carpenter exclaimed. 'It seems to me as if the walls of this famous old hall go in and out with the sound. I don't think any fighter in the history of boxing has ever had a reception into the ring like this man gets in Belfast.'

McGuigan was also dressed in red – with 'Young Barry The Clones Cyclone' emblazoned across the back of his gown – and he greeted his adoring fans by raising his arms. The crowd began to chant: 'Easy! Easy! Easy!'

There was nothing easy about fighting LaPorte. He absorbed McGuigan's punches and, from the outset, he was intent on hitting back even harder. After he had swallowed another ramrod jab, McGuigan stared at LaPorte. It looked as if the man from Brooklyn wanted to kill him. LaPorte was a solid fighter, with real snap to his punches, and he boxed with clinical purpose. McGuigan lifted the quality of his own work and shaded the first two rounds.

In the third, however, LaPorte hit him with a left hand that shocked McGuigan. He had never been hit so hard before. It was vital from then on that, as soon as he finished a combination, McGuigan moved his head and his feet to evade the booming counter-punches being fired at him.

McGuigan piled constant pressure on LaPorte to keep him at bay, and dominated rounds four to eight. He could feel LaPorte tiring when they were punching at close quarters and so McGuigan tried to quicken his work rate. But he was also feeling weary because he had never before fought at such a pace or against an opponent this skilled and treacherous.

LaPorte used lots of fighting tricks. A little shoulder roll would give him half an inch of space, which was enough for him to find the leverage to push McGuigan back. It was all he needed to then rip in a right uppercut and – *boom!* – McGuigan's head would rock on his neck before LaPorte crashed a left hook to the body. But McGuigan was in his absolute fighting prime, a few days from his 24th birthday, and he refused to wilt. He came back still harder at LaPorte and made him blink and wince with the ferocity of his assault. Near the end of round eight in a hard and gruelling fight, it looked – at least to some who weren't in the ring – as if the Irishman was strolling to victory.

Harry Carpenter suggested that, 'LaPorte looks sick at heart.

He really does. And there is no let-down in the pace of McGuigan. If anything he is getting faster.'

As more punches thudded into LaPorte, Carpenter said: 'He is being punished unmercifully by McGuigan. He may still be dangerous but it's becoming harder and harder for him to launch a counterattack under this incessant bombardment. And there was a smile on McGuigan's face just before the bell because he knew that he was in total command.'

The fighters retreated to their corners and, at ringside, Carpenter spoke down the line to Alan Minter, the former world middleweight champion who was watching the fight in the BBC's London studio with Des Lynam. 'This man is absolutely brilliant, isn't he?' he said of McGuigan.

Minter agreed but turned his attention on LaPorte. 'He's a former world champion but he's getting well beaten. I've got him losing every round but the fifth, which was even. I think he's gonna come out and he's got to try something new otherwise he's getting well spanked.'

A minute into the penultimate round, McGuigan aimed to use a ramrod jab to set up another combination. He threw the jab but, at that very moment, he saw a blur of red hurtling towards him. In that split second McGuigan thought a gush of blood might be spurting from LaPorte. He was wrong. It was the red of LaPorte's right glove exploding against his temple.

The shock inside McGuigan's head was profound. His brain was so scrambled by the shattering power of the blow that he lost all sense of time and place. McGuigan suddenly thought he was a small boy back in Clones. He had just left his mother's fruit and vegetable store on the Diamond and wandered down to Mrs Keenan's toy shop next door to the chemist's run by Cecil Chapman.

As LaPorte came after him for real, in his head little Barry was wandering around Mrs Keenan's shop looking at all the beautiful toys. He was lucky that LaPorte missed him with another huge right, but the next jab snapped McGuigan out of the toy shop and back into the King's Hall. 'What the fuck am I doing in Mrs Keenan's shop?' he asked himself as the noise washed over him in wave after wave. He was badly dazed and he tried to hold on to LaPorte or keep him at bay with a pawing jab. McGuigan did more clinching than punching, and referee Harry Gibbs kept barking: 'Break! McGuigan, you're holding, you're holding!'

McGuigan looked blearily at Gibbs and thought: 'For fuck's sake, Harry, what would you do, mate?' No one knew he had been knocked all the way to Clones and back.

There was no ninth-round stoppage and, in the corner, McGuigan slumped down on his stool. He threw back his head as Eddie Shaw went to work with a dripping sponge. Water ran in rivulets down McGuigan's face. He was tired but he felt his head begin to clear.

At the bell for the tenth and last round, he felt strong enough to jog from his corner and stretch out his left arm to touch gloves with LaPorte. The King's Hall crowd roared 'Easy … easy … easy!' with the indulgent bliss of spectators.

McGuigan was still intent on fighting and he outworked LaPorte for most of the round, landing the more punishing blows. The King's Hall sounded delirious in the last minute: 'Here we go … here we go … here we go!'

'Oh! He staggers LaPorte with a right hand,' Carpenter yelled, 'and LaPorte almost went! Unbelievable excitement in this place.'

LaPorte held on and the bell rang. 'It's all over and McGuigan is a runaway winner, no question about it,' Carpenter said. Gibbs immediately lifted McGuigan's hand to confirm his victory before he was swamped by his brother Dermot and his cornermen. Carpenter had to shout again above the bedlam: 'The most brilliant performance of his life against the most dangerous man he's ever met. McGuigan's done it on points and he's done it in style. The whole of Belfast will be celebrating tonight.'

An hour later, Hugh Russell was too exhausted to celebrate his final victory in the ring. He had also just won the Lonsdale Belt, his most cherished prize in boxing, after his third straight win in a British flyweight title fight. Russell had not only successfully defended his belt against Charlie Brown but he had knocked out the Glaswegian in the 12th round. At the start of that last round, both men had been so tired it looked as if they could barely stand. But Russell hurt Brown and the Scot went down. When Brown dragged himself up, Russell tore into him like a man possessed. It was hard to square such violence with the photographer who took such thoughtful and sensitive portraits of the Troubles.

He did not feel much like a winner in the dressing room. His fight had followed McGuigan's stunning performance against LaPorte, as the American TV producers wanted the featherweights on before the flyweights shed blood over the canvas. Sugar Ray Leonard had just left the dressing room, after he had congratulated McGuigan and assured him he would fight soon for the world title. But there was no stardust for the little flyweight champion.

Hugh stared forlornly at himself in the mirror. His face, cut to shreds, was a mess. Just as he had been to hospital after both Davy Larmour fights, Hugh knew he would be on his way to A&E as soon as he had showered and changed. He'd need at least another 30 stitches because his left cheekbone now featured a deep gash that would match the crescent-shaped scar on his right cheek. After they had sewn him up in hospital, his face would have absorbed over 100 stitches through all his years in boxing.

He could hardly believe he had struggled against Brown. They were both 25, but Hugh's record of 17–2 dwarfed Brown's mediocre five victories and four defeats. On an ordinary night Hugh would have outclassed Brown. But he had battled to make the flyweight limit and was a shadow of his fighting self. The nine-hour gap between the weigh-in and ducking through the ropes was nowhere near long enough for him to replenish his system. He knew that he cut more easily when he was dehydrated and that there was a much greater risk of damage being done when there was so little fluid around his brain.

Hugh had never considered going to university, and he mocked his own lack of erudition, but he was still bright. He was smart enough to know it was time to get out. If Charlie Brown could reduce him to such a grisly state, it was a warning he was no longer suited to professional boxing. The fact that he had just earned his biggest purse – close to ten grand – was immaterial. Hugh had never boxed for money. He had always been driven instead by glory.

Studying his gory face in the mirror, he forced himself to take the hardest but simplest decision of his career. It helped that he loved photography and he wanted to keep his hands steady and his gaze clear when he lifted the camera to his right eye. He could also feel proud that he remained undefeated, and a champion, in his natural weight category. His two defeats had both come at bantamweight – two divisions heavier than flyweight.

'What's up, wee man?' Barney Eastwood said when Hugh found him.

'Boss,' Hugh said to his promoter, 'I want to retire.'

Eastwood looked at Hugh Russell's cut-up face and heard the resolve in his voice. He knew his fighter had made a brave decision. He stood up and held out his hand.

'We've had a great ride, wee man,' Eastwood said. 'But you've got your camera now.'

A few months later, once his wounds had healed and he looked less like a fighter, Hugh was back in the press pack. He was a full-time snapper and one of the boys alongside all the hardened photographers who worked for the Belfast and Dublin papers, the English red-tops and broadsheets as well as the Pacemaker agency that supplied so many images to countries around the world. A few international photographers were also part of the pack and they all huddled together at the end of a road in Newry, nearly 40 miles from Belfast.

The woman at number 28 had just lost her husband. He had

been blown up by a bomb. It was almost certainly the worst moment of her life, but the press photographers knew it was time for a visit. This was the moment they hated more than any other.

Framing the shattered remnants of a body caught in such a blast, Hugh felt anguish when he captured the grief of the victim's relatives. Sometimes he would just see a mouth howling with the agony of loss; more often there was a muted numbness at the heart of distress too raw to have turned into mourning quite yet. His instinct was to look away or, even more humanely, to reach out and offer comfort. But it was Hugh's job to shut down his feelings until the work was done.

How could he neuter all emotion, however, when it came to the bleak task of collect work? When he was on a collect job he could not hide behind his camera. Instead, he had to pack it away in a bag and make the lonely walk to a house that had just suffered a death in the family. He would knock on the door gently and, when it finally opened, he would look into a tear-streaked face. Hugh would see a wife or a mother whose husband or son had just been murdered. He would see a father who had just lost his teenage daughter in a tragic shooting.

It was Hugh's job, or the mission of anyone in the pack who had been chosen to do the collect job, to offer his condolences before apologising for the intrusion. He would then explain that he was hoping to collect a small snapshot of the dead person that he could share with all his colleagues. In this way, every newspaper would be able to print a photograph of the victim that met with the approval of the family.

Most people, even in the depths of their hurt, understood when Hugh explained that it was a way to commemorate their loved one with a happy or proud photograph. Hugh knew that other snappers had been shouted at when they tried to collect a photo, or shoved away by a person crying in rage. The photographers understood. They could imagine themselves reacting with similar fury if they had just lost their wife or child and an unknown person knocked on the door and asked them to rummage through some old photo albums to find a suitable snapshot – just to satisfy the curiosity of newspaper readers who wanted to see what the victim had looked like before they were shot or blown to smithereens.

Since he had given up boxing and begun working full-time for the *Irish News*, Hugh noticed how the snappers always turned to him when it was time for another collect.

'You should go, wee man,' they said to Hugh. 'They'll know you're the boxer. They won't say no to you.'

They were right. People usually recognised him, even in their tangled shock and pain, and they asked him in while they went looking for a photo. Sometimes Hugh would sit down and have a cup of tea with them. He would try to be as sensitive as he could, and ask the right questions and, most of all, just be there to listen if they wanted to talk about the person they had lost to the madness of the Troubles.

The snappers were delighted when he came back with a family snap they could all share. It meant their picture editors would get off their backs. It also meant that they would ask Hugh to do the next collect. He was the youngest photographer, and the most famous, but it didn't seem fair that he should always be expected to fulfil the brutal demands of collect work. Hugh had not forgotten how some of the more bitter old hacks had tried to block him gaining a National Union of Journalists press card when he was still a fighter. The rules said you could only join the NUJ if journalism earned you two-thirds of your wages. That was clearly not the case when Hugh was making between five and ten grand a fight. Some jealous or resentful snappers complained when they heard about his application for a press pass. It was different now. He was a permanent staffer, and part of the pack.

'Go on, Hugh, you do this one,' someone urged him at the bottom of the road in Newry as they planned their next collect from the woman whose husband had been killed by a bomb.

Hugh felt drained and he was not sure if he could face the poor lady and ask her to help him. As he hesitated, another voice piped up: 'It has to be either you, Hugh, or Freddie ... the most famous or the smartest.'

Freddie Hoare worked for the *Daily Mirror* and, like many of the national papers, they insisted that he went to work in a suit. Hugh liked Freddie. He worked hard, took some great photos and looked dapper in his suit. Freddie had also done a large share of collects.

'Let's do this one together,' Freddie said to Hugh.

'Okay, Freddie,' Hugh said with a little smile and a nod. 'Let's go.'

The two of them walked down the road to a house shrouded in darkness. In the silence, and in their heads, they turned over all the words they could think of before they settled on the right combination. They would speak softly when the door opened. They would try hard not to add any upset when they asked if they might collect a small family photograph of a person who, earlier that day, had been alive and well and utterly oblivious to the fact that they were facing their last day on earth.

Hugh kept walking, bunching his right hand into a fist so he could rap his knuckles softly on the front door. He hoped they had been given the right address. His mouth was dry and he felt nervous. He was heartsore for what he was about to do. But this was his work now, this was his life. It felt important that the dead should be remembered, and honoured too.

CHAPTER 16

Shadows and Sunshine

Barry McGuigan woke early on the morning of Saturday 8 June 1985. He looked at the small clock next to his bed. It was just before 5.30am. His room in the Holiday Inn just off the Edgware Road in London was quiet ahead of the defining night of his life. Barry was 24 years old, at his fighting peak, but he was weary after a restless night. He was hungry and thirsty. It did not help his parched throat that the room was also hot and dry. Eddie Shaw had weighed him the previous night and Barry had been bang on the nine-stone featherweight limit. He still felt paranoid and wanted to dry off a few more ounces while he tried to sleep. Feeling so tight at the weight, he knew there was not much more he could lose – but he would not take a sip of water until they had completed the weigh-in at 10am.

Eusebio Pedroza was 30 years old and, at five foot ten, four inches taller than him. Barry took some comfort from the certainty that the older, bigger man would be feeling just as drained when waking on the morning of yet another fight. The champion had fought 42 times as a professional and almost half of those bouts had been successful defences of his WBA world featherweight title. Their bout at Loftus Road, home of Queens Park Rangers Football

Club in west London, would mark Pedroza's 20th title fight as the reigning champion.

Pedroza had refused to fight in Belfast. It seemed as if he was less worried about the Troubles than the intimidating atmosphere created by McGuigan's vociferous supporters, but at least he had agreed to bring his title to London. McGuigan had prepared hard for the most formidable challenge of his career. Juan LaPorte had provided a tough examination, but Pedroza had also beaten the Puerto Rican. Pedroza had not lost a fight since 1976 and he was the longest-reigning world champion in boxing.

Barney Eastwood had flown in two bruising Panamanian boxers to help McGuigan during his eight-week training camp in Bangor. Jose Marmolejo was ranked higher than McGuigan in the WBA world featherweight ratings. He was number three, while McGuigan was at five. Ezequiel Mosquera was a bigger man and Panama's lightweight champion. They were both hungry for well-paid sparring and so they tore into McGuigan day after day. He was not used to such relentlessly tough sparring and it was a daily battle to match Marmolejo and Mosquera. Nagging doubts rose up inside him again. If his sparring partners were such a test, how would he cope with a magnificent champion in Pedroza?

He felt a little better when Marmolejo, his fellow featherweight, got on the scales one day and weighed 143 pounds – which meant he was 17 pounds heavier than McGuigan. A couple of welter-weights, Davy Irving and Peppy Muir, were also part of the camp and McGuigan became more used to dealing with bigger rivals in sparring. As the fight was being held outside, Brian Eastwood, Barney's son, set up a ring in his garden. One sultry early-summer night in Belfast, McGuigan sparred 15 rounds as his training part-ners kept on replacing each other to remain fresh. His T-shirt was soon soaked with sweat but he kept it on so he could get used to the clammy humidity they expected him to endure under the hot lights against Pedroza.

As the days flew past in a blur of sweat and pain, McGuigan's old confidence began to surge through him. He was convinced now that he could beat Pedroza. Even when he hurt the tendons in his left arm during his very last sparring session, he proved resilient. He knew he would not be able to throw a punch again before he met Pedroza in 15 days, but he refused to believe his arm would give him any problems.

The last 12 days were spent in London. Apart from seeing Deborah Good, an excellent physio who worked daily on his arm, McGuigan received high-quality tuition from the boxing analyst Teddy Atlas, who worked with Mike Tyson, and Gerald Hayes who had fought Pedroza the previous June. Hayes had been stopped in the tenth round but he had hit Pedroza often. He kept encouraging Barry, saying: 'He's open to the right hand, man. You can nail him.' Hayes and Atlas agreed it would be extremely difficult because Pedroza was fantastic on the inside, but he preferred using his long reach while boxing at range. When the fighting got up close he was dirty. McGuigan was warned that Pedroza would hit him with his elbows and head. He would get fouled and roughed up and so he needed to sustain his aggressive pressure and keep close to Pedroza.

Not wanting word to slip out about his arm problem, McGuigan would pull on his sweat suit in his hotel room. He and Dermot would move the furniture and then he'd shadow-box for 30 minutes at a time. All the work had been done and so he was just ticking over. He felt ready.

Barry went over these thoughts on the morning of the weigh-in as a way to calm himself. He also remembered the message sent to him by Larry Holmes – the world heavyweight champion who had had as many successful title defences as Pedroza. Holmes wanted him to kick Pedroza's butt and break his long winning streak. Barry tried not to think about it, but he knew the whole of Ireland, both North and South, was also willing him on to victory. He had even more supporters in England and the fight's 27,000 tickets had been sold out for weeks.

At last it was time for him and Dermot to be driven to the Odeon cinema in Leicester Square for the weigh-in. It was less than three miles but the London traffic was so thick it took them 40 minutes to reach the venue. They discovered bedlam on their arrival. Three thousand McGuigan fans had crammed the cinema for the weigh-in. They looked and sounded as if they had been drinking all night. There was such uproar that McGuigan slipped onto the stage through a back door.

Eastwood was furious once the weigh-in began. Pedroza had got on the scales but stepped off so quickly that the marker, which seemed to indicate he was fractionally over the nine-stone limit, could not be properly checked. The champion then picked up a cup and seemed to drain it. Eastwood and his sons were convinced that the cup had been empty. They knew Pedroza would claim that the few extra ounces were because of his non-existent drink. But they could not even get the champion back on the scales. He refused and the WBA inspector, who was also from Panama, insisted that Pedroza had made weight.

The crowd's attention had now switched to McGuigan, chanting 'Ba-rry, Ba-rry, Ba-rry!' with deafening force, and Pedroza used the diversion to slink into the background.

McGuigan didn't care about Pedroza. He just wanted to get weighed so he could drink and eat again. His weight was fine – and he came in a quarter-pound under the nine-stone mark.

Pedroza ambled over to McGuigan. '*Número uno!*' he shouted, waving a long, bony finger in McGuigan's face. And then, just in case Barry's Spanish was not up to the mark, Pedroza did his own translation. 'Number one!' he shouted.

McGuigan smiled and offered his hand. He was all set to knock Pedroza off his top perch. They touched hands briefly.

Barry had already swallowed a large glass of flat Coke. He could feel the sugar zinging through his empty body. Barry followed it with two bottles of Lucozade, lots of water and a bowl of soup. He had been saying all week that he would murder a Big Mac as soon as he made the weigh-in but, in the middle of the morning, half a burger was all he could manage. A proper lunch would be better for him in a few hours.

He felt pensive and contemplative. His friend Sean McGivern, who had brought him the Big Mac, knew he needed spiritual nourishment. The two friends went often to church together. They did so quietly, discreetly, and were different to Barney Eastwood who was such a devout Catholic that they used to say he would eat the altar rails. Barry and Sean liked to keep their faith private. They walked through the back streets of Soho, Barry keeping his head down to avoid being recognised, until they found a church.

The front door was open. Religion, whose name had caused such grief in Northern Ireland, sustained Barry in these loneliest and most testing moments. He and Sean sat a little apart from each other in the back pew. Barry bowed his head and began to pray. The more he prayed, the more he thought of Young Ali. They were just one and a half miles from the Grosvenor House Hotel, where their tragic bout had unfolded, and Barry could not get the poor Nigerian boxer out of his head. He prayed for the dead man's family and he prayed for the safety of both Eusebio Pedroza and himself.

When he lifted his head he made a simple promise to himself and to God. If he could win that night, he would dedicate his world title victory to Young Ali. It felt important that he should remember the fallen fighter amid the certain fury and possible glory of the ring.

Gerry Storey walked through New Lodge an hour before the fight. His old neighbourhood and every other part of Belfast, it seemed, was empty. It reminded Gerry of the early 1970s when the city resembled a ghost town. Gunmen and bombers, at war with each other and the British army, were the reason Belfast had looked like a town in the Wild West. It was different now.

The streets were so quiet because everyone was at home or

already in the pub, tuned to BBC1 so they could watch McGuigan try to win the world title for all of them. Boxing had done it again. Boxing had brought down peace on a Saturday night and offered hope once more.

Gerry slipped into the corner shop and picked up the milk that Belle needed for the following morning and a few soft drinks for him to share with his sons. None of them drank alcohol, as they were boxing men to the core. But it was a night to raise a celebratory glass of juice or a fizzy drink in honour of boxing in Belfast and, he hoped, a new world champion in young Barry McGuigan.

His own son, Sam, would turn pro in another year and Gerry knew he was good enough also to become world champion. Sam had beaten Steve Collins in the final of the Irish Nationals in March 1985 – and Collins, who would win a world title himself and beat the likes of Chris Eubank and Nigel Benn, would admit to crying after he lost to Sam Storey in Dublin. Sam was a classy boxer, rather than a raw fighter, and he had the potential to follow McGuigan.

Gerry knew that fighters all around the city would be watching and willing on McGuigan. Hugh Russell had put down his camera for the night. He was relieved to be out of the fight game, but he still loved boxing. He had also shared many great nights with McGuigan at the Ulster Hall and the King's Hall – as well as when they were fellow amateurs boxing for Ireland on the Shankill Road or at the Moscow Olympics.

Hugh's old rival, Davy Larmour, was watching the fight with his great friend and former trainer, Paddy Maguire. The Protestant boxer from the Shankill Road and the Catholic fighter from the Falls Road were as close as ever. Davy had sparred more rounds against McGuigan than he could count, and he and Paddy wanted Barry to win for the sake of all of them.

'I thought you'd be in London with McGuigan,' the corner shop owner said to Gerry.

The trainer shook his head and explained that he had been

working with his Holy Family boys earlier in the day. They remained his priority.

'Do you think he'll win?' the man wondered as he prepared to close up for the night and get back in time for the fight.

Gerry smiled and nodded. 'I do,' he said. 'Pedroza's great, but I think McGuigan will do it. I always said he'd become a world champion. I think tonight's the night.'

Seventy miles away, in Derry, Charlie Nash also settled down for a night of boxing. He had driven through Derry earlier that evening, having spent the afternoon training young fighters at the gym, and the same hushed emptiness that gripped Belfast had taken hold of his city. Charlie remembered his first sparring session with Barry at St Mary's eight years earlier. He could still see Barry crying in the storeroom because he had been unable to land a glove on him. Barry had come a long way since then. Charlie felt certain that McGuigan winning the world title would lift Derry in a way it had not felt since long before Bloody Sunday.

He wished his brother, Willie, could watch the fight with him. Willie, who had been only 19 when he died, would have been 32. He would almost certainly have been married because most of the girls in Derry who knew him had loved the way that Stiff Nash danced so beautifully at clubs like the Borderland. If Willie had been alive, he might have brought his wife and kids over to watch the fight with Charlie and all his family.

Charlie knew that such thinking served no purpose and so, instead, he leant forward in his chair so that he could support his fellow boxer – just like he had done with his fighting friends, from Mousey Harkin to Damien McDermott, all those years ago.

Linking his boxer's hands together, almost as if in prayer, Charlie spoke softly to the gleaming television screen. He wished McGuigan might hear him as he prepared to make his lonely walk to the ring. 'C'mon, Barry,' Charlie urged, 'c'mon!'

Loftus Road, Shepherd's Bush, London, Saturday 8 June 1985

It took Barry McGuigan 12 minutes to walk from his dressing room to the ring. Twenty-seven thousand fans roared him on as he made his entrance. Ten days earlier, on 29 May 1985, 39 fans were crushed to death before the European Cup final between Liverpool and Juventus at the Heysel Stadium in Brussels. Less than a month before, 56 people had died during Bradford City's Third Division match against Lincoln City when a fire swept through a stand at Valley Parade. The security team at Loftus Road were, consequently, racked with paranoia. They were also the bane of the American and BBC television schedulers.

McGuigan knew even before he left the sanctuary of his dressing room that all the intricate plans of the television crew and their cameramen would never work. They had told him to follow the spotlights for 30 feet to his left before he cut across diagonally to the ring. The TV pictures would look stunning but McGuigan tried to tell them it was hopeless. At least 20,000 of the fans were Irish and he attempted to explain what would happen to the producers who had assured him his path to the ring would be cleared of spectators.

'The Irish don't listen to what you tell them,' McGuigan had stressed earlier that afternoon. 'You say: "You can't go there ... " And they say, "Right, no worries, mate ... " [McGuigan winked and gave a thumbs-up to emulate a typical fan] and they walk straight over there.'

A producer for ABC, the American network screening the fight live alongside the BBC, shook his head. They had planned it to perfection. 'Your fans are amazing!' he added. McGuigan could tell the man had no idea of the mayhem such passion engendered among his supporters.

There were many famous faces in the crowd – including George Best, Norman Whiteside, Willie John McBride, Pat Jennings, Mary Peters, Frank Bruno and Lucian Freud. Freud and his personal bookie, Alfie McLean from Belfast, were crazy about boxing. Alfie was intent on signing Sam Storey and backing him in the pro game.

Before he could get anywhere near the posh seats at ringside, McGuigan was engulfed by the police and security forces. They ignored the frantic television cameramen's pleading and, with the aisles jammed by hundreds of fans, they forced a different path through the crowd. The walk was slow and stressful but McGuigan calmed himself by saying his favourite little prayer over and over to himself:

Angel of God, my Guardian dear, to whom God's love commits me here; Ever this day, be at my side, to light and guard, to rule and guide.

The ring was crammed with people. McGuigan could see his father, Pat, whom he had asked to sing 'Danny Boy' after the Panamanian national anthem had been played. Even something as apparently simple as an anthem had to be considered carefully. Just as McGuigan wore trunks which were the same blue colour as the United Nations flag, with a dove of peace on the right leg, he was also adamant that he could not have the Irish anthem played for him in the ring. He came from Clones in the South, but playing '*Amhrán na bhFiann*' would be seen as an endorsement of the Republican movement.

'Danny Boy', instead, was a song that meant so much to Barry and his family. The melody wrapped around his heart, and the words – especially the happiness tinged with melancholia of 'in sunshine or in shadow' – tugged at him. His father singing the song was a gift to him just before he went into a dark place against Pedroza.

He knew how emotional it would be for his dad to sing these words for him, and to him, in a gesture that seemed so personal it hardly mattered that a record 20 million people were watching on the BBC. McGuigan kept his head down, not allowing himself to even wonder if his father would get through the song without breaking down and crying. He could see Pedroza less than ten feet away, staring at him, and so, instead of looking at his dad, he kept saying his Angel of God prayer.

The music began to swell and Pat McGuigan, his thick black moustache quivering, began to sing softly yet powerfully:

> *Oh, Danny boy, the pipes, the pipes are calling*
> *From glen to glen, and down the mountain side.*
> *The summer's gone, and all the roses falling,*
> *It's you, it's you must go and I must bide.*

The Loftus Road crowd joined the mass singing. Almost everyone knew the words. Men and women, the majority of whom originally came from Belfast and Derry, from Armagh or Dublin, lifted their heads. Their voices helped Pat McGuigan sing for his fighting son.

> *But come ye back when summer's in the meadow,*
> *Or when the valley's hushed and white with snow,*
> *It's I'll be here in sunshine or in shadow*

That last line seemed to catch at the back of so many throats. There was such feeling as the crowd sang 'in sunshine or in shadow', it was as if a muffled gasp ran through the throng. It was a communal recognition of the profound grief so many people had experienced for so many years – and yet it was mingled with the rare bursts of hope they felt on these extraordinary nights of boxing.

Pat McGuigan sang on, of the flowers that are dying, and asked that, 'If I am dead, as dead I well may be, You'll come and find the place where I am lying . . .'

People were crying openly, tears running down the faces of battered hard men who normally struggled to express love and compassion. The night filled with the sound of almost religious singing – and the final hope that, in a warm and sweet grave, 'I shall sleep in peace until you come to me.'

The ring was nearly empty as the two fighters, having been stripped of their gowns, looked at each other. The poignant fervour of communal song had been replaced by a surreal sight. 'A midget, an Irish midget, prances around the ring as McGuigan is announced,' an incredulous Harry Carpenter told his vast BBC audience as a tiny little man dressed in black pixie boots, white shorts, an emerald jacket and a matching green trilby gambolled across the canvas before doing a cartwheel. This had been Barney Eastwood's madcap idea because he had heard the Panamanians were superstitious and believed in black magic. Pedroza, however, appeared not even to notice the fake leprechaun. His gaze was fixed on his challenger skipping quietly in the opposite corner to him.

After the South African referee Stan Christodoulou brought Pedroza and McGuigan together for their final instructions, both champion and challenger retreated one last time to their corners. Pedroza knelt down on a knee to pray while McGuigan's feet danced and skipped.

As the lights outside the ring dimmed and the spectators bellowed, Carpenter asked a simple question: 'Can McGuigan do it in front of this astonishing crowd of people?'

During the opening four rounds, Pedroza slipped and slithered away from McGuigan with the guile of a veteran champion. McGuigan exerted fierce pressure. The action was stark and unremitting, but Pedroza's rangy left jab kept hammering home. He reddened McGuigan's Irish skin, but the challenger shrugged off the pain of being hit in the face and he pummelled Pedroza up close.

'What a marvellous fight,' Carpenter enthused just before the bell ended the fourth. 'McGuigan hurts him again. Heaven knows who is going to weaken first.'

Pedroza was ahead on the three judges' scorecards but

McGuigan boxed to a plan. He knew he would have to absorb many punches to slowly dent Pedroza.

The champion switched tactics in round five. He fought much more on the inside and he was just as effective at close quarters. But the changed strategy also suited McGuigan. He landed chopping short punches that encouraged the old 'Here we go, here we go, here we go!' chant from the crowd. And then, as he began to back up Pedroza, he sank a jolting left hook to the body. McGuigan heard a soft groan slip from Pedroza as the bell rang. A right hand from McGuigan landed fractionally late and Pedroza fired back. It was the third time that Christodoulou had to jump in and stop them fighting after the bell.

McGuigan turned to his corner feeling lifted. He knew now that he could hurt the champion even as Carpenter said, 'I've got them dead level.'

In the sixth, McGuigan rocked Pedroza again with a right hook and a left to the stomach – but the champion boxed well and landed eye-catching jabs. 'These are two great athletes and two great boxers,' Carpenter enthused. 'It's surpassing all expectations – the brilliance of it.'

Round seven was notable, initially, for the way Pedroza outboxed McGuigan with slick counters and sly movement. 'McGuigan's work has not been so effective in this round,' Carpenter said, 'he hasn't found the range.' At that very moment the challenger uncorked a big right hand. 'Oh, yes he has!' Carpenter suddenly yelped. 'He's got him with a right!'

Pedroza went down heavily, as McGuigan caught the top of his falling head with a left hook that missed the intended target of the champion's chin. McGuigan moved quickly to a neutral corner, looking calm in contrast to his trainer, promoter and cutman who were all leaping around. The referee counted to eight while Pedroza nodded at him on unsteady feet.

McGuigan came wading in, missing wildly while Pedroza weaved out of the way. The last 20 seconds of the round were messy but Pedroza made it back to his corner.

'I can hardly hear myself talk, amid this inferno of noise,' Carpenter yelled as Pedroza tried to regain his composure.

Pedroza came back strongly, like a true champion, and won the eighth – only to be hurt badly again in round nine. McGuigan nearly put him down for a second time when a left and a right hook to the temple shook Pedroza. He was so dominant and the crowd was so raucous that he landed three extra punches after the bell had rung. It was almost impossible for the fighters and the referee to hear anything above the roaring of: 'We love you, Barry, we do.'

The champion looked forlorn and weary. A mouse of a swelling under his left eye seemed tender to the touch as his trainer wiped his face gently. Pedroza looked ten years older than he had done at the start of the fight. Yet the Panamanian was tough and he won the next round, mixing grit and skill, only for McGuigan to take the 11th and the 12th.

Unlike British title fights, world championship bouts were still held over 15 rounds. The pressure McGuigan exerted, however, never lessened and, slowly, minute by minute, Pedroza wilted. He was backed up in the last 40 seconds of the 13th as, suddenly, McGuigan opened up with punches of terrible beauty. A long right hand and a sickening left hook wobbled Pedroza. Another left hook and a right almost knocked him down. McGuigan glanced at the referee, inviting him to spare a great champion any more suffering. Pedroza smacked a right hand in the challenger's face to remind him that they were still fighting. He then grabbed McGuigan in a clinch to recover. The bell completed his rescue.

His trainer talked urgently to him in Spanish, but Pedroza stared vacantly into the distance. Eventually the old fighter turned back to his trainer and began to nod as he drew in great gulps of breath to sustain him for the last two rounds.

After his epic 13th round, McGuigan sensed he would not be able to knock out Pedroza. But he still powered forward, hunting down Pedroza, throwing combinations with constant dedication. Pedroza's mouth was bleeding and the red trickle could be seen beneath his gumshield. He was still alert to an opening, however, and when McGuigan paused briefly and lowered his left hand, Pedroza caught him with a long right. He was not quite done yet.

Paddy Byrne, McGuigan's cutman, made his voice heard in the short break before the final round. 'You've got three minutes to beat the best featherweight champion this century.'

McGuigan looked up at him in surprise. 'Is this the last round?'

'Yes!' said Byrne. 'In three minutes you'll be the champion of the world!'

Pedroza's trainer was even more animated, yelling and bringing his hand down in a chopping motion as if to tell the champion that only a brutal knockout could save him now.

The two fighters came together in the centre of the ring. McGuigan stretched out his left glove and Pedroza, bowing his head respectfully, touched him with both hands.

'What a wonderful fight,' Carpenter crooned, 'and Barry McGuigan has raised British boxing to almost unprecedented heights.'

Despite all his careful efforts to remain neutral, McGuigan was being embraced as British even while, in Derry and Dublin, Belfast and Cork, his very Irishness was being exalted with drink and song in pubs and living rooms as the dream came closer to millions of his supporters.

In the fierce isolation of the ring, McGuigan's concentration remained intense. He focused remorselessly on Pedroza, hurting him again with a jolting combination.

'Here we go, here we go, here we go!' the crowd roared, as if they were going from crumbling old Loftus Road to a place filled with redemption and hope.

'Twenty-seven thousand people,' Carpenter purred, 'singing McGuigan home to victory.'

In the last minute, McGuigan lived up to his nickname of the Clones Cyclone. He came at Pedroza with natural fury, arms whirling and fists flying, as his punches whipped in with swirling impact. Pedroza sagged like an old willow tree bending and almost breaking at the end of a terrible storm. The Cyclone raged on, blowing all the way from Clones to Shepherd's Bush.

Chants of 'Champion, champion, champion!' reverberated as Pedroza clung on.

Pedroza ducked under a wild left hook from McGuigan, searching for his Hollywood ending, and punched back. They were firing blows at each other, in fitting tribute, as the bell sounded and the referee jumped between them.

The two men embraced and Pedroza leant down so he could say one line, in English, to McGuigan: 'You'll be a good champion.'

'You're a great champion,' McGuigan replied, just before he was swept up by his corner.

Dermot, his beloved brother, reached him first, his eyes brimming with tears, his mouth shouting words that Barry could not hear amid the madness. They lifted the new champion up on their shoulders and, while the verdict had yet to be announced, Barry raised his arms above his head.

He had done it. He had done it for himself and his family. But he had also done it for Clones and Belfast, for the North and the South, for every great boxing man who had gone before him, from Gerry Storey and Charlie Nash to Davy Larmour and Hugh Russell. He had proved that you could win a war in the ring and spread hope and happiness beyond the ropes – despite all the violence and murder, the hatred and grief.

Barry McGuigan looked calm as he was held high in the night sky. He gazed at the crowd, choosing neither to crow nor to shout, but drinking in the magnitude of the moment. Then, looking down at his brother and his father, he brought his red gloves to his lips and kissed them before dropping them down towards the men who loved him most, as if his kisses might follow them down.

'Unbelievable scenes,' Carpenter said. 'People are fighting to get into the ring, to get near to their hero.'

McGuigan wanted peace rather than any more fighting. As he

was lowered to the floor, he went in search of the valiant Pedroza. He pushed his way past people who wanted to hug and kiss him. It was important that he pay tribute to his opponent's courage and skill. The two fighters embraced and spoke soft words to each other that they could not hear above the noise. After they broke, Pedroza raised his arms to the crowd who duly acknowledged him.

People began to shout and say 'Sshhhhh!' before the announcement.

'Ladies and gentlemen,' the MC finally shouted. 'This is the result. A unanimous decision.'

Those last three words produced a huge rumble of cheering. Everyone knew then. There would be no mistakes or miscarriages of justice this time.

'Barry McGuigan is the new ...'

The rest of the sentence was lost in the roaring euphoria, in the jubilation that boomed around Loftus Road and was matched in Clones and Dublin and, most of all, in Derry and Belfast, on the Falls Road and in the Shankill Road, in Loyalist Tiger's Bay and Republican New Lodge. They all had one champion, the same man, the same dream, the same hope, the same happiness.

Harry Carpenter was in the ring. He put his arm around Barry and they began to discuss the fight on live television. Twenty million people watched and listened.

'I'm delighted to have beaten a renowned champion so well,' Barry said as he also remembered his private vow in church earlier that day. 'I'd like to take this opportunity to say one thing and I've been thinking about it all week ...'

The words snagged deep within his chest and he couldn't talk for a moment. He needed to draw in two breaths to push back the rising swell of his tears. 'I said if I won this world title I would dedicate it to a young lad who died when he fought me in 1982. I'd said at the start I'd like it to be not just an ordinary fighter that beat him, but a world champion ...'

Those two words, 'world champion', cracked him open. He

began to cry then. He could no longer talk. Barry could not say 'Young Ali' even though he wanted to honour his lost opponent with his fighting name. The tears took hold of him, running down his face and making his mouth twitch. He was helped by his father and by the commentator. As Pat McGuigan hugged his son, Harry Carpenter explained the significance of the tribute to his audience. Young Ali was remembered. He was honoured. He was back in the ring again.

Barry buried his face in his father's shoulder and let everything go. His pain and his relief, his sadness and his joy – both for Young Ali and himself, and even for Belfast and Clones – poured out of him. In such a public setting, in a moment of deep privacy, he knew how important it was to remember the shadows that had come before all this sudden sunshine.

'I'm here, son,' Pat McGuigan said quietly as he held the new world champion. 'I'm here.'

A Beautiful Wee Life

I feel like I have lived through the elation and the grief. I feel drained by the Troubles. I feel drained of them too. The Troubles are gone and Belfast is now warm and friendly. I have some favourite cafés and bars where I have watched this tough little city breathe in and out without the fear of another Bloody Friday. It is the same in the smaller world of Derry, where it is easy to see a city living in a new way with the belief there could never be another Bloody Sunday.

Yet every time I am in Belfast, and Derry too, it is impossible to ignore the past. In Belfast, the Troubles have become a tourist attraction. An hour-long drive in a black taxi will take you around the city, moving between Loyalist and Republican enclaves with a driver acting as an informed guide, detailing the milestones and tragedies of the Troubles. The taxi drivers are even-handed and patient in explaining a complicated story to visitors who want to learn more about this infamous conflict while stopping for a few selfies next to the murals. The drivers attempt to place the bloody strife into context and to offer insight into a battle that sometimes, from the outside, verged on madness.

There are other signs that the wounds of the conflict are not fully healed or resolved. Belfast's awkwardly named peace walls loom like giant symbols of enduring division. They remind me of how I feel every time I return to Johannesburg.

Twenty-five years have passed since Nelson Mandela was elected president in South Africa's first democratic elections. It is now possible to marvel at the easy mingling of black and white people. But I still remember those days when, while riding my bicycle as a boy over a bridge that crossed the railway line near my house, there was a partition. One side of the bridge was for 'Whites Only' while the other said 'Non-Whites'. There are no such bridges in South Africa today. There is neither detention without trial nor any whites-only schools, hotels and beaches. There is a one-person, one-vote system and a workable form of democracy.

Of course there is corruption, crime, violence and racism on both sides of the old divide. There are also graphic symbols of the past merging with the present. The gulf between the rich and the poor is probably wider than ever, and the walls and security fences in suburban white South Africa have become higher and more prolific. Armed security companies patrol the neighbourhoods as they attempt to keep out the desperate and the violent who have so much less in their lives. The demarcation of black and white remains vivid – which is not surprising when we remember the state of the country, and the embedded structures of racism, just 30 years ago. The bitterness and injustice of the past were never going to be washed away by marketing speak about the Rainbow Nation. The struggle for harmony and equality will grind on for decades.

I think of this when, away from the stylish cafés and bars, Belfast's scarred history rises up. The Good Friday Agreement, in April 1998, ushered in a multi-party devolved form of government in Northern Ireland. An uplifting if still tenuous peace has endured for the last 20 years, but some of the peace walls look so big and brutal, running like a giant barrier between Catholic and Protestant communities, that it is easy to wonder if anything has really changed.

Fifty years since the first peace walls emerged in Belfast, when temporary structures were built to form a physical barrier between the communities in 1969, it is jarring to see how many more exist now. One hundred and eight peace walls, or security fences, are found in Northern Ireland, with the overwhelming majority being in north and west Belfast. They are also seen in Derry, Portadown and Lurgan.

If all the peace walls in Northern Ireland were lined up they would stretch the divide for 21.1 miles. The longest wall extends for over three miles, while the highest structures are so tall it would be impossible to lob a petrol bomb over the top. Some have gates but they are usually locked at night. They remain in place because of the emotions stirred by official records declaring that 67 per cent of the fatalities suffered during the Troubles occurred within 1,600 feet of these walls.

It is striking that there are many more peace walls in place now than there were in the 1990s when the Troubles still simmered. Over a third of the walls have been built since the paramilitary ceasefire of 1994. The new structures since the Good Friday Agreement are also noticeably higher and longer than the older walls. That deal, brokered by the British and Irish governments, created a Nationalist and Unionist power-sharing government in Northern Ireland where previous sworn enemies like Martin McGuinness of the IRA and Ian Paisley of the DUP revelled in a real friendship and surreal status as the Chuckle Brothers. McGuinness and Paisley are both dead now, but the Northern Ireland Assembly at Stormont has committed tentatively to removing all the walls by 2023.

It is debatable whether this will happen because, in January 2017, the Northern Ireland Assembly collapsed and two years later remained in a state of suspension. The differences ran so deep that the amalgamated assembly seemed unable to sit down together and function as a basic form of government. The border between the South and the North also became an issue again during plans for Brexit.

So the problems of sectarianism and division have not disappeared and, by extension, it is easy to conclude that boxing had only a limited impact during the dark time it brought fresh hope. It also seems logical to argue that sport in my former country, South Africa, played a far more significant political role in bringing about change. The difference, however, is that it was a sports boycott of South Africa, by the international community, that cracked the resolute policies of apartheid. White South Africans were so crazy about sport, especially rugby, that the boycott from the late 1960s to the early 1990s forced them to question why the world reviled them and whether apartheid was worth the damage it also did to the privileged minority who yearned to see their teams on the international stage.

In contrast, a strange business like boxing inspired people in Northern Ireland, from all corners and sides, to believe that another way of living was possible. In the strict confines of the boxing ring and the gym, a man's religion and political persuasion did not matter when set against his courage, discipline and skill. Boxing did not stem the Troubles, or end the killings, but it offered shafts of light and hope. The full extent of its influence is impossible to measure, but fighters and trainers from opposite sides crossed borders and faced each other on equal terms. They respected and liked each other – and they were loved and even revered by both communities. They offered a template for the future.

My interaction with the five main characters in these pages means that I am more interested in the crumbling of walls within people themselves. There was such anger, hatred and sadness inside ordinary men and women during the Troubles that the hope offered by Gerry Storey, Barry McGuigan, Charlie Nash, Davy Larmour and Hugh Russell had a profound impact on me. Writing about paramilitary mayhem in the 1970s and '80s, and documenting a business as violent as boxing, is not really conducive to good cheer. But the paradox was established. I felt light and happy whenever I heard these stories of my boxing men as they forged their singular path of peace, despite devoting the prime of their lives to punching opponents into submission.

I still knew that it would be a mistake to argue that boxing, or even Storey or McGuigan, had altered the course of history. But at least their impact was acknowledged. McGuigan had, of course, been the BBC Sports Personality of the Year and been inducted into boxing's Hall of Fame. Storey had won the Laureus Sport for Good award in 2005 for his boxing work across the sectarian divide. The award was presented to him by McGuigan and Marvin Hagler and it meant a great deal to Gerry because his work was honoured just before he lost his wife, Belle, to cancer.

Gerry loved boxing, and his fighters, too much to focus on his own story. Despite him being such a welcoming man, it took me a long time to draw out his personal history. He prefers to deflect attention from himself. But of all the stories in this book it is Gerry's work in the Maze, just after the hunger strikes of 1981, that resonated deepest.

He helped me to meet two men who had been locked up in the Maze when he moved between the Loyalist and Republican cages and offered boxing tuition in a prison where stagnation and hopelessness dominated. Billy Hutchinson, who had worked so closely with Gusty Spence in the UVF cages, was different to Bik McFarlane, the IRA commander inside the prison when Bobby Sands and nine other hunger strikers starved themselves to death in 1981.

I met Hutchinson first, at his Progressive Unionist Party office in Mount Vernon, north Belfast. The PUP is a small party on the left of the Unionist spectrum, but Hutchinson had been an important paramilitary leader in the UVF. He had also been instrumental, alongside his colleague David Ervine, in sealing the Loyalist ceasefire in October 1994 and had gone on to become a central figure in the Good Friday Agreement negotiations.

It was riveting to hear him talk about the way in which a former gunman, Spence, helped him step back from paramilitary violence in the Maze – where Hutchinson had been sent after pleading guilty to his involvement in the murder of two Catholic workmen, Michael Loughran and Edward Morgan, in October 1974 when he was 19. I also liked hearing Hutchinson remember Mo Mowlam and how that singular British politician had rescued the Good Friday Agreement when she decided, without gaining clearance from Tony Blair, to meet with Loyalist leaders in the Maze. They were close to withdrawing from the peace process when Mowlam persuaded them to remain.

But I was captivated most by Hutchinson's memories of Gerry in the Maze – and how the trainer had lifted the men in the Loyalist cages. 'Gusty Spence [the UVF leader in the cages] had a great influence over me,' Hutchinson said. 'He taught me the importance of having principles and liking yourself. He would say if you hate yourself you will never be able to like others. He also got us to understand the importance of discipline and self-belief and how to work together. This is hard to do when you are in prison and self-hatred, a lack of discipline and petty squabbles sweep through the place. In 1981, Gusty knew we needed Gerry Storey. It did not matter that we were Loyalist prisoners and that Gerry came from the Republican side. We needed him to help our men exercise their minds and bodies. Gerry and boxing lifted us up.'

Hutchinson was no boxing aficionado, but he understood the power of Gerry Storey. 'We all knew who Gerry was and what he meant. Gerry is famous in boxing. But he is also famous for coming from the New Lodge and achieving so much by keeping young men away from paramilitary violence. We wanted him to bring those principles to our men, who were often serving life sentences without any hope. It was great that he lived up to everything we had heard about him.'

I asked if he had any doubts before meeting Gerry – considering the Storey family's involvement with the IRA. Hutchinson laughed. 'There were no misgivings with Gerry. There would have been if it had been someone else. But Gerry's narrative came before him. We all knew his interest was boxing. But he was also interested in building people's characters. It was not just about being a world or Olympic champion. It was about finding the best character in everyone – how boxing could build their confidence. He stayed away from sectarianism and boxing politics. There was always infighting and backstabbing, but Gerry rose above it. We noticed this about him – how he offered hope to everyone he met.'

Hutchinson paused and looked up. 'How do you measure the depth of that hope?' he asked. 'How do you measure the way that Gerry and boxing changed society for the better? You can't. It's too difficult. All I know is what I saw with my own eyes and I felt it with every fibre of my being. He showed us a better way to live. The impact on us was profound.'

I told Hutchinson how striking it seemed that, through Gerry, the Loyalist and Republican cages shared their boxing equipment and looked out for each other. It showed grace amid such gloom. 'It did,' he agreed. 'It also helped in later years when we had to negotiate peace deals. We had got used to thinking of each other as people. I remember that conversation we had with Gerry and him telling me and Gusty that the IRA boys did not have much boxing equipment. We offered our stuff for them to use. One of the interesting things about Long Kesh [as Hutchinson still called the Maze] is that all the groups kept in touch. We would check how each other were doing. "We're doing x, y and z in regard to the prison governors. What are you doing?" It was like one group of politicians talking to another. Gerry helped break down those walls.

'The fact that he moved between the Loyalist and the Republican cages made me think, at first, that Gerry was either very stupid or brave. But I soon realised he was the opposite of stupid – and he was more than just courageous. He was just a genuine human being, and the goodness shone out of him. He was entitled to have worked only with the Republicans, who were his people, but he didn't live life like that. He wanted to bring boxing to both sides. He never asked people about their religion or political affiliations. He just saw us as people.

'Other people came into the cages – politicians and the press. But they came with their own agenda. It was like they were visiting a zoo and they saw us as animals. But Gerry just saw us as people who belonged to his boxing club – which just happened to be in a prison.

'I remember doing my postgraduate degree in geography and this woman came in as a tutor once a week. She was always nervous meeting me in the Nissen hut even though the prison officer would be there. One sunny afternoon the tutor came in with my exam, which she'd marked. I'd got good marks so I was happy. The officer said, "Right, Hutchie, I might as well go outside and sit in the sun." I could see the panic in this woman once he left. I could see her fear. I tried to calm her by talking about the subject. Eventually I said: "He's outside the door. Nothing's going to happen. I'm only interested in my education." She eased up a bit. She said it was very strange as it wasn't the prison they saw on TV – where everyone was violent.

'Ten years after I had been released, as the last man out of Long Kesh, I was in the city centre. I walked into a café. This woman was there. I didn't see her at first. But when I turned round and saw her, I said her name. She said, "You're that William Hutchinson. Sit down." She said when she'd started at the prison she had been told we were all animals. We'd kill or rape her. She said: "That day I was terrified but I realised you were trying to put me at ease."

'This woman was very middle class, academic and had probably not worked with anyone like me. Gerry is a working-class man and so he was very comfortable with us. He had no fear. He was totally non-judgemental and he would have ignored whatever the prison officers told him. We forged a great rapport and I felt very privileged to know him. He is still a legend. The debt we all owe him, and boxing, is immeasurable.'

The following morning, Gerry and I went to see Bik McFarlane.

We met in a café and spoke about Gerry's miraculous work. I did not tape our discussion as the pain of the hunger strike and Bobby Sands was too personal. Gerry's nephew, Bobby Storey, and McFarlane had also led the escape of 37 Republican prisoners from the Maze in 1983. McFarlane preferred to talk about the way Gerry still used boxing as a force for good 35 years later at the Holy Family.

'He's like no one else I know,' McFarlane said simply, shaking his head in admiration.

'Gerry, Gerry!' they shouted, clamouring for his attention one evening in January 2018. Three small girls and two boys, ranging in age from eight to 13, crowded around him at the Holy Family. Each one of them had an urgent question for the trainer. Could they get in the ring? Could they go on the pads? Could they spar soon? Could they go for a quick pee?

'Hold on, hold on,' Gerry Storey said calmly, smiling at his latest recruits. The Holy Family was heaving again on a Monday night. I counted 30 kids, the two oldest being a couple of aspiring Olympians showing steely dedication. Inside the ring, the best of them worked with Seamus McCann, a former Holy Family boxer who is now one of Gerry's main assistant trainers. McCann, a ferociously fit man, pushed the oldest boys hard, encouraging them to whip combinations into the shuddering pads he held on his hands. The seriousness of their punching stood in contrast to the enthusiasm of the kids around Gerry.

Once Gerry had reminded the little boy to take off his gloves and wash his hands after going to the toilet, he sent them to various parts of the gym to continue training with his assistants – one of whom is a barrister, Kevin Morgan, who helps out often at the Holy Family.

Gerry stood with me on the apron of his ring, pointing out which of his wee fighters were progressing the fastest. He loved the fact that so many girls were now learning how to box.

'It's tough being a young girl out there,' he said quietly.

After an hour you get used to the heat of the Holy Family. The oppressive intensity when you first walk in, accompanied by the familiar stench of a busy boxing gym, starts to feel ordinary. Gerry and I tried to work out how many evening sessions of training I'd watched over the years, but all my visits had begun to blur even though each one was made distinct by a new story or a new character.

The walls were still dripping with sweat when the last of the boxers came over to shake hands with us. Seamus was closing in on 50. He had been coming to the Holy Family since the early 1980s. 'When I joined the club as a kid it was full of champions,' he said. 'Hugh Russell, Davy Larmour, Barry McGuigan. Soon after that, Sam Storey went all the way to the Olympics and to fighting Chris Eubank for a world title in the '90s. It's always been special.

'In my early days you'd have gunplay outside. Inside it was like it is today – full of kids keen to box and soak up knowledge from Gerry. But outside, every kind of madness was going on. You'd come out of the Holy Family on a dark winter night, like tonight, and you would have heard gunfire, explosions, screaming and running. Everything that turns your blood cold.

'My own kids have never really understood the Troubles. They've never experienced what we felt. There was a huge sectarian divide. But in boxing there was no divide. Boxing gave us freedom whether you were a Protestant or a Catholic. No matter who was getting murdered, you clung to boxing. My father was blown up by a bomb when I was a kid. Right here in New Lodge. He survived it, but it was terrifying. Boxing gave me the hope that we would, one day, get to a better place. And so we did – eventually.'

Gerry listened quietly as Seamus spoke. The younger man then pointed to him. 'He might not like me saying it but the real hero of the Troubles is sitting next to us right now. I would say all of New Lodge, the whole of Belfast, everywhere in Northern Ireland, owes a thank you to Gerry Storey. Before anyone else he saw a way to bring people together. He saw a way to get over the hate and prejudice. It was because of Gerry that I felt no bitterness after my father got blown up. It was because of Gerry I could be friends with Protestant kids. It was because of Gerry we kept going, we kept trying and laughing, even when someone would get killed every night of the week.'

'Shamey,' Gerry said, 'remember going into Maghaberry Prison to box?'

Maghaberry Prison, not far from the Maze on the outskirts of Lisburn, was another bleak and labyrinthine place of confinement. Eight hundred prisoners, from both Loyalist and Republican backgrounds, were kept behind the towering walls and barbed-wire fences. Their cells ran along pale-green corridors and were sealed shut by steel doors with observation shutters to enable the wardens to peer in at the inmates at any time of day or night. It was a relatively new jail but it already seemed a desolate place when, in the late 1980s, Gerry was asked if he could spread his boxing magic.

He suggested bringing in a squad of Holy Family fighters. They would put on a show of ten bouts for the prisoners. His usual stipulation – that there should be no sectarian divide – had already been met. The prison governor even agreed that women from the adjoining Mourne House detention centre would be allowed in to watch the boxing.

'It was fun,' Gerry said as Seamus grinned. 'I was surprised to find some of my old Protestant friends inside. People like Silver Wilson. What a character. Before the Troubles I mixed with Protestants and Catholics alike. Silver Wilson and Fat Hobbs would have been two of my closest Protestant friends. And there we were, 30 years later – Silver was a prisoner and I was the boxing trainer bringing in kids like Seamus to put on a show for them.

'It was like going into a dance hall except it was full of Republican and Loyalist paramilitaries and gangsters. Although it was regimental, the women prisoners were there. I got such a big laugh in Maghaberry because the women were shouting at some of the men and boxing boys: "Big fella, you can have me any day!" It was all good fun. And what a reception they gave to Seamus and the boys. They loved having us there. So we went back.'

The stories flowed as we looked around the Holy Family, picking out all the familiar faces from the old fight posters and photographs. 'There's wee Cue,' Gerry said of Hugh Russell.

'He was one of your favourite fighters, wasn't he?' I said.

'I didn't allow myself favourites,' Gerry replied. 'I treated Davy Larmour just as well as I treated Cue. It was important to be fair to everyone. There was so much prejudice and unfairness outside that I liked everyone here to feel as if they mattered just as much as each other. They all got a fair crack in the Holy Family. That's why they got along so well – even when trying to knock each other out. They were all special to me.'

The next day I met Davy Larmour and Hugh Russell again. Almost 35 years had passed since their mighty battles in the ring, and each man still had scars from those bloody nights. Davy no longer worked on the docks or drove a taxi. In his mid-sixties, he had retired but he was still busy doing boxing work around the clubs in Belfast. We spent the morning talking about the fight game then and now. Davy remained at the heart of boxing in the city – as did Hugh Russell, who worked as a boxing official on big fight nights in Belfast while still being a photographer for the *Irish News*.

After work that evening, Hugh and I met in the Cathedral Quarter. He had brought his laptop because he was about to download a selection of his photographs onto a memory stick for me. These included one taken by his mentor, Brendan Murphy, of Hugh leaning over the ropes to kiss his mother just moments after he had beaten Davy in their first fight. Another was of Edgar Graham, Hugh's 'first body', and the photograph that captured the young Unionist politician lying dead next to his briefcase.

Hugh's most famous photograph absorbed us. 'This is Gerry Conlon, one of the Guildford Four,' Hugh said as he tapped the black-and-white image on his screen. Conlon, Paul Hill, Paddy Armstrong and Carole Richardson were wrongly convicted of carrying out the Guildford pub bombing that killed five people and injured 65 more on 5 October 1974. These four innocent people spent 15 years in jail before they were finally cleared at the Old Bailey in London on 19 October 1989.

Hugh looked down at the photograph as if greeting an old friend. 'That's Gerry Conlon coming out of the old building. That's probably the most famous one I've taken. It would have been in the *New York Times*. It was the first photograph of their first moment of freedom – and I got it. I was picked out by the families. It was crazy outside the Old Bailey with hundreds of photographers waiting for that one shot. But they saw me. They said, "Aren't you the wee boxer?" It was well over four years since I'd been in the ring but people still knew me. They asked me to come out of the crowd and follow them. No one else knew what was going on. But they did. They wanted me to take the first photo before anyone else. So I got given that chance and I was told exactly where to stand. It meant the first shot was mine.'

In the photograph, Conlon leaves court with his right arm raised in triumph. His sister wraps her left arm around him while her right hand is also held high. Her mouth is a scream of joy, while Conlon's pursed lips make a more quizzical shape as if it is too soon for him to start smiling. His other sister clutches Conlon's wrist while her other arm waves in delight. A heavily moustached British bobby looks on stoically.

'It makes me smile to think that I only got the photo because of boxing. I owe that to Gerry Storey ... just as me and so many other fighters owe so much more to Gerry.'

We spoke for a long time about the legacy of Gerry Storey before we returned to that sight of freedom. 'Conlon liked the photograph, which is the main thing,' Hugh said. 'I got to know him well later and he was a lovely guy. They suffered a great miscarriage of justice for 15 years. I was just glad that, because I was the "wee boxer", I got that moment in history.'

Later that week, back in Derry, Charlie Nash looked older and more frail. His memory had begun to fade, but we still relived another terrible miscarriage of justice – and the vindication he and his family finally felt when, on 15 June 2010, 38 and a half years after Bloody Sunday, the Saville Inquiry was made public and the British Prime Minister apologised in parliament.

Charlie's sister, Kate, who had helped lead the campaign to overturn the lies of Bloody Sunday, represented the Nash family at Guildhall where a selection of people were allowed to read the Saville Report before David Cameron made his apology.

The rest of the city seemed to turn out that day, retracing the steps of the march that resulted in the death of Willie Nash and 13 other people. There was tension on that summery afternoon as the city waited for news of a definitive report that had taken years to compile. Eventually, a hand appeared through the Guildhall window grilles. Another followed, and another, and then another until ten hands were in the air. It took a while for the crowd to understand. But, slowly, the murmuring turned to joyful shouting.

Each hand had upturned its thumb. The crowd understood, at last, that Lord Saville had vindicated the victims. The dead and the injured were all innocent. The tragedy had been caused by the British army and its support company of the 1st Battalion, the Parachute Regiment – a fact that the British government had concealed for 38 years.

In the sunlit square outside Guildhall, people danced and hugged and cried. They only fell silent when, a few minutes later, the British Prime Minister's speech was broadcast live from Westminster on a big screen. 'Mr Speaker,' David Cameron said, 'I am deeply patriotic, I never want to believe anything bad about our country. I never want to call into question the behaviour of our soldiers and our army, who I believe to be the finest in the world. Mr Speaker, these are shocking conclusions to read and shocking words to say. There's no doubt, there's nothing equivocal, there are no ambiguities. What happened on Bloody Sunday was both unjustified and unjustifiable. Lord Saville says the immediate responsibility for the deaths and injuries on Bloody Sunday lies with those members of Support Company whose unjustifiable firing was the cause of these deaths. The government is ultimately responsible for the conduct of the armed forces, and therefore on behalf of the government, on behalf of our country, I am deeply sorry.'

An immense silence filled the square before, suddenly, decades of pain exploded in disbelief, relief and then joy. A family representative of each person who had died then made a short speech to the city below. Every speech, including the powerful oratory of Kate Nash, ended with the speaker shouting out a single word: 'Innocent!'

At home, more than seven years on, Charlie Nash smiled sadly. 'I was so proud of Kate and all the people who fought to clear the names of Willie and the others,' he said. 'It was a good day but, still, I just wish none of it had ever happened.'

In March 2019, the Nash family were devastated when Northern Ireland's Public Prosecution Service decided that only one former British paratrooper – Solider F – would stand trial for the murder of James Wray and William McKinney, and for the attempted murders of Joseph Friel, Michael Quinn, Joe Mahon and Patrick O'Donnell. 'In respect of the other 18 suspects,' said Stephen Herron, the director of public prosecutions, 'it has been concluded that the available evidence is insufficient to provide a reasonable prospect of conviction.'

The killing of William Nash and 12 other people on Bloody Sunday would not be examined in a trial quite yet. Kate Nash reiterated her family's commitment to continuing the fight for justice, and she lamented the testimony of one of the paratroopers who insisted that he and his fellow soldiers had carried out 'a job well done.' For Kate and Charlie, it was 'very cold, very brutal.'

Charlie was happier when we got back to boxing. Sitting in his room where he kept all his trophies and photographs, he smiled. There was no sadness now. 'Oh, we loved the boxing,' he said simply.

I thought of Charlie again when Barry McGuigan, his fleeting sparring partner all those years ago, and I completed our second-last interview for this book in September 2018. We spent four hours together one morning in Wandsworth, south-west London, across the road from the gym he and his three sons – Shane, Blain and Jake – had built up. Sandra, his wife of 36 years, was working in the office on their next boxing promotion. At the end I asked Barry about 'Danny Boy' and becoming world champion.

'It meant so much that my dad sang that song before I beat Pedroza,' he said, 'but it's bittersweet. I've since lost my dad and I've lost Dermot, my brother. There has been a lot of grief. But at least they were with me that night. When he sang the song for me as our anthem, he was telling me how much he loved me as I went into battle. The song is both uplifting and melancholic. It's the same for boxing, and life itself. There is sunshine and there are shadows wherever we go, whoever you are. It just seems especially true for boxing and the Troubles.'

A month later, I met Barry and Sandra in the same pub. Sandra relived those years from her perspective as a Protestant girl in Clones and then as the wife of the most famous fighter during the Troubles. Barry wanted to highlight the significance of Storey again – and to stress that boxing's unique role in spreading hope in the Troubles was down to its hardness and coldness chiming with the experiences of the paramilitary gunmen. They gave the fighters and trainers leeway to travel across sectarian borders without fear.

Sandra was clearer in underlining Barry's impact on both boxing and the Troubles. 'I think it was his personality. I genuinely think that only Barry could appeal to such a wide spectrum of society.

Before Barry we had George Best, who was massive but he was a drinker. Alex Higgins was massive, but he was a drinker. Barry was bigger than both of them because, away from sports fans and boxing fans and the paramilitaries, he attracted the mums, the parents, the grandparents. He was warm and sincere and he was a huge star at a time when there were only four television channels. Everyone could identify with Barry and he was able to offer such hope through boxing.'

Barry pointed out that Storey had done so much before him. 'Yes, he did,' Sandra said, 'but it needed someone with your personality to bring boxing to the masses. Fate played a huge part. If you had not been left out of the Irish squad for the European under-19 championships in 1978, after you had beaten Michael Holmes in Dublin, none of this would have happened in the same way. You would have kept boxing for Ireland. But they picked Holmes ahead of you and you boxed for Northern Ireland instead.

'You were this Catholic kid from Clones who won a Commonwealth gold medal for Northern Ireland. It would have had nowhere near the same impact if you'd boxed for Ireland. The fact you won it for Northern Ireland and they played "Danny Boy" as your anthem, and you cried over that sunshine and shadow line, set the template for your whole career. Your personality and that particular twist of fate meant you had a platform to spread hope – and the hope was real. It was true. It helped bring about some change. It was important.'

On my last day of research in Belfast I spent most of the morning in the Republican neighbourhood of Ardoyne with the former boxer Eamonn Magee, who had won the WBU version of the world middleweight title in 2003. Fifteen years on, Magee described himself as a high-functioning alcoholic. He opened the front door in his dressing gown and with a beer in his hand. It was just after 11 on a Monday morning and the former boxer was cut and bruised from being attacked the night before. His left hand was swollen and an obviously broken finger made him wince whenever it brushed against his can of Carling.

Such pain was fleeting compared with the deeper hurt that ran through him. His life in Ardoyne has been scarred by violent sectarianism and tragedy. He said 'more sectarian shit' had caused his latest problems after he had been attacked on successive nights. Exception had been taken to his biography – in which he detailed many horrendous incidents stretching from Republican politics to drink and drugs.

Magee waved his bust hand at me and took another slug of beer. 'I've had a beautiful wee life,' he said. 'I wouldn't change a thing.'

I asked him if he knew Gerry Storey. 'Aye, Gerry's a gentleman,' he said softly. 'He chose the right path. I went the other way.' Magee's battered, 46-year-old face crinkled and the lump under his left eye looked even more like a purple mouse as he echoed himself: 'It's still been a beautiful wee life.'

A trip to the Ardoyne, into the troubled world of Eamonn Magee, was a reminder that some Belfast boxing men were different to Storey and McGuigan, to Russell and Larmour. It was also salutary to remember that Belfast was still haunted by sectarianism and danger in 2018.

I had felt calm when I took the call that told me about Magee's latest scrap. My mood remained the same in the cab rumbling through the familiar streets of Belfast, passing the Republican murals and the high peace walls. I even felt okay when, after I rang the bell, two pit bulls next door leapt at the fence, barking fiercely. 'They're wee nippers,' their owner warned as he pulled the dogs away.

It was harder to feel serene once Magee told me that some Republican hard cases had threatened to shoot him in the next few days. I also twitched each time Magee's phone interrupted us with its 'Who Let the Dogs Out?' ringtone. I scanned his beaten-up face, wondering if it was a call to tell him a paramilitary gunman was on his way. I didn't feel too hopeful at the prospect of Magee, in his dressing gown, and I talking our way out of trouble.

Magee offered me a beer but I declined. Did he ever wish he could kick the bottle?

'I tried rehab,' he said, pausing with comic timing before breaking into the Amy Winehouse song. 'And I said, "No, no, no!"'

I laughed with him but I also knew that, beneath all his scars, the internal wounds had not healed. Magee told me a chilling story of how, during internment raids in the 1970s, he and his three brothers would be turned out of the two beds they shared. British soldiers marched them downstairs and they had to kneel, hands behind their heads, while their photographs were taken for no apparent reason.

'Oh fuck, where are we starting?' Magee said as he remembered the impact that internment had on Catholic families. 'My dad was a through-and-through Republican and had a proper understanding of the war. It wasn't about bothering Protestants. The war was against the British army in Ireland. But my dad was a smashing man. The Brits imprisoned him in Long Kesh and the Irish Republicans had a bus run because in them days people couldn't afford anything else. So we would take the bus up to Long Kesh. I was a wee nuisance and carried in letters written on cigarette papers. I folded them and hid them under my tongue.'

Sitting in his dead father's house, I was upset by his memory of how, once his dad had fallen out with the IRA and been banished to England, he snuck back into Ardoyne and was hidden away in his attic. Magee, his mum and his brothers lived in fear of his dad being discovered. They hid him in the attic for 18 months – which contributed to Magee Sr's acute depression and alcoholism.

'I didn't get over that,' Magee said. 'My mum would have a wee drink and Dad would sit in there all night. I'd go in and slip him a tin or a fag. Nobody else ever knew he was there.'

Later, when Magee had become one of the most accomplished amateur boxers in Ireland, his father saved his career. Magee had joined the IRA's youth wing because he loved rioting, but he also began taking and dealing drugs. An IRA punishment shooting usually entailed being shot in the kneecap or worse, but his dad reminded the paramilitaries that Eamonn was fighting in the Irish championships.

'If my dad hadn't stepped in they were talking about me getting the six-pack – elbows, knees and ankles. But my father convinced them to only give me one bullet.'

How did Magee feel, waiting for the knock on the door before he took a bullet in his calf? He shrugged. 'It had to be dealt with. I knew it was going to be a flesh wound, so hurry the fuck up. When he took me down an alleyway, I asked: "What's it like getting shot?" He said: "Like a hot poker going in your leg."'

Magee won the vacant WBU welterweight title by beating the journeyman Jimmy Vincent in December 2003. He retained his world title until May 2006, but he had only had two fights in that troubled time. Magee had fallen out with a respected figure in Republican circles and, in a gruesome attack in 2004, his left leg was clubbed to a pulp. He suffered a compound fracture of his tibia and fibia, a shattered knee and a punctured lung. They called him the Miracle Man when he returned to the ring.

Magee's legs poked out of his dressing gown and the lumps and scars provided graphic proof of that terrible beating. 'It still gives me pain,' he said, balancing a beer on his damaged knee. 'The doctor thought I'd never walk again, but I was in the gym a year later.'

Rather than waiting inside for a knock on the door, I suggested we went for a walk around the neighbourhood. Magee agreed but, first, we remembered his son who was stabbed to death in May 2015 by the jealous ex-husband of his girlfriend. Eamonn Jr was so different to him, studying engineering at university while also boxing, and the grief became too much. Magee started to cry, a muffled ache falling from him as tears rolled down his face.

He squeezed my hand, only to curse the pain in his broken finger, before wiping his eyes. He went upstairs to get dressed. When he returned, wearing a hat straight out of *Peaky Blinders*, he looked dapper. The old fighter sank the dregs of his beer. We walked outside and he took me on a tour of the murals. Afterwards he hugged me in the street, calling me a gentleman and a scholar.

'Stay for a drink,' he said. 'We can talk boxing and the Troubles.'

We both laughed, but I shook my head. 'I'm off to the Holy Family,' I explained.

'Ah, you're seeing the king? Gerry Storey ... what a man. Tell him I said hello.'

Magee lifted his broken hand in a stately wave when my taxi drove away. It was time to return to more familiar terrain.

I head back now to the New Lodge. I take my usual short cut up North Queen Street, passing the McGurk's Bomb memorial and reaching the walkway round the back. After my morning with Magee, I almost smile to see that the brick wall is still painted white, with green and orange trim completing the colours of the Irish flag. In its left-hand corner, an IRA gunman in a balaclava still looks down at the rifle that has slipped from his hands. Opposite him a hooded IRA soldier still stands to attention with his bowed head and gun. The same words remain, echoing the bloody history of this city.

> *I don't care if I fall*
> *As long as someone else picks up my gun and keeps on shooting.*

The adjoining mural still shows three gunmen, dressed in black, aiming their rifles at a blue sky. *Tiocfaidh Ár Lá* (Our Day Will Come) and *Saoirse* (Freedom) are still painted in shimmering white.

I walk more quickly now. In less than a minute I am inside the red-brick building of the North Street Community Centre. I climb the stairs to the Holy Family gym on the top floor. As always, especially when empty in the daytime, it fills me with light and calm. It is steeped in discipline and pain, but it is also an oasis of peace.

Gerry Storey is already there, sitting on a chair next to the blue ring. He shouts out my name and says, 'Bang on time!'

I settle down with a sigh, feeling safe again, as if I have reached home. Gerry listens, smiles and shakes his head as I tell him about my morning with Magee.

In the heart of gritty old Belfast, alongside a boxing man who survived three assassination attempts and fought so hard for peace and tolerance, it feels like a miracle that the Troubles really are over. I spend another two hours in the gym, not wanting to leave, lingering over the old stories and the photographs that hang from the sweat-soaked walls.

Joe Frazier, who fought three titanic battles with Muhammad Ali, in a trilogy of fights that damaged both men while making the rest of us exalt in the majesty of boxing at its greatest, smiles down from some black-framed photos. Joe and Gerry were close friends. At the invitation of Smokin' Joe, Gerry often took teams from the Holy Family to fight in Philadelphia. Joe wanted Gerry to move to Philly.

Billy Conn was another great American fighter who tried to lure Gerry away from Belfast. Conn, who moved up a division and came so close to beating Joe Louis for the world heavyweight title in 1941, had worked hard to persuade Gerry to leave Belfast in the 1970s so that he could train young fighters in America. The Troubles were at their darkest pitch then but, despite the substantial increase in salary he was offered, Gerry refused to walk away.

I already know his answer but I ask him again why he chose not to leave for America where he would have made so much more money and found probable fame.

'What would have happened to Belfast,' he asks simply, 'if all the good people had left?'

When we meet again, just before Christmas in 2018, the miraculous work of Gerry Storey continues. A letter has arrived at the Holy Family. It contains confirmation from the court that a teenager will be spared incarceration in a detention centre if he is willing to begin training three times a week at the Holy Family under the guidance of Storey. The magistrate has decided that boxing offers more education and hope than a spell in a juvenile jail.

Gerry nods. The decision is so obvious he wonders why there might have been any debate. The boy will be welcome. There is little doubt that the Holy Family will work its magic and save another soul. This work means so much more to Gerry than the millions he might have made if he had moved to America and into professional boxing.

'This is good news,' Gerry says, waving the letter gently as if a sudden breakthrough has been achieved. 'We will keep working. We will keep fighting.'

In the hushed gym, on a peaceful December afternoon, the great old man of boxing sinks back in his chair and smiles. We talk a little longer, about his sons and some of his fighters, from Russell and Larmour to McGuigan and Nash. Gerry also calls Big Bobby Storey, his nephew, to tell him that we have finally completed the book.

It is time to leave and, with a little regret that we really have reached the end, I offer my hand and my thanks to Gerry. The 81-year-old walks me down the stairs and out into New Lodge.

'Now, Don,' he says, looking surprisingly serious, 'are you going to be all right getting back?'

Of course, I reply, for the surrounding streets are familiar and tranquil. I know the way to my usual hotel.

'Okay,' he says with a wink. 'Come back to the gym tonight, at seven, and you'll meet some cracking wee fighters. And if you get any bother tell them you're a friend of Gerry Storey. They all know I walk with the angels.'

The champion trainer laughs as we shake hands. Gerry begins to walk away before, slowly, he turns around. He lifts his hand to wave goodbye. On an afternoon of faint winter sunshine he looks like a man who really has lived a beautiful wee life.

Prologue: The Holy Family

The opening pages of the book are built around my many trips to Belfast and they are supplemented by my interviews with Gerry Storey and Barry McGuigan between 2011 and 2018. Towards the end of my research, I was fortunate enough to also interview Trevor Ringland and Willie John McBride, two great rugby men from Ulster who come from a Protestant background but played for Ireland and the British Lions. Ringland, in particular, was invaluable on the role in which sport plays in Northern Ireland and how boxing and rugby allow a 'relaxing of identities' and a blurring of backgrounds. He told me: 'I'm a Belfast man and an Ulsterman. I'm British and I'm Irish. I'm Northern Irish and I'm European. I'm a long-suffering Leeds United supporter. These identities are interchangeable and anyone who demeans any one part demeans me as a person. A multi-layered identity challenges the extremists.' It was unsurprising to hear of Ringland's admiration for the work done at the Holy Family, and he praised Storey's commitment to crossing the sectarian divide.

Before I began writing, it was especially helpful to read Teddy Jamieson's *Whose Side Are You On? Sport, the Troubles and Me*, Susan McKay's *Bear in Mind These Dead* and Mark Carruthers' *Alternative Ulsters: Conversations on Identity*.

Chapter 1: Bloody Sunday

I spent a considerable amount of time in Derry interviewing Charlie Nash and Damien McDermott. Their memories shape this chapter and Charlie, of course, helped my writing about Bloody Sunday and his brother Willie. Damien supplemented these insights with his clear recollections of the day and their journey back from Dublin while the carnage unfolded.

I read Charlie's unpublished writing about Willie, the build-up and aftermath of Bloody Sunday, and enjoyed seeing his photographs of his brother and wider family.

I often visited the Free Derry Museum, which is an invaluable source of archival material and witness accounts, in both visual and audio form, of Bloody Sunday. The work done by the Bloody Sunday Trust, which opened the museum in 2007, has done much to ensure that the events of that terrible day on 30 January 1972 will never be forgotten.

It was also important to read key extracts from the contrasting Widgery Report of 1973 and the Saville Enquiry of 2010 to understand how the truth was distorted and then uncovered decades later. I also spent many days at the British Newspaper Library, reading the English newspaper accounts, and at the Belfast Newspaper Library, which houses all the major archives from newspapers in Northern Ireland and the Republic of Ireland.

There are some excellent British and Irish television documentaries about Bloody Sunday and the following books were of real value to my research: David McKittrick and David McVea's *Making Sense of the Troubles*; Eammon McCann's *The Bloody Sunday Inquiry*; Douglas Murray's *Bloody Sunday*; and Adrian Kerr's *Free Derry: Protest and Resistance*. The magisterial *Lost Lives* – by David McKittrick, Seamus Kelters, Brian Feeney, Chris Thornton and David McVea – documents the stories of every man, woman and child who died in the Troubles. The section on Bloody Sunday is typically informative and illuminating.

Charlie Nash's unpublished memoir was also useful in underpinning his and Damien's memories of the death of Martin Harkin – whose tragic demise after an amateur fight is also recounted briefly in Barry Flynn's *The Little Book of Irish Boxing*.

In writing about Derry City, it helped to re-read Jamieson's *Whose Side Are You On?*

I enjoyed reading John Bradley's writing about Derry in the 1970s and '80s – and I also interviewed John about growing up in Derry both before and after Bloody Sunday.

Chapter 2: Two Bombs

Damien McDermott and Charlie Nash shape the first section of this chapter – and their interviews are supplemented by the newspaper archives.

Interviews with Gerry Storey and Davy Larmour are instrumental to the rest of this chapter, and both men were painstaking and generous in helping me establish the facts that drive the narrative.

Lost Lives, *Making Sense of the Troubles*, *Bear in Mind These Dead*, Peter Taylor's *Provos: The IRA & Sinn Féin* and Ed Moloney's *Voices from the Grave* were all useful – as were documentaries and online resources linked to the McGurk's Bar and Balmoral Showroom bombings.

But Larmour and, most of all, Storey provided the key information in this chapter.

Chapter 3: The Shankill Road Summit

Interviews with Gerry Storey, Charlie Nash and Davy Larmour provided the framework and the detail. Additional interviews with Willie John McBride and Damien McDermott added supplementary information.

Barry Flynn's *Legends of Irish Boxing* has some fine chapters on Gerry Storey, Charlie Nash, Davy Larmour and Hugh Russell – and I benefited from reading about Neil McLaughlin too.

Chapter 4: The Darkest Year

Charlie Nash's unpublished writing about 1972, and our detailed interviews, are at the heart of this chapter. Gerry Storey and Charlie Nash shared their memories of the Munich Olympics and I read various books and visited newspaper archives to learn more about the massacre, as well as the success of Mary Peters. I watched a number of documentaries about Bloody Friday, and focused on the *Irish News* and *Irish Times* coverage in the aftermath of the bombing.

The account of Charlie meeting Betty comes from our interviews.

Davy Larmour's unpublished memoir of his life helped enormously and I appreciated him sharing the hundreds of pages with me. They were especially useful in this chapter as a supplement to our interviews.

Damien McDermott shared his powerful and distressing memories of a punishment shooting and instances where women were tarred and feathered in Derry.

Gerry Storey, with much amusement in his voice, remembered how it could resemble the Wild West – with 'gunplay' on ordinary weekday afternoons outside the Holy Family – and how the army began to suspect he was a high-ranking IRA official because there was a 'ceasefire' whenever he appeared.

Chapter 5: Crossing Borders

Information in this chapter was gathered primarily from my interviews with Gerry Storey, Davy Lamour and Barry McGuigan. After my interviews with Barry, I re-read his books *Barry McGuigan: The Untold Story* and *Cyclone.*

Colm Tóibín's *Bad Blood: A Walk Along the Irish Border* and *Stepping Stones* by Seamus Heaney also helped me understand Clones and the borders and differences, as well as the similarities, between the North and the South more clearly. *Lost Lives* was, again, invaluable in confirming key details.

Chapter 6: The Clint Eastwood of Belfast

I interviewed Davy Larmour, Gerry Storey, Sam Storey, Charlie Nash, Paddy Maguire and Hugh Russell for this chapter. The unpublished writings of Larmour and Nash provided an additional perspective.

Chapter 7: Turning the Shankill Road Green

This chapter is again built on my first-person interviews with Barry McGuigan, Gerry Storey, Davy Larmour, Charlie Nash and Hugh Russell.

Lost Lives, Bear in Mind These Dead, Provos and Jim Cusack and Henry McDonald's *UVF* all added to my research.

Boxing archive film was given to me by George Zeleny.

Chapter 8: A Second Warning

Interviews with Gerry Storey, Charlie Nash, Barry McGuigan, Davy Larmour, Paddy Maguire and Sandra McGuigan gave me the bulk of information in this chapter.

The Belfast Newspaper Archive and fight footage supplied by George Zeleny added to my research.

Chapter 9: The Camera

George Zeleny supplied complete fight footage of Charlie Nash v Ken Buchanan on DVD.

I completed detailed interviews as research for this chapter with Charlie, Gerry Storey, Barry McGuigan and Hugh Russell.

Lost Lives provided some key details.

Hugh's photographic archive and Brendan Murphy's brilliant book of photography, *Eyewitness*, helped with the latter stages of the chapter.

Chapter 10: Hunger

There are numerous powerful documentaries about the hunger strikes – and I also watched *66 Days*, a 2016 documentary about Bobby Sands. I saw Steve McQueen's *Hunger*, a cinematic recreation of the 1981 Hunger Strikes, again. My primary source material, however, for this chapter came from newspaper archives and some key books – most notably *Ten Men Dead* by David Beresford and Brendan Hughes' account in *Voices from the Grave*. I also read Richard O'Rawe's *Blanketmen* and *Afterlives*.

Interviews were carried out with Gerry Storey and Barry McGuigan, who were both extremely powerful.

Chapter 11: A Funeral and a Wedding

The books and newspaper archive mentioned in the previous chapter were again of great help – as were first-person interviews with Gerry Storey, Charlie Nash and Barry McGuigan.

George Zeleny supplied complete fight footage of Jim Watt v Charlie Nash, McGuigan's professional debut and McGuigan v Jean-Marc Renard.

Paddy Maguire and Davy Larmour recalled the funeral scene for me – while Barry and Sandra McGuigan relieved their wedding. Hugh Russell was an additional key interview for me.

Chapter 12: Into the Maze

In our lengthy and compelling interviews, Gerry Storey captured his work in the Maze prison. Billy Hutchinson was also a gripping and invaluable interviewee about Gutsy Spence and the Maze. *UVF* and Roy Garland's *Gusty Spence* were useful, while I especially liked Donovan Wylie's *Maze* with its stark and haunting photographs and descriptions of the prison.

Barry McGuigan was a compassionate and unflinching witness to his tragic fight against Young Ali. I also spoke to Hugh Russell and Sandra McGuigan about this night and its distressing aftermath.

Chapter 13: A Bloody Battle

Davy Larmour and Hugh Russell described to me, in detailed interviews, the build-up to their first fight, the bloody battle itself and travelling to hospital together. Barry McGuigan relived his emotions and the action of his return to the ring against Jimmy Duncan. George Zeleny supplied the fight footage.

Chapter 14: The Body and the Briefcase

Details from Davy Larmour's unpublished writing and our vivid interviews about the rematch with Hugh Russell are the cornerstone of this chapter – with additional material from Hugh and, also, Paddy Maguire. George Zeleny provided a DVD of the entire fight as well as Barry McGuigan v Vernon Penprase. Charlie Nash, Gerry and Sam Storey were also interviewed.

Hugh spoke poignantly about Edgar Graham, and his photograph after the murder of the Unionist politician. I also appreciated the insights offered by Diane Drennan into the political impact of Graham. A family friend of the Grahams, Diane spoke with real care and consideration. I also read a great deal of newspaper archive material about this political assassination – in particular from the *Irish News*.

Chapter 15: Collect Work

Hugh Russell and Paul Faith, another Belfast photographer who covered the Troubles, helped me understand the delicate nature of collect work. I also enjoyed the documentary, featuring Paul, about Pacemaker, the photographic agency. The key interviews, again, were with Hugh, who described his decision to retire as a boxer in vivid detail.

I also interviewed Gerry and Sam Storey for this chapter.

Barry McGuigan and Juan LaPorte both spoke evocatively about their fight – and George Zeleny again gave me a copy of the entire bout on DVD.

Chapter 16: Shadows and Sunshine

Barry McGuigan was my key interviewee for the final chapter. I was also helped by Sandra McGuigan, Gerry Storey, Sam Storey, Hugh Russell, Davy Larmour and Charlie Nash. My descriptions of the fight are taken from the DVD recorded by George Zeleny.

Epilogue: A Beautiful Wee Life

Billy Hutchinson, Eamonn Magee, Barry McGuigan, Charlie Nash, Davy Larmour, Hugh Russell, Seamus McCann and Gerry Storey were all interviewed for these final pages. Paddy Armstrong's *Life after Life* helped my research into the wrongful arrest of the Guildford Four, and Hugh's photographic archive was of great assistance. The Magee interview was written first for *The Guardian* in May 2018. Jonathan Drennan, Paul Gibson and Trevor Ringland helped me with their additional thoughts and comments about life in Belfast and Northern Ireland today.

ACKNOWLEDGEMENTS

This book could never have been written without the generous help and involvement of Gerry Storey, Charlie Nash, Davy Larmour, Hugh Russell and Barry McGuigan. They all gave me so much of their time and never complained when I returned for yet another long and detailed interview. Instead, they took us back to often dark and difficult times in their lives – and spoke with such warmth and humour that our conversations always felt uplifting.

Gerry gave me more time than anyone and I loved visiting him at the Holy Family over the years. Whether it was quiet and empty in the day or seething with noise and aspiring young boxers in the evening, it always seemed like a place of hope to me. Gerry is one of the kindest and most interesting men I have met – as well as the most self-effacing. It has been an honour to spend so much time with him. Thanks to the great man.

Charlie and his family suffered terribly after the loss of his brother, Willie, on Bloody Sunday. Yet, on every visit I paid to his home in Derry, Charlie was kind and welcoming. He shared so much with me and I valued the fact that he even allowed me to read his unpublished writing. His words to me after he finished reading this book will stay with me forever. Thank you to Charlie and his wife Betty.

I first met Davy Larmour at the Ulster Hall. He was with his great friend Paddy Maguire. We soon established a pattern where Hugh,

Paddy and I would meet up whenever I was in Belfast. Paddy was great company and many of his memories appear in the preceding pages. Thanks go to him. Davy's story is compelling and, in an attempt to do it justice, we decided on a concentrated burst of interviews. We must have done at least a dozen long 1-2-1 sessions which were fascinating and inspiring. I also appreciated Davy sharing his unpublished memoir with me and always being there when I needed to check another fact. He has been a good friend.

I always felt grateful that, after a long day of work at the *Irish News*, Hugh Russell would give me as long as I needed to talk to him. We met in the Cathedral Quarter and I especially loved those evenings when Hugh would bring along his laptop and we would look at his photographic archive. Thanks to Hugh for all the memories, the photos and all our interviews. I also understood the depth of his kindness when he allowed free use of his photographs in this book.

I have been friends with Barry McGuigan since our first interview in Kent in 2011. It was just after a wake for Henry Cooper and Barry gave me such a riveting interview that, in many ways, it sparked this book. We forged a bond that day and I have interviewed and written about him many times since then for *The Guardian* and *Boxing News*. His story has been told before and, among the main characters in this book, Barry is by far the most famous. Yet I was touched by his willingness to spend so much time with me for the purposes of this book so that we could try to tell his story in a fresh way alongside the four other boxing men I feature. I appreciated all our interviews – whether they were at home in Kent, in Belfast or across the road from his gym in Wandsworth. Thank you to Barry, again, and also to Sandra, his wife, who helped me so much when I interviewed her.

Sam Storey, Gerry's son, became a good friend. He was a great help to me in the latter stages of writing and I always had such fun talking to Sam about his dad and his own career. I was very happy when, early in 2019, Sam asked me if I would write a little tribute to his dad that could be read out at the Ulster finals. It felt like we had come full circle and Sam and I enjoyed talking about the words we could use when reflecting the mighty contribution of Gerry Storey.

At the Holy Family, I loved talking to Seamus McCann, Gerry Storey Jr and Paddy Barnes Sr. Thanks, too, to Seamus for our interview. His electrifying words lit up a winter night.

In Derry, Damien McDermott was so helpful and friendly. I really appreciated the interviews we did – whether in the gym, where he and Charlie still help train young fighters, or at home.

Thanks to Billy Hutchinson for the long and involving interview he gave me about his time in Long Kesh and for his insights into the work of Gerry Storey. They meant a lot. I also valued meeting Brendan 'Bik' McFarlane with Gerry Storey. Thanks also to Bobby Storey.

Trevor Ringland gave me a wonderful interview for a *Guardian* feature I wrote about Irish rugby – and his understanding of identity in Northern Ireland and the role of sport helped greatly when I was revising this book. Thanks to Trevor and also to Willie John McBride who spoke to me about rugby during the Troubles and his memories of Bloody Friday.

Outside of all those I have written about, no one has given more time to this book than Jonathan Drennan. A fellow writer and boxing fan, Jonathan comes from Belfast and he was the first person I wrote to in detail about the broad ideas for this book. He has been a great friend and a wonderful source of information and insight. Thanks to Jonathan for all his enthusiasm, hard work and helpful suggestions. He has read two early drafts of this book and made considerable improvements.

His parents, Neil and Diane, have also become friends of mine and they read the book so carefully and thoughtfully. Their considered and balanced views were invaluable and I enjoyed talking to them about Belfast and Northern Ireland – even though they had to relive some upsetting memories.

Hugh O'Halloran was also introduced to me by Jonathan Drennan – and my research in Belfast began on a memorable day when Hugh, who is such an expert on the city's boxing history, drove me around, from one interview to the next. Hugh also set up many of the interviews at the outset and introduced me to Davy Larmour and Paddy Maguire. I will always remember his generosity.

Thanks to Tom Jenkins – yet again – for taking the photographs of Davy Larmour and Hugh Russell. Tom also took the photo of Barry McGuigan on one of our many joint assignments. I appreciated our being able to use Margaret McLaughlin's photograph of Charlie Nash.

Ciaran Bradley helped me over the years with his insights into Irish history and politics and he also introduced me to his dad, John, who grew up in Derry. John and Ciaran both read a draft of the book and made many useful suggestions. Thanks to them both.

It meant a lot to read such a generous and uplifting email from my friend Elliot Worsell, who is such a fine boxing writer, after he completed an early draft of the book. He also made some helpful suggestions.

I valued the considered views of Paul Gibson who read an early draft. He made some instructive points and so thanks to Paul whose book on Eammon Magee was such a revelation.

Charlotte Atyeo was an inspired choice as the book's copyeditor. She offered a fine close reading of the text and made some excellent general points that improved the final edition.

My editor, Ian Marshall, at Simon & Schuster, has been a great ally of my writing yet again. Thank you to Ian for believing in the book and also for his scrupulous editing and hard work on so many facets of its publication. He helped me greatly and I look forward to our working together on many more books. Thanks, too, to Ian Chapman at S&S for his unwavering support – and to everyone else at Simon & Schuster, with a special nod of appreciation to Sue Stephens and to Craig Fraser for his excellent work on the cover.

Thanks to Amanda Kelley for reading a draft of the book and for all her ideas on the cover – which helped produce the eventual concept. Amanda, who painted the cover of a new US edition of my book *Dark Trade* in 2019, has a great knowledge of boxing and an eye for design which helped so much here.

Jonny Geller, my agent, was yet again an invaluable support and a fount of interesting ideas. Here's to the next book we work on together.

George Zeleny, who has also done this for two of my previous books, tracked down the boxing film footage I needed. Some of these were very obscure but George did the business again. I always love having the excuse to talk to George about boxing in the pub.

Kim Whyte, Hilton Tanchum and Anita Matzdorff all did sterling work when it came to transcribing my interviews and documentaries.

Bill Campbell, my first publisher, came to the rescue when I could not track down a copy of the monumental *Lost Lives*. He had published the book for Mainstream and kindly sent me a copy from his own personal collection. Cheers, Bill, as always.

Thanks also to Andy Lee, Paul Faith, Glenn Speers, Declan Heaney and Tim Musgrave.

I owe a great deal, as always, to my family. They put up with me being away so much, and working almost every day, with understanding and good humour. Jack and Emma have the best Irish accents in the house, so much so that we know them as Seamus and Saoirse now. I'll take them to Paddy McGinty's one day. Bella, whose great writing talent is already obvious, also did a wonderful editing job on one of my final drafts. Her attention to detail and use of language stunned me all over again. Alison, my wife, read the first two drafts and saved me from my worst excesses many times. She has helped edit eleven out of the 12 books I've written so far and gets better at it every time. Thanks to Alison, too, for her constant support and understanding of my strange old writing life and for all her help in a year, 2018, when I lost my sister and my mother fell ill with cancer.

My parents, Ian and Jess, did more than anyone to help me become a writer. Through every stage of my life they have been an unbreakable support to me. Even now, amid ill health and the loss of my sister, Heather Simpson, who died in September 2018, they have always wanted to hear about my writing progress. I am proud to dedicate this book to them, and to Heather. Thanks to all three of them for everything they did for me.

INDEX